essential

MONEY

essential

MONEY

Everything You Need to Manage Your Personal Finances Wisely

Peter Sander, M.B.A.

Adams Media
Avon, Massachusetts

I dedicate this book to my parents, Jerry and Betty Sander, who are no longer with us but taught me enduring lessons of personal finance at a very early age.

Published by Adams Media, an F+W Publications Company
57 Littlefield Street, Avon, MA 02322 U.S.A.
www.adamsmedia.com

ISBN: 1-59869-072-8
Printed by KHL Printing Co Pte Ltd, in Singapore

J I H G F E D C B A

Previously published as The Everything® Personal Finance Book
Copyright ©2003, F+W Publications, Inc.

Contents

Acknowledgments

I would like to thank the practitioner-instructors of the University of California–Davis Personal Financial Planning program, notably J. Jeffrey Lambert, CFP and chairman, and instructors Steve Bertino, CLU/CEBU/MBA, and Gary Paul, CFP, for expanding my perspective. I would also like to recognize my wife, Jennifer Basye Sander, for her continual support of my writing and financial-planning endeavors (and for living on a budget!), and to Mary Ann Ziakas, who did a great job of taking care of our wonderful children, Julian and Jonathan, so that I could have more time to write.

Top Ten Personal Finance Tips

1. It's not what you make, it's what you keep. Even a substantial income is not likely to help you achieve your goals if it's spent frivolously.
2. Know who you are, financially, and understand your spending and saving habits.
3. Get a grip on your income, expenses, assets, and liabilities. You can't know where you're going unless you know where you are.
4. Create a budget and make sure that your entire family agrees to follow it.
5. Avoid the following purchases: pleasure boats, RVs, vacation homes, swimming pools, timeshares, and sports cars. Cost to purchase and cost of ownership are usually underestimated. Don't buy until other financial goals are met.
6. Always work to *maximize* available credit and credit rating and to *minimize* the amount of debt outstanding. Remember, it's the amount of debt—not the interest rate—that's important.
7. Put your assets to work for you by investing wisely and taking advantage of compounded growth.
8. Take advantage of the greatest long-term wealth accumulation device available for most families—buy a home.
9. Plan future needs rationally and create specific plans to achieve those sums. Don't just "save for college" or "save for retirement" without precise goals in mind.
10. Know where you're going and practice *awareness, commitment*, and *control* in each financial decision you make. Get help if you feel you can't do it alone.

Introduction

▶WHEN IT COMES TO FINANCES, times are tough. You know you should save more for retirement. You should save for your kids' college education. You should save in case you get laid off. We are constantly bombarded by news that the market is down, inflation is rising, unemployment is rising, insurance costs are skyrocketing, and Social Security might not be around much longer. There's so much information to process, and it sounds so scary. And yes, it does pertain to you, and you do have a reason to care.

Many of these factors are beyond our control, but many more are actually our responsibility. Today, we all have more control over our financial destinies, a power that is both good and bad. Deregulation and the Internet have made it easier to manage assets, but they also make it easier to spend more money more quickly—and even to get a loan to finance those expenditures.

The job market is more fast-paced, too—the constant shifts in the economy create thousands of new jobs and make others obsolete. Companies no longer want you for life—and they won't be there to sponsor your retirement. The popular 401(k) retirement savings plans may be great, but guess what? They transfer the burden of growing your retirement assets *to you.* If you make bad investments and lose your money, you are on your own. And whether any money gets into that savings plan in the first place is entirely up to you. You have control, and that can be great; however, for a great many individuals and families, the level of financial knowledge hasn't kept up with the responsibility and the opportunities for "do it yourself" personal finance. People don't know what they don't know, and they aren't good at applying what they *do* know.

The process of managing your personal finances requires you to take an objective look at where you are and to deal with financial issues objectively. It's never too late to learn how to effectively manage your own finances. You must gain control of your daily, weekly, and monthly living expenses. Getting to the point where your finances are clear and stable may take some serious financial "remodeling," but once you build a solid foundation, you can then start to think about accumulating wealth and achieving your long-term financial goals.

All along the way, you will need to set goals and monitor your performance against those goals. Because financial prosperity requires a team effort from the entire family, you will also need to build awareness and get commitment from others in your household. To learn how to manage your personal finances, you'll need to learn five main elements:

1. Controlling day-to-day finances.
2. Accumulating wealth.
3. Protecting what you own.
4. Achieving specific financial goals.
5. Building a financial plan.

Keep in mind that when you understand yourself and your own finances, you can set good goals and tie the proper strategies and tactics to those goals. As you read on, you'll gain a better understanding of the elements of personal finance, and how to apply them to the benefit of you and your family.

Chapter 1

Money, Wealth, and Personal Finance

The process starts with understanding what personal finance *is*. It is *personal* (about you), and it is *finance* (about money). Personal finance isn't just about cashing checks, paying bills, and meeting your monthly obligations. It is about accumulating enough wealth to achieve family goals and aspirations through the application of sound financial principles and behavior.

It's a Question of Money

According to the Bible, money "answereth all things" and the "love of money is the root of all evil." And then, as the Beatles later put it, money can't buy you love. So what is money? And what does it mean to us? Is it good or evil? Does it give us happiness or misery? Is it something we should strive for or a goal in itself?

Regardless of your personal feelings and approach to money, at the very least you could hardly question that it is a means to an end. Unless you are able to build your own house, farm your own food, and make your own clothes, money is the vehicle to basic sustenance. Beyond that, we can all agree that money helps to achieve education, allow you to travel, and give you the ability to spend time doing things other than work. That is, money *can* make your life better and easier. And that's what personal finance is all about—managing money with an end in mind of achieving goals, while avoiding the problems that arise when there isn't enough money.

Money Is Not Wealth

In economics, money is just a commodity. This may sound kind of strange—as if money could be traded around in bushels, barrels, or boxes; stored in silos and warehouses; or sold in lots and shipped in rail cars to the highest bidder. Well, that's actually true—though in a figurative, not a literal, sense. Money is "stuff" just like the "stuff" we buy with it. We use it to receive the value of what we produce (by working, selling, or investing) and to transfer that value to something else (food, transportation, clothing, shelter, or pleasure) that we need or want. Having money, by itself, doesn't really mean anything about wealth; as we know, you can have money in your pocket but owe $3,000 on your credit card bill.

E ALERT!

Personal finance "literacy" is becoming more and more important. Financial illiteracy is increasingly a handicap. It is not only important to pay attention to all facets of your personal finances; but also to be able to talk to professionals if you don't do your own financial planning.

Take Charge of Your Personal Finances

There must be a reason why you decided to spend your hard-earned money for this book. Perhaps your finances are out of control, and you find there is always "too much month at the end of your money." You want to "get a rope" around your current finances, to stay afloat month to month, and to be prepared for those unexpected expenses—when your car suddenly breaks down or when you get those insurance bills (which shouldn't be unexpected anyway). Or perhaps you are in decent financial shape, financially "fit" as it were, and you want to fine-tune your finances and build wealth towards achieving some *aspirational* goals.

The following are some of the most common personal finance issues:

- **Overspending:** Almost everyone succumbs to the temptation to overspend at one time or another, but chronic overspending is a serious problem. Debts pile up quickly and form a barrier to achieving other financial and personal goals.
- **Surprises:** Failing to plan in advance can give you an unpleasant surprise as you suddenly find yourself struggling to pay those "surprise" insurance and utility bills at the end of the month. Remember: Lack of awareness creates overspending—and debt.
- **Procrastination:** People tend to put things off, particularly for long-term goals and needs. Saving for retirement or college is more effective if you start earlier rather than later, even if you start in small increments.
- **Using emotion, not reason:** Allowing your emotions to cloud your mind can result in poor financial decision-making. Deals that look too good to be true usually are. Four-day weekends are fun and necessary at times, but are they really worth a thousand dollars? Reason must accompany emotions and feelings.
- **Financial personality clashes:** What do you do if you are a spender and your spouse is a saver? You build a workable financial plan that relies on each person's strengths to carry it out.

Whatever your issues, this book will help you solve them and to develop a personal finance system combining tools and techniques with habits and behavior to achieve your objectives.

Knowing What You're up Against

To begin, you need to have a good working definition of what personal finance is.

Personal finance is the management of individual or family financial resources to create enough wealth to achieve the basic needs, chosen lifestyle, and aspirational goals of the individual or family.

The objective of managing your finances is to reach your and your family's goals, in terms of both keeping what you have and obtaining what you want. When it comes to personal finances, your family is in charge—each family member is both the manager and the beneficiary. What does this mean? In a business situation, the managers and the beneficiaries (shareholders) are different parties. Managers manage business finance with the aim of achieving shareholder wealth. In government, officials manage finances for the benefit of the public. In the case of personal finance, you manage your own finances for your own benefit. Nobody does it for you. The process works better if everybody in the "entity" participates in this assignment. This also means someone will have to take charge as a leader.

Become Your Own Chief Financial Officer

This all sounds a lot like business, doesn't it? A business must be actively managed to maintain its course and to adjust to changes. Discipline, diligence, and commitment are important. The business manager who neglects the business or refuses to adapt to change doesn't last long.

QUESTION?

Are you "in business" to manage your own personal finances? You bet. Someone has to take charge and lead the family. You are, in the words of Jennifer Openshaw, founder of the Women's Financial Network, "your own CFO" (or Chief Financial Officer). Congratulations on the promotion—it's an important job.

Tools and Rules—And Beyond

Personal finance uses a system of tools and techniques to achieve financial reward. You are undoubtedly already familiar with many of them—banking, investments, insurance, and retirement plans. Information describing these tools and how they work is widely available. However, successful personal finance means being able to put all the tools together to build a solid financial plan. Successful personal finance also means having the right attitude and discipline in daily life to carry out your plan. Tools without a plan won't work, and a plan without execution won't work either.

A Few Basic Principles

What is "personal finance" as a subject of study? A lengthy compendium of numbers, laws, and planning tools, tricks, and techniques? Yes—for the professional practitioner, anyway. This book, however, is not intended to prepare you for personal finance as a profession. Rather, it is intended to prepare you for personal finance in life. Three principles form the basic thread of personal finance:

1. **Money, income, and wealth aren't the same.** Personal finance isn't just about money or how much you make—it's about how much you *keep.* Personal finance is concerned with wealth and the *accumulation, preservation,* and *distribution* of that wealth.
2. **Personal finance isn't just about the tools—it's about behavior.** Again, it requires the right set of behaviors to make the tools and techniques work.
3. **Personal finance is a full-time job.** Personal finance is more than just sitting down once a month to pay bills. You must be aware of your responsibilities all the time—otherwise all that you strive for is liable to be wrecked in an instant.

Wealth and Financial Aspirations

Accumulating wealth means accumulating money beyond the obligations against that money. That is, wealth is having something left over after you pay all your bills and cover all your expenses. You will need this "something left over" to conquer long-term obligations, like your children's college education or your retirement plan. Beyond that, wealth can provide for your aspirations—goals wrapped around things you want, whether it's a bigger house, a nicer car, a better retirement, or starting a business.

ESSENTIAL

If you are in debt, you obviously have some work to do before you start accumulating wealth. Still, wealth should be the real objective of any personal finance-savvy individual or family. Active personal finance sets a mark, or goal, then provides the tools, techniques, and behaviors to reach that goal.

But Isn't Income Important?

Yes, income is important. No common financial scenario can succeed without it. But it's surprising how much income is overemphasized. Let's say that I ask you, "So how are you doing, money-wise?" Ninety percent of the time, the answer sounds something like this: "I just got a raise, and now I'm making $80,000 a year." Okay, that sounds like a plausible answer. It's specific, anyway.

But did it answer the question? Does the fact that you make $80,000 a year really tell me anything? What if you're spending $90,000? What if you have $20,000 in personal debt and a negative net worth? What if you have three kids, aged four years apart, the first of whom is about to start college next year? Income is a great thing, and if you can get more of it, so much the better, but it cannot serve as an indication of your financial health.

Most people can't control income on a day-to-day basis, but they can control their expenses. Accumulating wealth has as much (or more!) to do with how much you let out as how much you put in.

At the end of the day, personal finance is about strategies to accumulate, preserve, and distribute wealth. *Accumulating* wealth means putting in more than you take out and growing what you have through sound financial management and investing. *Preserving* wealth means controlling the outflow but also protecting your financial base. Finally, *distributing* wealth means managing the outflow towards achieving objectives—spending to meet goals.

QUESTION?

What is net worth?

Your net worth is your assets (what you have) minus liabilities (what you owe or spend). Net worth is a bottom-line measure of wealth. Think of it this way: Money is accumulated into wealth, wealth achieves goals, net worth measures wealth. Do you know what your net worth is?

A Brief Tour Through the Toolbox

If you think personal finance involves more than balancing the checkbook and trading stock online, you're right. Conceptually, it's the planned application of tools and behavior toward a goal of accumulating, preserving, and distributing wealth. Let's look at a short list of some of the specific tools and strategies you will encounter as you manage your finances:

- **Budgeting and spending:** Budgeting is a short-term plan for managing financial flows. Closely related is spending. You ask: is "spending" a "financial tool"? Not really—but as already pointed out, the effective management of spending is critical.
- **Banking and credit:** These are tools to manage finances on a day-to-day basis; they may be used in wealth accumulation, preservation, and distribution. To use these tools effectively, you need to be aware that the banking system can work for or against you.
- **Investing:** Investing is the other half of the accumulation game. Growing your accumulated wealth through productive investments augments your income contributions; investing may consist of intangible (securities) and real (property and collectibles) investments.
- **Insurance and risk management:** Insurance and risk management are preservation techniques. Once you have assets and income, you need to preserve and protect them from certain types of risk. Loss of income and assets resulting from death, disability, and casualty (fire, theft, and so forth) are some of the major areas of risk, and insurance products are a major—but not the only way—to manage these risks.

- **Contingency planning:** Aside from random, insurable events, personal life events can devastate finances. If you get laid off or have to care for a sick parent, what will you do? Minimize risks in advance, and have a ready plan to combat any problems you might face.
- **College and retirement planning:** There are several tools to help you accumulate the funds to send your kids to college and to prepare a retirement plan to meet financial needs in old age.
- **Estate planning:** The wealth that you do not consume in your lifetime will be left to others. It's important to know how to do this according to your wishes, providing for the needs of your heirs without paying too much in inheritance and gift taxes.

Good financial planning involves a combination of these tools, depending on your particular situation and the phases of life. In the earlier stages of life, accumulation is more important; as we get older, distribution comes more into play. To borrow from Lincoln, you won't use all of the tools all of the time, but you can use some of the tools all of the time and all of the tools some of the time. It isn't just about the tools—they won't work without some cooperation from you.

On Your Best Behavior

Financial principles, tools, and techniques won't work by themselves. Sure, they can help produce and preserve wealth, but no tool can work effectively if you aren't in charge. Good personal finance blends tools and techniques with attitude and behavior. Managing something implies watching it and controlling it when necessary. Awareness and control are part of what we call the financial "persona," or conscience, the part of you that watches everything and keeps it in order.

A Financial *What?*

"Financial persona"—sounds funny, doesn't it? Like it might refer to greedy money people who prefer an in-depth reading of the stock page of the newspaper to a dinner with a best friend, those folks who think about money all the time. Fortunately, that's really not the case. The financial persona is a personality and a lifestyle, a set of attitudes and behaviors essential to achieving your financial goals and financial success.

ESSENTIAL

Avoiding injury in driving or in sports is as much a function of behavior and mindset as it is a function of devices and rules. The same approach should be applied to personal finance. There are dozens of excellent financial "devices and rules" that can help lead you to personal financial success, but they can't work if you don't develop the right mindset to go with them.

Let's review some of the characteristics of an effective financial persona:

- **Awareness:** You need to be aware of your current financial situation at all times. Somewhere in the back of your mind you should have a good notion of your net worth, debts, this month's expenses, current credit card balances, and income you can count on receiving. You don't have to write everything down, of course, and there is no need to keep a "mileage log" of all your minor purchases. However, you should be organized enough to know where to get that information if you do need it. A business CFO doesn't know the dollars and cents of every asset or income account in the business, but he or she could give you the highlights in an instant; in the same way, you should be aware of the highlights of your financial situation.
- **Control:** You should be able to control your expenses and financial transactions. If you buy that new shirt on sale, will you exceed the monthly personal allowance you have set for yourself? Maybe it's a good idea anyway, because you need a shirt and the price is 50 percent off. Eventually, you will begin to realize that without awareness there's no control, and without control, awareness doesn't help, either.
- **Commitment:** Commitment is the combination of diligence and persistence needed to get in control and stay there. Plans fail when you or your family members are only committed some of the time to achieving some of the results. Commitment implies agreement,

follow-through, and rewards—when things go right.

- **Risk tolerance:** Everybody has a different tolerance for risk. While it always makes sense to keep some wealth in reserve to meet unexpected or unplanned contingencies, some people will naturally want a bigger cushion than others. This has to do with each individual's comfort level, security, and, to some extent, outlook on life. If you are one of those "If something can go wrong, it will" people, it's hard to change that notion—it's easier to create a financial reserve accordingly.

FACT

Risk tolerance plays a big role in investing. The amount of growth achieved has a lot to do with amount of risk taken ("no pain, no gain" remains the popular expression). Your financial persona governs the amount of risk taken.

Your financial habits are the outward signs of an effective financial persona. Keeping track and occasionally checking your savings, investments, and net worth balances is a good habit. Keeping mental notes of money spent during the month and especially charges to credit cards is another. Holding off big purchases until funds are accumulated—or at least until budget impact is understood—is still another. Good financial habits are good management skills that include being aware, being in control, working with the people involved to achieve desired outcomes, making rational decisions, and adjusting to change.

The Persona Is Individual

You can't delegate a financial persona, although many tasks can be delegated to other family members. Awareness, commitment, and control can't be delegated.

It won't work if one family member practices awareness and control, and the other spends freely. Everyone in the family unit must have and use a well-grounded financial persona, even though a single family member may take on the task of determining the budget, paying the bills, and monitoring wealth. Each family member must exercise the persona, and agreement among all on the details—goals, strategies, and objectives—is required so that the persona can work effectively in tandem.

ESSENTIAL

This book will help you gain knowledge and insight into the tools and practice of personal finance and evolve your financial persona to apply those tools and manage your finances on a daily basis. At the end of the day, you'll be able to set realistic goals, make a plan to achieve them, and make that achievement part of your lifestyle.

It's a Full-Time Job

Once you adopt your financial persona, you must adhere to it at all times. It just won't work if you leave it behind when you drive off to the mall. It should be present in "back of mind" for all financial decisions.

Your financial persona manifests itself as a *set of financial habits.* It can help you counteract the impulses and emotions of a moment and keep an eye on such important things as how much you've charged so far that month, whether you've paid the day-care bill yet, and how you would handle that $500 car repair, should your transmission break down tomorrow. An active financial persona takes stewardship of your finances, almost on an up-to-the-minute basis. This stewardship is necessary to keep your plan from disintegrating and your wealth-creation in progress.

Like Any Job, You Must Learn It

As you set out to bring good personal finance into your life, don't get overwhelmed by the size and complexity of the task. As long as you devote attention to it, you will have no problems achieving a financially productive lifestyle. Start simple, and you will grow. Sooner or later, the things that took a lot of effort in the beginning—like budgeting—will become second nature. The *amount* of attention you should have to devote should decline as your financial plan and persona evolve. Eventually, you won't even need to write your budget down. It will simply become part of your financial persona operating in the back of your mind.

Chapter 2

A Look in the Financial Mirror

To get started in developing a financial plan, the first, absolutely critical step is to understand who you are and where you are financially. This chapter explores *who* you are (your financial "type") and *where* you are—your current financial status in terms of numbers like net worth and net cash flow. Combined, these assessments represent the starting point from which your financial plan and set of goals can evolve.

Common Personality Types

Psychologists classify personalities into dozens, even hundreds, of personality types. Such classifications help individuals to better understand themselves and to figure out the best path to self-improvement. Specifically, there are *financial* personality types as well. Don't confuse a financial personality with a financial persona. The personality type is the end result of how you apply (or don't apply) a combination of tools and your financial persona to your lifestyle.

E ALERT!

The personalities presented here are a few broad financial types. Conceivably, extensive research and testing could uncover more, but this approach keeps it simple. It would not be surprising if you and most of your friends fell—loosely, at least—into one of the three described below.

He Who Dies with the Most Toys Wins

We all know this type. These people buy the latest television and audio equipment, wear the latest fashions, have the most kitchen gadgets, and furnish their homes with fancy countertops and pool tables. Some of these folks can afford to acquire all this stuff, but others can't. The bottom line: Wealth is converted to physical assets.

That's okay if there is enough left over to achieve other goals, or if other financial goals are modest–suppose there is a locked-in retirement pension, a family trust, or no kids to send to college. But in the majority of cases, the Most Toys Wins type is spending every last dollar of potential wealth to acquire these assets, and often they are spending money they don't really have. Consequently, high debt and negative net worth are common among people of this financial personality type. The Most Toys Wins folks frequently put off financial responsibilities, such as retirement and college planning, until it is too late. They also tend to forget that their toys lose value over time and cannot be thought of as investment. Their financial persona is but a small, lost, powerless sliver of their overall personality.

The Check Writer

"Sure, I do personal finance. I sit down every month and pay the bills." This is how the Check Writer defines personal finance. Check Writers do have a degree of financial conscience. They talk about money and have at least an idea of what they earn, what they spend, and how much things cost. But the Check Writer's involvement in personal finance usually stops with the monthly bill-paying cycle. Write a few checks, pay a few bills in full, and wait for next month's mail. If they don't have enough this month, that's okay—pay a little and wait, next month will be better.

ESSENTIAL

Check Writers do have some vague long-term financial goals, but they usually lack a good plan or a disciplined approach to achieving their goals. They are analogous to the "C and E" (Christmas and Easter) churchgoer, who goes to church on major holidays but doesn't "live the religion" every day.

The Check Writers live hand-to-mouth and generally spend everything that they have, although they are less prone to excessive spending than the Most Toys Wins personalities. They do know what things cost, and they do a good job keeping track of their short-term financial situation. They are unlikely to accumulate huge debts but may have a negative net worth. The Check Writers may run halfway across town to save six cents per gallon of gas in an effort to be frugal, then blow the savings on a candy bar, magazine, and a Coke at the adjoining convenience store.

The Millionaire Next Door

The Millionaire Next Door—a concept and phrase made popular by the best-selling book of the same name by researchers Thomas Stanley and William Danko—may only have a net worth of $50,000, but it's the approach to life and finances that earns him or her this title. Millionaires Next Door aren't necessarily millionaires, but they do think and act like them.

Millionaires Next Door personality types are keenly aware of all aspects of their financial situation. They are more than willing to sacrifice today's pleasures to achieve long-term goals and may even be compulsive savers. Millionaires Next Door think wealth is more important than income and act to "make it, keep it, and grow it," not just "make it and spend it." The Millionaires Next Door minimize consumption and get the most value for what they purchase and what they own. They get excited every time their odometer turns another 10,000 miles—not because they are that much closer to their next new car but because they have gotten yet more value from their original investment and have put off paying sales tax on a new car for yet another year.

The Millionaires Next Door seldom go to the mall, and when they do they are happiest when they resist temptation and come home with nothing. Yet these folks aren't penny-wise and dollar-foolish—no trips halfway across town to save six cents a gallon on gas for them. They value time as much as money. In short, the Millionaire Next Door applies the maximum awareness, commitment, and control.

FACT

In 2001, there were over 7.2 million individuals worldwide with over $1 million in net worth. Despite the 2000/2001 economic downturn, wealth among these individuals actually increased by 6 percent.

And Which One of These Fits You?

Although it may not be a perfect fit, it is likely that you fall into one of these three categories. You may live your life as it comes, without regard to your finances; you may be deeply committed to a life of financial propriety, day in and day out: or maybe you're an occasion-driven "C-and-E" believer who pays homage to financial issues at the appropriate times but may drift from "the Way" at others. Of course, the Most Toys Wins, Check Writer, and Millionaire Next Door types probably won't fit you exactly; indeed, you may exhibit qualities of two or all three types. Different members of your family, in all likelihood, exhibit different characteristics as well. It's a good exercise to do an assessment for yourself and all family members. As a family unit, your personal finance challenge is greater if a Most Toys Wins and a Millionaire Next Door live under the same roof.

Take the Test

In everyday life, some of you may skydive and hang glide, or fly private planes, while others are wary of the height from the door of your SUV to the ground. As people have different tolerances for risk in every life, they also differ in risk tolerance in their financial life.

To learn more about your financial risk profile, you can fill out a personal finance questionnaire to assess your financial personality and style. One such questionnaire is listed in Appendix B; others are available online. One example of an in-depth assessment is the Financial Checkup posted on the Intuit Corporation's Quicken Web site at *www.quicken.com*. (Intuit produces Quicken personal finance software.)

QUESTION?

What is your financial risk tolerance?
Different people have different levels of financial risk tolerance. When it comes to investing, the higher the risk, the greater the potential profits. Financially conservative investors avoid risk and accept lower returns, while financially aggressive investors take the risk in order to achieve higher returns. Once you know your risk profile (that is, how well you tolerate risk), you can create a financial plan that will work best for you.

Appraising Your Financial Position

Now that you know what your financial personality is, you also need to take stock of your financial position. A clear, honest picture of your financial position should include your current level of wealth, measured by *net worth*. Additionally, a close look at true *net cash flow* (how much is going in and how much is going out) provides a better understanding of the dynamics of your financial position.

The first step is to learn and understand the four major quadrants of personal finance and how they relate to each other. The four quadrants each represent assets, liabilities, income, and expenses. The relationship between these quadrants defines such critical financial elements as net worth, net cash flow, and net savings, so it's also important to know how these quadrants work together.

FIGURE 2-1

▲ The four quadrants of personal finance.

Let's define the quadrants:

1. **Income** is what you *earn*. It is what you bring in from your job or profession and what you receive from other sources. Earned income normally comes from jobs or self-employment, while investment income comes from your asset base. Earned income usually comes in regular intervals—monthly, weekly, twice a month, and so on.
2. **Expenses** are what you *spend*, whether on a regular basis or as one-time expenditures. Virtually any check you write or cash you pay out is some kind of expense. Expenses may also arise out of ownership of assets, such as expenses associated with investment in real estate.
3. **Assets** are items of value that you *own*. Assets can be tangible, such as real estate, personal property, cash, and collectibles. They can also be intangible; these include stocks, bonds, business interests, and other nonphysical assets.
4. **Liabilities** are amounts that you *owe*. Some liabilities are tied directly to assets, such as a mortgage on a home. Other liabilities, like unpaid bills, are tied to expenses. Debt is an accumulated liability resulting

either from an accumulation of assets and the loans used to acquire those assets or from an abundance of expenses and the loans acquired to pay those expenses.

It is important to understand the nature of the income and expense quadrants as compared to the asset and liability quadrants. Income and expense categories measure activity over a specific period of time–a month, three months, and so forth. Asset and liability categories are "snapshots" of specific points in time. It follows, then, that if you wanted to assess your situation at a particular point, you would look at your assets and liabilities. And if you wanted to examine how you've been doing this past month, you would look at your income and expenses.

ESSENTIAL

Once you are aware of what your income, expenses, assets, and liabilities are, you can return to your diagram on an ongoing basis to modify those numbers. For most people, a quarterly examination of the complete financial picture—the quadrants—makes sense.

Assets Minus Liabilities Equals Net Worth

This is the fundamental equation of personal finance. What you're worth financially is *what you own* minus *what you owe*. It doesn't matter what your income is, how many rooms your house has, or how long your boat is. Your financial worth is measured by the value of those assets minus the money owed to purchase them and sustain your lifestyle.

Income Minus Expenses Equals Net Cash Flow

This equation determines whether you end up saving or getting into debt. If the net cash flow result is positive, you are saving money. If it is negative, you are in financial difficulty. Cumulative savings become assets, while cumulative debt becomes a liability. We can state this another way: *Income without expenses becomes an asset; expenses without income become a liability.* The easiest way to look at expenses and liabilities in practice is to examine cash flow–that is, what comes in and goes out of your financial household.

Time out for Financial Forensics

Now that you understand what the four personal finance quadrants represent, you can fill them in with your own numbers. It may take a little detective work–something that might be called "financial forensics"–to figure it all out, but once this information is collected, you can then do a quick appraisal of your financial position.

If you don't already have good records, you may have to piece it together and make some educated guesses. Information on assets will come from bank statements, brokerage statements, insurance policies, and so forth. Real estate values require more creativity–you can guess from looking at prices for comparable properties in your area or talking to a realtor. Liability details come from bank and mortgage statements. You can find records of income in your paycheck stubs and list of deposits on your bank statements. Tracking down expenses can be a little more challenging, as many cash transactions have no written record and the sheer number of transactions can be large. As you keep doing it, though, you'll learn to keep good financial records, making the job of evaluating your finances in the future much easier.

Our Typical Family

As you go on to examine your financial position (Appendix A contains blank forms that will help you calculate your assets, liabilities, income, and expenses), you can use some calculations done for a hypothetical household to illustrate these financial concepts.

Don and Susan Stone are a typical suburban couple. They have one son, Sam, who is ten years old. Both Don and Susan work; he is a store manager, and she is a marketing communications specialist. He makes $30,000 a year; she makes $35,000. He is forty-five years old, she is forty-two. They own their home, which they bought last year with a thirty-year mortgage. The house was new at the time of purchase and required landscaping, decorating, and furnishing. Don and Susan own two cars, valued at approximately $15,000 and $5,000, respectively.

First, you will examine your net worth (assets minus liabilities), and then you will go on to examine cash flow (income minus expenses).

Calculating Net Worth

Net worth is the basic measurement of financial situation, financial success, and goal potential. Aside from providing a base point for developing a financial plan and a budget, knowing your net worth brings to light financial problems, suggests changes, and can even help with things like getting proper insurance coverage. Finally, it just feels good for most of us to be able to measure our achievement.

And yet very few Americans actually know their net worth number. Why? Because it takes some effort to calculate. You don't get a monthly or weekly summary statement. You have many different types of assets and liabilities, and many different banks and financial service companies may hold your assets or debts.

First, Let's Examine Assets

Assets may be broken down into four categories: non-retirement financial assets, retirement assets, real property (which includes real estate, collectibles, jewelry, cars, and other possessions), and business interests. Within each category, there are a number of specific line items. Some values, such as personal property, can be educated guesses (such as the value of your cars or coin collection), but if you can get precise data, that's so much the better. Remember that assets represent what you own, regardless of how much you owe on them.

FACT

Each asset has different uses and different levels of *liquidity*—the ability and ease with which you can convert an asset into cash. Money in a regular savings account is liquid, while wealth tied up in real estate or collectibles is illiquid. Because of taxes and penalties for cash conversion prior to age fifty-nine-and-a-half, retirement assets are usually considered illiquid. Having sufficient liquid assets to meet unexpected needs is a common financial planning objective.

Let's use the Stone family's finances to illustrate the four categories of assets.

Non-Retirement Assets (NRAs)

Non-retirement financial assets include cash and any other asset that can be readily converted into cash to meet a current need without undue penalty or tax.

FIGURE 2-2

Net Worth Worksheet				
Don & Susan Stone		Date:	1/1/03	
ASSETS				
Non-retirement current assets (NRAs)				
	Cash, checking	$ 1,200		
	Savings, credit union	$ 6,500		
	Securities, brokerage accounts	$ 5,300		
	Mutual funds	$ 14,400		
	Life insurance, cash value	$ 2,000		
	College savings, savings plans	$ -		
	Other	$ -		
	Total NRAs			$ 29,400

▲ Non-retirement financial assets.

Notice that the non-retirement assets worksheet in **FIGURE 2-2** is created for a specific point in time: January 1, 2003. Although there is no need to be devastatingly accurate about the exact hour in which you sat down to figure out your assets, you should keep in mind that this worksheet only shows your assets on a particular day. While absolute precision isn't necessary, glaring omissions and exaggerations are also no good.

Retirement Assets (RAs)

Retirement assets are assets committed to a retirement plan, such as an IRA or a 401(k). **FIGURE 2-3** shows a sample retirement assets worksheet.

FIGURE 2-3

Retirement assets (RAs)				
401(k)			$ 45,000	
IRA(s)			$ 4,000	
Other RAs current value			$ -	
	Total RAs			$ 49,000

▲ Retirement assets.

You should have statements available for most retirement plans. If you have a pension or some other plan in which you don't have a specific account, retrieving the data may be harder but should be available as some form of estimate from your plan administrator.

Real Property

Real property is physical, tangible property. You can touch it, feel it, or stand on (or in) it. For instance, the Stones' real properties include their home, a set of valuable baseball cards (classified as collectibles), and other personal property including two cars, household items, jewelry, and electronics (as shown in **FIGURE 2-4**). The total number of real-property assets may look large for this family, but keep in mind that there is a mortgage as well as installment loan liabilities that will bring the "net" asset value down.

FIGURE 2-4

Real property				
Home			$ 160,000	
Second home			$ -	
Investment property			$ -	
Collectibles			$ 5,000	
Personal property			$ 30,000	
Other				
	Total real property			$ 195,000

▲ Real property.

The tricky part of real property is arriving at fair value. For real estate, you can get a sense from looking at comparable sales or from talking to real estate professionals. For cars, the *Kelley Blue Book* (which is now online at *www.kbb.com*) or another Web site will get you close to an answer. For collectibles, visit eBay.com or another auction site to get estimates for what your particular items may be worth.

ALERT!

Don't fool yourself by misrepresenting the true value of an asset. Just because you paid $20,000 for that car doesn't mean that it's worth $20,000 today. You need to know your car's fair market value—the value at which you would be able to sell your car today.

Business Interests and Other Assets

Business interests reflect your ownership in all of or part of a business. Like real property, it can be hard to evaluate, and may require professional assistance. In our example, Don and Susan have no business interests or other assets, as shown in **FIGURE 2-5**.

FIGURE 2-5

Business interests			$ -	
			$ -	
	Total business interests/other			$ -

▲ Business interests and other assets.

Total Assets

Once you have figured out what your assets are for each category, you can add up the four numbers, arriving at a number that represents your total asset base. In the case of the Stones, their assets amount to $255,400. Again, although it seems like a hefty figure, keep in mind that assets do not equal net worth. However, you can't have wealth without assets, so this family is on the right track so far. The next step is to examine the liabilities.

Financial Liabilities

If assets are the good news, then liabilities are the bad news. Remember, net worth is the number you get when you subtract your liabilities from your assets. Most families have two types of liabilities: current and long-term.

Current liabilities are what you owe now. They are usually due and payable in a relatively short period of time, from thirty days to five years. They are often—but not always—tied to current expenses and depreciating forms of real property, such as cars and furniture.

FIGURE 2-6

Current liabilities		
Credit cards	$ 4,400	
Installment debt (car loans, etc.)	$ 12,400	
Home equity loans/credit lines	$ 7,700	
Student loans	$ -	
Margin loans	$ -	
Other	$ -	
Total current liabilities		$ 24,500

▲ Current liabilities.

The Stone family owns two cars with a combined value of $20,000. As you can see from **FIGURE 2-6**, their installment debt amounts to $12,400. Therefore, the net worth of their cars is $7,600 ($20,000 minus $12,400).

Long-term liabilities are longer than five years and are usually secured (or backed) by an asset you own. Mortgages are the typical long-term liability for most families. According to **FIGURE 2-7**, the Stone family owes $130,000 on their house, a liability that tempers the value of the $160,000 asset value shown in **FIGURE 2-4** (real property assets). That means the net worth of the house is $30,000.

FIGURE 2-7

Long-term liabilities		
Home mortgage	$ 130,000	
Second home mortgage	$ -	
Investment property mortgage	$ -	
Business loan or share	$ -	
Other	$ -	
Total long-term liabilities		$ 130,000

▲ Long-term liabilities.

Putting It Together

Once you figure out what your liabilities are, you can calculate your net worth. For the Stone family, their liabilities of $24,500 (current) plus $130,000 (long-term) add up to $154,500 (total liabilities). Hence, $255,400 (assets) minus $154,500 equal to $100,900 in net worth.

Capturing Cash Flow

Cash flow analysis is designed to capture your income and expenses. Understanding your net cash flow (or net earnings) is critical in determining whether you're building net worth.

The "financial forensics" around calculating cash flow can be particularly tedious. Not all expenses can be easily tracked, and both income and expenses may be irregular. As you conduct your research, it's a good idea to look at a full year's time frame to capture irregularities such as property taxes, owners' or renters' insurance, car repairs, annual dues and subscriptions, medical expenses, and the like. Good financial forensics may even go back a few years to capture better estimates for these items.

E ALERT!

Watch out for irregular income—if you are self-employed or derive income from bonuses or commissions, it's easy to lose sight of the timing and true amount of your income.

Again, we'll use the Stone family's finances as an example and examine their cash flow over a period of one year. As you look at specific worksheets, keep in mind that your personal situation may be simpler, or it may be more complex. In fact, your finances may require a more detailed worksheet, so feel free to add items–it's important to be thorough. Also keep in mind that your income and expenses need to be measured over a specific period, not at one point in time.

Calculating Income

First, let's look at income–any funds brought into the household on a regular or fairly regular basis. Don't worry about large capital gains, inheritance, or insurance settlements here. The focus should be on ordinary sources of income from work, investments, retirement, and other forms of entitlement.

Earned Income

Earned income, which includes regular salary as well as bonuses and commission, is earned through ordinary work for an employer. Other sources of earned income are tips and gratuities. **FIGURE 2-8** demonstrates Don and Susan Stone's earned income during the year 2002.

FIGURE 2-8

Cash Flow Worksheet			Year:
Don & Susan Stone			2002
			TOTAL
Income			
Earned income			
	Salary, wages (regular)		$ 65,000
	Bonuses, commissions (irregular)		$ -
	Tips		$ -
	Other		$ -
		Total earned income	$ 65,000

▲ Earned income.

Self-Employment Income

If you are self-employed—on either part-time or full-time basis—make sure *that* income is included. Whether you own a construction company or make beeswax candles on the side, this is important. Income from tenants (if you are a landlord) as well as royalties should be treated as self-employment income.

Note that the amount here should really be net income, that is, income after all expenses involved in producing that income are subtracted.

FIGURE 2-9

Self-employment income		
Own business	$	-
Freelance income	$	1,000
Income from partnerships	$	-
Rental income	$	-
Royalties	$	-
Other	$	-
Total SE income	$	1,000

▲ Self-employment income.

Investment Income

Investment income is any cash flow received from bank and securities investments, typically as interest or dividends, or as irregular capital gain distributions found with mutual funds. Again, remember that the investment income figures that appear in **FIGURE 2-10** represent the annual investment income of the Stone family.

FIGURE 2-10

Investment income		
Interest	$	700
Dividends	$	1,400
Capital gain distributions	$	500
Other		
Total investment income	$	2,600

▲ Investment income.

Retirement and Other Income

This section can help you track income received from Social Security or retirement benefits, alimony or child support, or any other type of income you have not yet accounted for. As **FIGURE 2-11** shows, the Stones are a young family and do not have any income that would apply here.

FIGURE 2-11

Retirement income & other	
Social security	$ -
Pension	$ -
Income from other retirement plans	$ -
Alimony	$ -
Child support	$ -
Family trust(s)	$ -
Disability or other insurance	$ -
Other	$ -
Total retirement/other	$ -

▲ Retirement and other income.

Total Income

Adding up earned, self-employment, investment, and retirement/other income will give you the amount of your total income. The Stones' total annual income is $68,600.

At this point, also consider doing a breakdown of your income month by month. It might be valuable for you to examine your income in more detail and to see whether that number fluctuates during particular months.

Calculating Your Expenses

Expenses are cash outflows, the money you spend and that leaves your household. As you figure out what your expenses are, try to capture the reasons why you have these expenses.

You can break down your expenses into four categories: obligations, necessities, discretionary expenses, and "small stuff."

Obligations

Obligations are expenses that must be paid regularly without fail or with severe penalty for omission. Most obligations are contractual. They include mortgages, rent payments, insurance premiums, utility bills, and taxes. There is little you can do, outside of a major lifestyle change, to alter or control your obligations. They must be paid.

These line items are fairly self-explanatory, but they will still take some work to collect. The largest expense for most households is the house payment itself, whether that means rent or a mortgage (see **FIGURE 2-12**).

FIGURE 2-12

Obligations (fixed)			
Home (mortgage or rent)			$ 10,800
Installment loans			
	Car loans		$ 1,600
Student loan payments			$ -
Other loan payments (not credit cards)			$ -
Credit card interest			$ 720
Household operation			
	Utilities		
		Energy	$ 1,200
		Telecom	$ 800
		Water/sewer/disp	$ 440
	Insurance premiums		
		Auto	$ 1,100
		Life	$ 540
		Home/renters	$ 500
		Health/dental	$ 480
		Disability/LTC	$ -
	Taxes		
		Federal	$ 6,000
		State	$ 800
		Property	$ 2,200
		Vehicle	$ 400
		Self-employment	$ -
		Other	$ -
Dues, owners' association			$ 600
Other			
	Total obligations		$ 28,180

▲ Obligations.

FIGURE 2-13

Necessities (manageable)				
Food			$	5,200
Clothing			$	1,500
Transportation				
	Auto			
		Gas	$	900
		Maintenance/repair	$	1,500
		Parking, tolls	$	400
	Non-auto			
		Fares	$	-
		Other	$	-
Household				
	Maintenance, repair		$	2,400
	Home improvement		$	2,000
	Furnishings, fixtures		$	600
	Garden		$	500
	Supplies		$	800
	Other		$	2,000
Child care & tuition				
	Day care		$	3,600
	Tuition		$	1,300
	Summer school/camp		$	1,200
	Babysitting		$	300
Financial/professional services				
	Accountant		$	150
	Legal		$	-
	Bank fees, etc		$	250
	Other		$	-
Medical care (not covered by insurance)				
	Co-pays		$	180
	Dental		$	700
	Eyeglasses,contacts, etc.		$	600
	Other		$	-
Personal care				
	Haircuts, styling		$	600
	Cosmetics		$	400
	Other personal care		$	300
	Total necessities		$	27,380

▲ Necessities.

QUESTION?

Why isn't credit card debt an obligation?
Simply because credit card debt isn't an expense! It's a liability. For the purpose of understanding your finances, it's okay to track interest costs as an "obligation," but to see what's really going on, we need to look at the expense that caused the debt.

Necessities

These expenses are necessary for life and the standard of living you choose. However, they are not obligatory because you have some control over what you spend. Food is a good example. Every individual and family needs food, but you can practice discretion in terms of what kind of food you buy and where you buy it. Careful shopping can save money, so your food expenses can be controlled, though not eliminated.

FIGURE 2-13 on page 31 shows the necessary expenses of the Stone family. Depending on your situation, you may not have some of these expenses—and you may have many others.

FIGURE 2-14

Discretionary		
Recreation and entertainment		
	Health, other clubs	$ -
	Restaurants	$ 2,500
	Subscriptions	$ 200
	Other/miscellaneous	$ 600
Recreational equipment		
	Purchase	$ 500
	Maintenance/upkeep	$ 1,000
	Supplies	$ 350
Travel and vacations		$ 3,100
Charitable contributions, incl. church		$ 900
Other		$ -
	Total discretionary	$ 9,150

▲ Discretionary expenses.

Discretionary Expenses

Discretionary expenses are a matter of choice. In fact, it's possible to have no discretionary expenses at all. For most people, entertainment, recreation, and travel are discretionary—even if they refuse to believe so themselves!

Small Stuff

These include small purchases that may be obligatory, necessary, or "extra" and that are too small to track individually. You can go nuts trying to keep track of every coffee or Coke you've ever purchased. The idea is to estimate the total amount you spend on the small stuff and budget accordingly. Another option is to label these your "ATM" expenses.

FIGURE 2-15

Small stuff				
		Meals at work	$	1,500
		Small family expenses	$	1,200
		Small individual expenses	$	1,600
		Total small stuff	$	4,300

▲ Small stuff.

And Now, Ring up the Total

Adding up the expense items and combining the result with your total income produces net income, or cash flow. In the case of the Stone family, their total annual expenses are $69,010. If you subtract these expenses from the income of $68,600, the resulting number—their net earnings or cash flow—is actually in the negative of $410. This isn't too bad, especially if there had been unforeseen expenses to take care of, but if the family's cash flow doesn't increase, eventually debts are likely to pile up.

A Time of Reckoning

At this point, you should have a better picture of your financial personality. Likewise, you should now have a more detailed, objective accounting of your situation. You know your net worth and cash flows. You know the key components that drive those important totals—the "quadrants"—of your personal finances. Knowing these details is a good investment in itself, with a "return" that will become more apparent as you read the rest of this book. In the next chapter, you'll learn how to interpret some of this information and use it to start setting personal financial goals.

It is important to be as honest as possible in assessing your assets, liabilities, income, and expenses. Cheating on the value of your assets, omitting expenses, overestimating income, or sweeping debts under the rug will do you no good. This exercise isn't for someone else—it's for *you*.

Chapter 3

E The State of Your Financial Affairs

You've collected your financial data. You know your net worth and your net cash flow. Now, what are these indicators telling you? Are there areas that need your urgent attention? Are there other areas where you've done a good job and deserve a pat on the back? Are you on a wealth-accumulation track? This chapter will help you form some conclusions in regards to your financial state of affairs.

Just the Facts, Ma'am

You're about to compare important indicators of your financial position against a set of good-practice standards used by many financial planners. But before you can do this exercise, it's a good idea to bring forward the important numbers from your appraisal done in Chapter 2. Again, let's use the Stone family as an example. **FIGURE 3-1** illustrates the summary of their finances, as they have been presented in the previous chapter.

We know that the Stone family has a net worth of nearly $120,000. According to their 2002 cash flow number, they are not currently building up their net worth—in fact, they are depleting it just slightly to the tune of $410 each year. What else should we look for?

Making the Financial Grade

This chapter will allow you to grade yourself on the way you handle your finances. As with any large set of numbers, you can look at your financial analysis and dissect it until the proverbial cows come home. There is no one way to do it; in fact, it's doubtful that any two financial planners would grade anyone's finances the same way. However, there are a few basic themes or subjects that you should examine and evaluate. This chapter provides one way of analyzing your financial data using the following points of evaluation:

- **Amount of wealth:** It should be no surprise that the amount of wealth you have is important. However, it is even more important that your wealth matches your income. Ask yourself: Is your wealth consistent with your earning ability and your lifestyle? If you make $1 million each year but you have a net worth of only $100,000, something in your finances is not working right. If, on the other hand, you have accumulated the same $100,000 on an annual income of $20,000 and you're only thirty years old, clearly you are doing well.
- **Quality of wealth:** The quality of wealth is the form in which your wealth exists. Cash in the bank is usually "better" wealth than cars or other personal properties that quickly depreciate (lose their market value). Furthermore, you don't want all your wealth to be tied up in the same thing, so the best option is to have a mix of different forms of wealth.

FIGURE 3-1

Financial Summary				Net worth
Don & Susan Stone				1/1/03
				Net Cash Flow
				2002
Assets				
	Non-retirement assets (NRAs)			$ 29,400
	Retirement assets			$ 49,000
	Real property			$ 195,000
		Home	160,000	
		Collectibles	5,000	
		Personal property	30,000	
		Total ASSETS		$ 273,400
Liabilities				
	Current liabilities			$ 24,500
	Long-term liabilities			$ 130,000
		Total LIABILITIES		$ 154,500
NET WORTH				$ 118,900
Income				
	Earned income			$ 65,000
	Self employment income			$ 1,000
	Investment income			$ 2,600
		Total INCOME		$ 68,600
Expenses				
	Obligations			$ 28,180
		Debt service	13,120	$ -
	Necessities			$ 27,380
	Discretionary			$ 9,150
	Small Stuff			$ 4,300
		Total EXPENSES		$ 69,010
NET INCOME (CASH FLOW)				$ (410)

▲ Summary of Stone family finances.

- **Debt:** Debt is debt—it never goes away. It must be paid off someday; without proper attention or resources, it can get out of control. Debt is expensive and can breed more debt.
- **Adequate reserves:** A good financial standing should give you the ability to meet emergencies, honor major commitments like your

child's college tuition payments, and prepare for retirement. If wealth isn't sufficient to provide these reserves, it's time to make some improvements.

- **Wealth accumulation rate:** You also need to examine how much wealth you are accumulating. If there is no "inflow" to your wealth base, adjustments may be necessary.
- **Wealth return rate:** If the wealth base you have isn't producing investment returns in its own right, it isn't "pulling its weight." Some adjustments may be needed.

Amount of Wealth

At the end of the day, the amount of wealth you have should be proportional to your income. The amount you do have depends on your particular situation as well as on your financial habits. Although people's wealth is usually dictated more by their habits than by their financial contingencies, it is also true that long-term illness, disability, layoffs, and dependent elderly parents can have a great effect on the state of your wealth.

QUESTION?

What if I have negative net worth?
You cannot meet your financial goals if you have more liabilities than assets; worse, if you don't change your financial standing soon, you could end up going bankrupt. Any individual or family with a sound financial persona and a minimum of good luck should have a positive net worth.

A Wealth Yardstick

Arguably the best tool for measuring wealth available today was provided by Thomas Stanley and William Danko in *The Millionaire Next Door.* According to Stanley and Danko, one study compared wealth (net worth) to income and found that the average household wealth was a function of age and income. Here's the formula they came up with.

Average net worth = (Age × Annual Income) ÷ 10

So for our sample family, the Stones, basing the calculation solely on Mr. Stone's age and on his and his wife's steady wages, expected net worth would be 45 × 65,000 ÷ 10 = $292,500. That is, if they accumulated wealth at a rate representative of most Americans, that's where they would be. As they have a net worth of $100,900, they are behind, but not out of the race.

Stanley and Danko went on to examine the top and bottom of the wealth range, and they came up with two additional wealth standards:

- **Prodigious accumulator of wealth (PAW):** If your net worth is twice the "average wealth" standard for your age and income, you are a PAW. Your wealth is in the top 25 percent of all people in your situation. You deserve an "A."
- **Under-accumulator of wealth (UAW):** The "UAW" has less than half of the average for his or her age and income group. The Stone family falls into the UAW category, though not by much ($100,900 versus $292,500 ÷ 2 or $146,250), so their grade is probably a "D." Note how the Stones' ages influence this calculation.

Quality of Wealth

If your personal balance sheet shows assets and a positive net worth, but those assets have questionable value or cannot be easily converted to cash to meet other needs, you may have a "wealth quality" problem. A closer look at the types of assets you have and the mix of those assets is in order.

Assets That Don't Fly

If many of your assets are tied up in property that may be difficult to sell—or sell at a reasonable price—you may have an asset-quality problem. Some assets—like new cars, RVs, boats (and in some years, securities)—depreciate in value at an incredible rate. Other assets cost more than they are worth in the long run to maintain and/or sell.

FACT

Ideally, personal property—aside from your home, if you own yours—should be no higher than 10 percent of your total net worth or asset base. This area of finances is problematic for the Stone family, which has about 30 percent ($30,000) of their assets in personal property. Furthermore, there are significant liabilities—loans—associated with these assets.

The Right Mix Makes the Cake Rise

As in many facets of life, better results come from "covering all your bases" and "not putting all your eggs in one basket." It makes sense to have a well-rounded asset base. Too much real property can cause liquidity problems (that is, an inability to convert assets quickly to cash) and may drain your cash at the least opportune moments. Too much in retirement assets can cause the same problem—hard to convert without additional expense and penalties. Likewise, too much in current assets (that is, NRAs) may mean too much in more volatile securities investments, low-paying bank deposits, and not enough in tax-favored retirement plans.

Financial planners all have different advice to offer on diversifying your assets. One good idea is to divide net worth into equal thirds among NRAs, RAs, and real property (if you have business property, you'll have to figure out how it will relate to the three other categories). Notice that in calculating real property, you should use the net value of your home, not its total value before the mortgage.

The Stones are doing a pretty good job in diversifying their assets. If you look at their assets, you will see that $26,400 is in NRAs, $34,000 in RAs, and $41,000 is net property ($195,000 minus the debt of $154,500). The distribution is not perfect, but it will do—the Stone family deserves a solid "C." To improve their grade, they should focus on growing NRAs and keep from replacing personal property too hastily.

When It Comes to Debt

In today's world, debt is easy to acquire and sometimes may appear to come cheap. In 2002, interest rates were at a thirty-year low. It may be getting easier to borrow money, but it is never easy to pay it back. Debts drain your income with high interest and even higher late charges. Even worse, it reduces flexibility—your ability to borrow money for more important reasons and to make new purchases.

Debt avoidance is not always possible. Mortgages make sense for most people and college loans can make sense for a lot of people. It is easier to borrow for college than for retirement! The key is to try and minimize your debts as much as possible, particularly for unnecessary expenditures.

What's Your Current Ratio?

Both corporate and personal financiers recognize a measure called "current ratio," which is simply the ratio of current assets to current liabilities. Strictly speaking, if the ratio is greater than 1.0, your current assets (in our terms, NRAs or non-retirement assets) are sufficient to cover your current debts (or liabilities). Of course, having a ratio of 2.0 or higher is even better. Just to compare, the Stone family has a current ratio of 1.08 (26,400 ÷ 24,500)—not great, but not a disaster, either.

ALERT!

Be careful not to overlook certain types of debt or debt payments. For certain types of loans, the payment may be "interest only," or a loan may even be devoid of payments, with the "imputed" payment instead being added to the value of the loan. Brokerage margin loans work this way. In a more careful evaluation, you would add the full value of this debt service to the debt-service ratio calculations.

Even if your ratio is high enough, you still need to make sure you have the ability to use your assets to pay off your debts. Which part of your income will "service" them? Calculate your debt service (the portion of money you should apply to paying off your debts) by taking the amount you would have to pay to service all debts (including your mortgage, installment loans, and credit card interest and minimum payments), and dividing that total into your gross income. You should also make a separate debt-service calculation for your mortgage (or your housing cost, if renting). Financial planners use a limit of 28 percent for mortgage debt service and 38 percent for total debt service. If your percentiles are lower, you are in good shape.

In our example, the Stone family is paying a mortgage (principal and interest only) of $10,800 each year, with a total wage income of $65,000. (Using wage income is a more conservative approach because it is a more dependable figure.) Their debt service is thus 17 percent of their income. If you add in the car loans and credit card interest payments, they are still at 20 percent, well within the standards.

ESSENTIAL

Depending on where you live, you may be entitled to a little "grace" on your debt service ratios. In places where housing is particularly expensive, like San Francisco, New York, or Silicon Valley, financial planners would accept 40 or even as much as 50 percent of gross income for the all-inclusive debt service measure.

Adequate Financial Reserves

Different people have different financial situations, and opinions on what it means to have adequate financial reserves do vary. Still, there are some specific measures you can use to check your financial standing.

Your Emergency Vehicle

One way of assessing your financial health is to imagine yourself losing all your income and then calculating how long it would take until you used up all your resources. This approach measures how much of your wealth you can rely on in an emergency by figuring out the emergency fund ratio (EFR).

Calculating your EFR is simple: All you need to do is divide your current liquid assets by your monthly nondiscretionary expenses. Current liquid assets are represented by your NRAs, while monthly nondiscretionary expenses show up in your cash flow statement as obligations and necessities. The Stone family has $26,400 in NRAs, $28,180 worth of annual obligations, and $27,380 worth of annual necessities. To get the monthly nondiscretionary expenses, add up the annual obligations and necessities and divide by 12 (for months in the year): $28,180 + $27,380 = $55,560; $55,560 ÷ 12 = $4,630. To calculate the Stone family's EFR, divide $4,630 into $26,400; the result is 5.7, the number of months that this family can survive without any additional income.

QUESTION?

What is a reasonable emergency fund?
Many financial planners like to see at least six months of expenses in a current asset base for a mature household. For a household just starting out, three months is a good goal.

Off to College?

If you are a parent, you probably want your kids to have a bright future, and one way you can help your kids start out their lives right is by making sure they receive a good education. Although it may be years before your children grow up and are ready to head off to college, you need to start preparing financially well in advance.

You need to know in advance how you will come up with the money to pay for your children's college tuition as well as other educational expenses. The best option is to rely on your non-retirement assets. Although it's tempting—especially for older parents—to tap retirement assets to fund college, financial planners like to remind people that they can borrow to pay the college tuition, but there is no such thing as a retirement loan. If at all possible, plan to keep your retirement assets intact. And what about personal property? Some parents may sell their house and "downsize," but this is a difficult choice and often not a practical solution.

ESSENTIAL

How much you need to save depends on a lot of factors—what school your children will attend (and whether it's public or private), whether they will earn scholarships or qualify for other financial aid, and whether there are other people (grandparents, for instance) who will help you with educational expenses.

Your financial planning will of course depend on how many kids you have, when you expect them to begin their college education, and what type of education you are prepared to pay for. Just to give an example, suppose you need $40,000 to pay for your daughter's college education ten years from now. Without getting into the details, let's assume that with a 5 percent annual return on investments, you need to invest just over $24,500 today to have $40,000 in ten years. Does the Stone family have that sum ready for their child to go to college in ten years? Yes—but only if you include their emergency funds into that figure. If they get lucky and never need the emergency funds, they should be fine, and their son should be able to go off to college. But should they experience any financial trouble, their son's education will be jeopardized.

You may have noticed that the financial assessment and planning process used here focuses on *needs*. Smart personal finance means evaluating your financial needs first and then looking for the products (insurance, investment plans, and so forth) to fulfill them.

Preparing for Retirement

Preparations for retirement vary dramatically from person to person, and the options will be explored in greater detail in Chapter 20. Evaluate your retirement plans in terms of your financial preparedness. Let's use the Stone family's example to illustrate what you need to consider. The Stones have at least twenty years to go before retirement. They expect to live for at least twenty years after they retire on 80 percent of their current income. If you assume an 8 percent return before retirement and a 5 percent return in a more conservatively invested "during-retirement" portfolio, they would need $104,000 (including Social Security) in current retirement savings. Right now, the Stones only have $34,000 in retirement assets (RAs). That means they are falling short of their retirement expectations. They need to increase their retirement savings and investment returns, and they should perhaps reduce their retirement expectations as well.

Wealth Accumulation Rate

Wealth accumulation rate (WAR) is a fancy term that represents the rate at which you increase your savings by setting aside a portion of your income to build your net worth. If you're making $50,000 a year, and you manage to put $10,000 away into your retirement savings plan and NRAs, you have an excellent wealth accumulation rate of 20 percent. Most financial planners recommend the initial goal of 10 percent, with an ideal WAR of 20 percent. And there are families with a much higher WAR—in the 40 to 50 percent range.

The Stone family's net cash flow is in the negative (by $410), so they aren't putting any money away. Evidently the Stones were better at one time—they did manage to accumulate $34,000 of retirement savings, even though they are currently not making any contributions to their retirement accounts.

ESSENTIAL

Although your financial situation may be complicated, you need to try and make sense of as much as you can, and then act to maintain your successes and try and improve your shortcomings. Don't punish yourself for "failures"; very few people have finances that are in perfect standing.

Wealth Return Rate

As the popular expression goes, nothing ventured, nothing gained. If you have investment assets (whether they are NRAs, RAs, or even real property), you should be receiving returns on them. Assets invested productively should give you interest, dividends, or growth of capital (often represented as "capital gains").

Why is this so important? It's important because many longer-term goals, such as retirement or the ability to pay college tuition, require not only a committed influx of funds but also a growth of those funds through productive investment. Financially conscious individuals should measure these returns and see if their investments are up to snuff.

The acceptable rate of return depends in part on your risk profile—what risks you are willing to take. Today, an 8 percent return on average risk investments would be considered quite good. Conservative investors would expect 5 percent, and more aggressive investors would expect a return of 10 percent. Aside from risk, acceptable returns also depend on the investment (or market) climate.

The Stones' financial worksheet didn't give a complete breakdown of all investment returns. We don't know what they earned in their retirement account. But on the NRA portion of their financials, they managed to earn $2,600 combined interest, dividends, and capital gains on a base of $26,400—a rate of return of almost 10 percent.

The More You Know

When exploring complex topics, it's easy to throw your arms up into the air and exclaim, "The more you know, the more you *don't* know." And it's true—every avenue explored has a few side streets, an alley or two, that will require further exploration. It's easy to lose yourself on those small streets and alleys. You think, if only I cut down on those mocha lattes, I can save $2.50 each day! And you work so hard on eliminating those little expenses that you forget about that $800 weekend getaway or maintaining your car in good condition so that you can drive it for a few extra years and avoid the expense of buying a new one. And avoiding coffee may arguably improve your health, but it won't help you when it's time to retire and you discover that you don't have a retirement income.

Instead of worrying about the details, consider making a gradual shift in your lifestyle. Think about becoming more financially responsible and keeping your eye on the larger, longer-term goals, rather than obsessing over buying the latest gadget.

Chapter 4

A Small Dose of Personal Finance Math

Certain aspects of personal finance require understanding of a few very specific and highly applicable mathematical principles. You don't need fluency in calculus or statistics to take control of your finances. Sure, you can run your own calculations, but there are also tools that can help you—the point is that you should be able to understand the principles behind the calculations. In this chapter, you'll learn about taxes, inflation, and the time value of money, as well as a few easy ways to apply these principles.

Inflation: Depreciation of Currency

Inflation could be defined as the erosion in the purchase value of currency. Inflation renders each dollar (or whichever currency you use) less valuable—it purchases fewer goods and services than it did before. Does this affect your personal finances? It does, but not so much as you might think—if it is slow, steady, and predictable.

Inflation means prices go up over time. If you have long-term goals, such as college and retirement, that sounds ominous—what will that trip to Paris cost twenty years from now, anyway? What makes it less of a concern is that, as a wage earner, your wages—the "price" paid for your labor—should also go up to keep pace. Will you lose buying power? Unless you work for a government, nonprofit, or other concern that is forced to freeze wages due to hardship or publicity, you shouldn't lose too much buying power. Where's the problem, then? It is where you are relying on economic wealth or income supplied *other than* by wages. Here is where inflation affects you the most:

- **Money assets:** If your assets are in the form of cash or are based on the dollar, you are exposed to declines in dollar value. If you had $10,000 in the bank, and next year's inflation rate turned out to be 5 percent, at the end of next year you would have about $9,500 in equivalent purchasing power.
- **Return rate:** If you are counting on an 8 percent growth in your asset base, and inflation is 3 percent, you must earn an 11 percent rate of return, in dollars, to achieve an 8 percent real growth. Otherwise, your wealth won't buy you as much in the future as you were counting on. When projecting the growth of your assets, you must always adjust for inflation and keep in mind both a "before inflation" and an "after inflation" figure.
- **Interest rates:** Interest rates are driven in part by inflation and in part by *expectations* of inflation. That is, if inflation is at 10 percent, a person lending you money would expect to get a "real" return on their money, plus an adjustment for the inflation that occurred while their precious dollars depreciated in your hands. So even the best interest rates at that time might be 14 or 15 percent. Does that affect

your personal finances? You bet. You need to keep track of inflation, because that may tell you which way interest rates are heading.

ESSENTIAL

You don't need to worry a great deal about inflation unless you have significant dollar assets, are counting heavily on future investment returns, or are concerned about future interest rates. But you should always keep inflation in mind and be prepared to adjust your figures accordingly.

Taxes—Here to Stay

You've heard it before. People think that if they get a raise, they'll just lose that difference to taxes. Or they think they can spend more money because they can write it off. Those thoughts are true–to an extent. You will get those tax deductions from a mortgage and you will pay more taxes if you get a raise, but it's not a one-to-one ratio. You don't get taxed a dollar on every dollar earned, nor do you save a dollar of taxes on every dollar spent.

The trick is to always be aware of the residual left over after taxes are paid. And that's where the formula (1 – t) comes in. This simple formula, where "t" equals the total marginal tax rate, allows you to figure out how much of your income will be left after income taxes. All you need to do is multiply the amount of money to be taxed by (1 – t) where "t" is the marginal (that is, highest applicable) tax rate.

Suppose the marginal tax rate (t) is 35 percent. What does that mean? Well, at that rate, for every new dollar you earn, you will lose 35 cents to taxes. Let's say you get a $1,000 raise. To figure taxes on that amount of money at this tax rate, use the formula like so: 1 – .35 = .65; multiply .65 by the amount of your raise, $1,000, and you find that after taxes, you are only getting $650. Likewise, for every dollar you spend on a deductible expense, you will reduce your taxes by 35 cents, so if you spend $1,000 a month on deductible home-mortgage interest, the real cost of that mortgage to you is $650 a month.

Federal and State Taxes

How did we arrive at a total "t" of 35 percent? For a majority of readers, the federal marginal tax rate (as of 2002) is 27 percent; that is, every incremental taxable dollar is taxed to the tune of 27 cents. Many of you also have state and local income taxes, which would account for an additional 5 to 10 percent. You can figure your federal and state/local tax total like this. Let's say your state/local tax rate is 10 percent. To figure your total tax rate, subtract 10 percent of the federal tax rate from the rate itself: 27 – 2.7 = 24.3. Add the state/local rate, and we arrive at a full t = 34.3 percent (24.3 + 10 = 34.3).

E ALERT!

Note that the marginal tax rate (t) changes as you move up the income ladder. Income taxes are progressive—rates go up as income levels rise. If you earn (or expect to earn) $300,000 next year, your total marginal tax rate will be far higher than 27 percent—perhaps as high as 45 or 50 percent, depending on what state you live in.

The Time Value of Money

Money has time value. A dollar in your possession today isn't worth the same as a dollar you may get tomorrow, next month, next year, or twenty years from now. Why? First, the dollar you have today allows you to do something or buy something *today*. Right now. And for most of us, not having to wait translates to value. Secondly, as just explored, inflation will reduce the purchasing power of the future dollar.

A person lending us money to use today is giving up his/her right to use it today, and wants compensation for that. What do we call that? Interest. *Interest* is a time-based fee or price paid for the use of money. As time goes on, interest payments accumulate with an investment. At the end of that period of time, the interest accumulated represents the value received for time committed to the investment. A sum invested today will retrieve the original investment *plus* the interest accumulated at the end of the time period. If you need a sum of money twenty years from now, you need only invest a smaller sum of money today, and let the interest received build up to the desired twenty-year total.

Value—Present and Future

Suppose you have $1 today. You invest it at an annual rate of return (let's say, from interest) of 10 percent. After one year, you will have $1.10 (original investment plus 10 percent of that investment). At the beginning of year two, the entire $1.10 is invested, still at 10 percent. So at the end of year two, you will have $1.21 ($1.10 + 10 percent of $1.10). And so forth. If you're standing here at Day One looking forward, the original $1 is your *present value*, and the $1.21 is the *future value* at the end of two years.

The principle of *compounding* is one of the most important principles in both personal and business finance. Compounding was just illustrated: a sum of money $1 received a percentage return (10 percent) in the first year. The entire balance was left for another year, still at 10 percent, receiving the return not only on original principal but on last year's interest, too. Each year's golden eggs become part of the next year's goose, which in turn lays *still more* golden eggs. And after a number of years and with a good rate of return or "yield," that flock of geese can become quite large.

Bringing the Future Back to the Present

In the previous example, a present value of $1 was invested and allowed to compound into a future value of $1.21 in two years at a rate of 10 percent. But what if all we need is $1, two years from now? What if $1 is our down-the-road objective?

Simply, we need to calculate what amount of money, if *invested today*, would *compound to* $1 two years from now. That figure will be obviously less than $1 (it'll be 82.6 cents, if you want to be exact).

Why would we need such a figure? Suppose we decide we need $500,000 to retire twenty years from now. What amount would we have to have today to reach that goal? It's the same principle–what number, if invested at 10 percent (or whatever rate you want) would become half a million twenty years from now? For those wanting an answer, it is $74,500. Yes, a mere $74,500 invested at 10 percent for twenty years would indeed become half a million, without a dime additional being added. Is this interesting? You bet. It illustrates both the time value of money and the incredible power of compounding. What follows is a deeper dive into the world of compounding and some quick tools to help you evaluate and harness its power.

Here is the basic formula for calculating the future value of money:

$$FV = PV \times (1 + i)^n$$

FV = future value
PV = present value
i = interest rate
n = number of years

Now you have a better understanding of time value of money, and how the present and future values of money are related. However, you don't actually have to do the calculations yourself every time. All you need to do is learn how to use the tables provided for you here in this book.

ESSENTIAL

Another option is to use a financial calculator. Hewlett-Packard's HP-12C is the venerable favorite among finance professionals. Just enter your data, and the HP-12C calculates present value, future value, payments, and a variety of other useful financial calculations.

Calculating Future Value

You can use **FIGURE 4-1** to figure out the future value of money at a particular interest rate and over a particular time period. The values presented here are for every dollar invested. So let's take an example and say that you would like to invest $10,000 for twenty years at a 6 percent interest rate.

FIGURE 4-1

Interest Rate % / Number of Years	1	2	5	10	15	20	30	40
4.0%	$ 1.04	$ 1.08	$ 1.22	$ 1.48	$ 1.80	$ 2.19	$ 3.24	$ 4.80
5.0%	$ 1.05	$ 1.10	$ 1.28	$ 1.63	$ 2.08	$ 2.65	$ 4.32	$ 7.04
6.0%	$ 1.06	$ 1.12	$ 1.34	$ 1.79	$ 2.40	$ 3.21	$ 5.74	$ 10.29
7.0%	$ 1.07	$ 1.14	$ 1.40	$ 1.97	$ 2.76	$ 3.87	$ 7.61	$ 14.97
8.0%	$ 1.08	$ 1.17	$ 1.47	$ 2.16	$ 3.17	$ 4.66	$ 10.06	$ 21.72
9.0%	$ 1.09	$ 1.19	$ 1.54	$ 2.37	$ 3.64	$ 5.60	$ 13.27	$ 31.41
10.0%	$ 1.10	$ 1.21	$ 1.61	$ 2.59	$ 4.18	$ 6.73	$ 17.45	$ 45.26
12.0%	$ 1.12	$ 1.25	$ 1.76	$ 3.11	$ 5.47	$ 9.65	$ 29.96	$ 93.05
15.0%	$ 1.15	$ 1.32	$ 2.01	$ 4.05	$ 8.14	$ 16.37	$ 66.21	$ 267.86
20.0%	$ 1.20	$ 1.44	$ 2.49	$ 6.19	$ 15.41	$ 38.34	$ 237.38	$ 1,469.77
25.0%	$ 1.25	$ 1.56	$ 3.05	$ 9.31	$ 28.42	$ 86.74	$ 807.79	$ 7,523.16

▲ Calculating future value.

If you look up "6 percent" and "twenty years," you'll get a future-value factor of 3.21. This means that for every dollar you invest at 6 percent, you will get $3.21 at the end of twenty years. To get your answer, all you need to do is multiply the factor by the amount of money you plan to invest: If you multiply 3.21 by $10,000, you end up with $32,100 at the end of twenty years. It's that simple—no special calculators or exponents required.

FACT

Remember Warren Buffett? Through his Berkshire Hathaway insurance and investment conglomerate, he achieved compounded annual returns exceeding 25 percent for forty years. Little wonder he is worth over $30 billion today, and shares of Berkshire Hathaway have appreciated from $10 to more than $70,000 each in that time.

Present Value of a Future Return

Suppose you need a certain sum of money in twenty years; that is, you need a specific future value. How much do you need to deposit today? You can work backwards to the present to figure out the *present value*—the sum you would need to deposit today to achieve that future value. Use the table in **FIGURE 4-2** to determine what to invest.

FIGURE 4-2

Interest Rate % / Number of Years	1	2	5	10	15	20	30	40
4.0%	$ 0.962	$ 0.925	$ 0.822	$ 0.676	$ 0.555	$ 0.456	$ 0.308	$ 0.208
5.0%	$ 0.952	$ 0.907	$ 0.784	$ 0.614	$ 0.481	$ 0.377	$ 0.231	$ 0.142
6.0%	$ 0.943	$ 0.890	$ 0.747	$ 0.558	$ 0.417	$ 0.312	$ 0.174	$ 0.097
7.0%	$ 0.935	$ 0.873	$ 0.713	$ 0.508	$ 0.362	$ 0.258	$ 0.131	$ 0.067
8.0%	$ 0.926	$ 0.857	$ 0.681	$ 0.463	$ 0.315	$ 0.215	$ 0.099	$ 0.046
9.0%	$ 0.917	$ 0.842	$ 0.650	$ 0.422	$ 0.275	$ 0.178	$ 0.075	$ 0.032
10.0%	$ 0.909	$ 0.826	$ 0.621	$ 0.386	$ 0.239	$ 0.149	$ 0.057	$ 0.022
12.0%	$ 0.893	$ 0.797	$ 0.567	$ 0.322	$ 0.183	$ 0.104	$ 0.033	$ 0.011
15.0%	$ 0.870	$ 0.756	$ 0.497	$ 0.247	$ 0.123	$ 0.061	$ 0.015	$ 0.004
20.0%	$ 0.833	$ 0.694	$ 0.402	$ 0.162	$ 0.065	$ 0.026	$ 0.004	$ 0.001
25.0%	$ 0.800	$ 0.640	$ 0.328	$ 0.107	$ 0.035	$ 0.012	$ 0.001	$ 0.000

▲ Calculating present value.

For example, let's say you need $100,000 for a college education. Your son is now three years old, so you have about fifteen years to accumulate that sum of money. How much do you need to invest now if you can get a 9 percent rate of return? According to **FIGURE 4-2**, your factor is 0.275, which means that you need to come up with $27,500 (0.275 × $100,000). As you can see, $27,500 wisely invested today will give you $100,000 to spend on your son's college tuition in just fifteen years.

The Rule of 72

The rule of 72 is a computational shortcut that can help you to estimate time value of money. Divide 72 by the return rate, and you get the number of years it takes for your investment to double. Or divide 72 by the number of years you plan to invest your money, and you get the return rate it would require to double the sum in that number of years. Consider the following examples:

- If the interest rate is 6 percent, your money will double in twelve years (72 ÷ 6 = 12).
- If you need your money to double in nine years, you need to earn an 8 percent return rate to make that happen (72 ÷ 9 = 8).

Accumulation Annuities

Suppose you need $100,000 for college in fifteen years, but what if you don't yet have the $27,500 necessary to invest? In this case, your best alternative is to set aside money over a period of time. This is called an *accumulation annuity*.

FACT

An accumulation annuity is a stream of equal payments over a defined period of time set aside to grow into a lump sum of money. As such, it is a basic model for a savings plan. Accumulation annuity calculations are used to figure out just how much you'll have to save each month or each year to reach a financial goal.

Of course, it means setting aside more than just $27,500, but you will still end up having to save less than the full $100,000. Suppose you save $100 each month for five years. What would you have at the end of five years? You'd have the "original" $6,000, the money you have contributed over the past sixty months. But you would also have earned interest in ever-larger increments as each new $100 bill landed in that account, and interest on the interest. The sum representing the total of payments plus the interest received for the ever-growing balance is an accumulation annuity.

Avoiding the Formula

Although there is a formula to help you calculate how much you would need to invest each month in order to arrive at a particular figure in a specific period of time, it's much easier to use the table in **FIGURE 4-3**.

To go back to the college-education example, let's say that you will need $100,000 in fifteen years and you are willing to choose a relatively aggressive investment plan that will give you an 8 percent return. To calculate how much you will need to contribute each month, you need to look up the factor for 15 years and 8 percent, which happens to be 27.2, and divide your desired sum ($100,000) by that factor. The result is $3,676.47 per year, or about $306 each month.

FIGURE 4-3

Interest Rate %	Number of Years: 1	2	5	10	15	20	30	40
4.0%	1.0	2.0	5.4	12.0	20.0	29.8	56.1	95.0
5.0%	1.0	2.1	5.5	12.6	21.6	33.1	66.4	120.8
6.0%	1.0	2.1	5.6	13.2	23.3	36.8	79.1	154.8
7.0%	1.0	2.1	5.8	13.8	25.1	41.0	94.5	199.6
8.0%	1.0	2.1	5.9	14.5	27.2	45.8	113.3	259.1
10.0%	1.0	2.1	6.1	15.9	31.8	57.3	164.5	442.6
12.0%	1.0	2.1	6.4	17.5	37.3	72.1	241.3	767.1
15.0%	1.0	2.2	6.7	20.3	47.6	102.4	434.7	1779.1
20.0%	1.0	2.2	7.4	26.0	72.0	186.7	1181.9	7343.9

▲ Calculating accumulation annuities.

Suppose you don't want to invest your money as aggressively. If you choose a more conservative investment strategy providing returns of 6 percent per year, your factor would be 23.3. To get $100,000 you would need to invest $4,291.84 per year or about $360 each month. With less risk you get less return, so you have to pull a little more of the sled.

ESSENTIAL

With monthly compounding, your principal earns just a little more than annual compounding. That's because the interest is added to principal every month, instead of at the end of every year. So if you want to save $100,000 in fifteen years, you would need to invest $306 a month for interest compounded annually and $303 a month for interest compounded monthly. These differences get larger at higher interest rates, but the annual approximation is usually good enough.

You can also project future sums based on a current savings level. Suppose you're putting $500 away each month in a mutual fund earning 8 percent. That money is meant to be your retirement fund and you plan to retire thirty years from now. (Thirty years at 8 percent gives you a factor of 113.3.) Now, since you're working toward a particular lump sum, you need to multiply $6,000 ($500 per month × 12 months) by 113.3. The result is $679,800, a healthy sum for retirement.

Distribution Annuities

A distribution annuity works like a pension except that it is set for a definite period. It is a sum of money that is distributed in equal increments (or decrements, to be more precise). You can work forward to figure out how much you could withdraw each month from a sum you already have, or you can work backwards to figure out what you would need to establish as the lump sum in order to receive a desired monthly or annual income stream.

Understanding distribution annuities is useful if you want to pay yourself a supplemental pension when you retire. Suppose you decide that you want to pay yourself—to distribute—$10,000 a year for the next fifteen years. A $10,000 withdrawal will occur at the end of each year; in the meantime, whatever principal is left in your original investment will earn interest (in the following example, let's assume the interest is set at 6 percent). What sum of money would you need to start out with in order to achieve that payout?

To figure it out, simply find the factor for the time value of distribution annuities (from the table shown in **FIGURE 4-4**) at twenty years and 6 percent. Then multiply that figure (11.5) by the expected payout ($10,000) to get the sum that you will need to start out with: $115,000. Invest $115,000 at 6 percent, and you will be able to withdraw $10,000 each year for twenty years. Sounds pretty good, huh? Put in $117,000, and you get $200,000. That's the power of compounding.

FIGURE 4-4

Interest Rate % \ Number of Years	1	2	5	10	15	20	30	40
4.0%	1.0	1.9	4.5	8.1	11.1	13.6	17.3	19.8
5.0%	1.0	1.9	4.3	7.7	10.4	12.5	15.4	17.2
6.0%	0.9	1.8	4.2	7.4	9.7	11.5	13.8	15.0
7.0%	0.9	1.8	4.1	7.0	9.1	10.6	12.4	13.3
8.0%	0.9	1.8	4.0	6.7	8.6	9.8	11.3	11.9
10.0%	0.9	1.7	3.8	6.1	7.6	8.5	9.4	9.8
12.0%	0.9	1.7	3.6	5.7	6.8	7.5	8.1	8.2
15.0%	0.9	1.6	3.4	5.0	5.8	6.3	6.6	6.6
20.0%	0.8	1.5	3.0	4.2	4.7	4.9	5.0	5.0

▲ Calculating distribution annuities.

Now That You've Got What It Takes

You have now seen some of the basic math principles used in financial planning. They aren't too complicated, but they are immensely useful in helping you both to build your goals and to decide on the means to achieve them. You don't need to be able to quote the tables listed in this chapter verbatim, but you should be able to understand the concepts of inflation, compounding, and annuity as well as how they work.

The goals you set in your personal finances, and the means to achieve those goals, become much better defined when you "put the numbers" to them. Once the numbers are in place, you can save, budget, and invest with a clear purpose.

Chapter 5

Budgeting and Reducing Debt

Before building your financial "house," you must have a firm foundation, and that means getting out of debt. Building a budget is a handy tool to defeat the "debt monster." But it also serves well beyond that—a good budget will keep you out of debt and help you start accumulating wealth.

How Do Most People Get into Debt?

Getting into debt is a constant danger. Offers of credit cards with high interest rates swamp our mailboxes. We are flooded with television, radio, and magazine ads that try to convince us to buy expensive goods and services. "No money down, zero interest for six months, then only forty-eight payments of $69.99 per month. . . ." These companies know that it's easy to charge now and worry about paying later. It works, for the national consumer (nonmortgage) debt is a whopping 1.7 trillion dollars, or an astounding $6,742 per person.

FACT

You could argue that our economy runs on debt. If consumers bought only as much as they could afford, our gross domestic product figures wouldn't grow—current purchases wouldn't happen now but out in the future. For the United States, and really for the capitalist world, debt fuels the economy.

Credit—the instrument we use to go into debt—is readily available everywhere. Just go into a department store to buy a bunch of new clothes. Don't have a credit card with that store? A driver's license will do. You fill out a short application, the clerk makes a simple phone call, and—voilà—you have a new credit card and you are ready to spend.

The causes of excessive debt actually go deeper than the ubiquitous availability of credit. How you manage your finances has a lot to do with whether scenarios like the above happen and are allowed to become a habit. Let's explore some more common reasons why people and households get into debt.

Asleep at the Switch

Debt happens when you (or your family members) lose awareness and control and begin to spend freely, without regard to how much debt piles up. The "unaware" person can tell you exactly how much gas costs at ten filling stations close to their house, but if asked to guess their current credit card balances, wouldn't come within a 50 percent range.

Spending to Your Heart's Content

Excessive spending is a big problem for many. We live in a consumer society, and all the temptations are out there–stores, shopping malls, Web sites that let you purchase goods online or participate in auctions, and so forth. Meanwhile, there's another airfare sale to Europe, you find low interest rates for purchasing a new car, and your favorite department store has a special sale to honor yet another holiday. As a result, people continue to buy, often purchasing goods that they don't really need.

Caught by Surprise—Again

Many people have a pretty good grasp of what they make and spend on a regular basis. They can list their expenses, how much they pay for mortgage, utilities, food, gas, day care, and other "small stuff." They make ends meet–most of the time.

But then the air conditioner goes out on the car. Eight hundred dollars later, they're in debt. They start paying that, and then Christmas comes. Did they budget $500 for gifts? Another $200 for cards, parties, and so forth? And how about that wedding present for their niece?

The only way they know for dealing with surprise expenses is to charge them and somehow pay them off later. And charging is not always a bad decision; the problem is that most often these debts don't get paid off in a timely manner, and they incur additional debts.

ALERT!

People in debt lose sight of total costs, and they are inclined to repeat their mistakes. If you have trouble paying off your debts, you need to make a conscious effort not to give in to the temptations that are out there. Keep yourself on the right path with constant reminders of what it will mean to get into debt (like the information in the following section).

Paying the Price for Debt

Debt doesn't come cheap. The two main costs associated with debt are interest and flexibility. Interest is the fee for the use of someone else's money. It is the direct, obvious, and measurable cost of debt. Most lenders charge interest periodically (usually monthly) on the balance owed. Moreover, interest on debt is usually compounded, so that your balance will grow over time.

The second cost of debt, the loss of flexibility and purchasing power, is more conceptual. Your purchasing power could be loosely defined as that which you can buy with funds you have plus funds you can borrow. The availability of debt, or credit, is a resource available to all of us in varying amounts. But once this resource is used, it's gone. Buying power is diminished forever, until the debt is repaid. That isn't a big deal so long as debt is under control, but as the debt burden increases, suddenly you may find yourself unable to purchase things you really do need.

Isn't That Interest-ing?

Many consumers fool themselves into believing that interest doesn't cost much and that interest rates don't matter. But the reality is that even in years with very favorable interest rates, the rates you will end up paying, particularly on "installment" debt, are still quite high. Even when "prime" lending and mortgage rates are in the 6–8 percent range, you are most likely paying at least 10 percent and perhaps as much as 20 or 22 percent for installment debt.

Most credit card and installment lenders "get" you not only with high rates but with low minimum payments too. As a result, you pay a lot of interest, and you pay it for a long time. Once the effect of compounding kicks in, you begin to also pay interest on previous interest. Instead of reducing debt, minimum payments tend to keep balances intact. Worse, if you continue spending, you go further and further into debt.

Suppose you have a $4,000 credit card balance on a card that offers an annual interest rate of 21.5 percent. Nominally, it costs $71.66 each month to "service" (pay) the interest on this balance (21.5 percent ÷ 12 months × $4,000). Your credit card company probably requests a minimum payment of $75, which approximates a fifteen-year payoff. Not bad—that $75 a month fits well into your budget.

But if you stick to that payment—and charge no more, guess how much interest you will pay over the fifteen years as you pay off the original $4,000? A hefty $9,450—over two times the original balance! That's because out of that $75 payment, you're only paying $3.34 toward your debt. The rest of the payment is to cover your interest. If you stick to that $75 payment for just a year, you will end up paying $856 in interest and only $40.51 of the balance. You will still owe $3,959.49 at the end of the year!

The Virtues of Saving

Here is another example to illustrate how hurtful debt is to your financial health. Suppose one family invests $5,000 every year at 8 percent. (Let's ignore tax effects for now—assume the money is invested in a qualified retirement plan.) At the end of thirty years, this family will accumulate $611,729.

FACT

It's possible to have "good credit" and a lot of debt. In fact, the credit-card companies will love to have you as a customer if you charge a lot and conscientiously keep on sending in your minimum payments. Those high interest rates they are charging you are increasing their profits.

Now suppose the family next door went out and spent all their money *plus* charged $5,000 on their credit cards. Suppose the average interest rate offered by their credit cards is 18.9 percent each year, and suppose they made only minimum payments, and on top of that let's suppose they also charged another $5,000 each year to their balance. At the end of thirty years, do you know what their financial situation would be? They would have paid $439,425 in interest (with no tax benefit, since this is ordinary consumer debt). And they would still owe a little less (because of minimum payment portion allocated to principal) than $150,000 as a balance. As illustrated in **FIGURE 5-1**, the net worth divergence between $611,729 in accumulated wealth for the "saver" family and $589,425 in debt and interest for the "spender" family is $1,201,154. In personal finance, style can be everything!

FIGURE 5-1

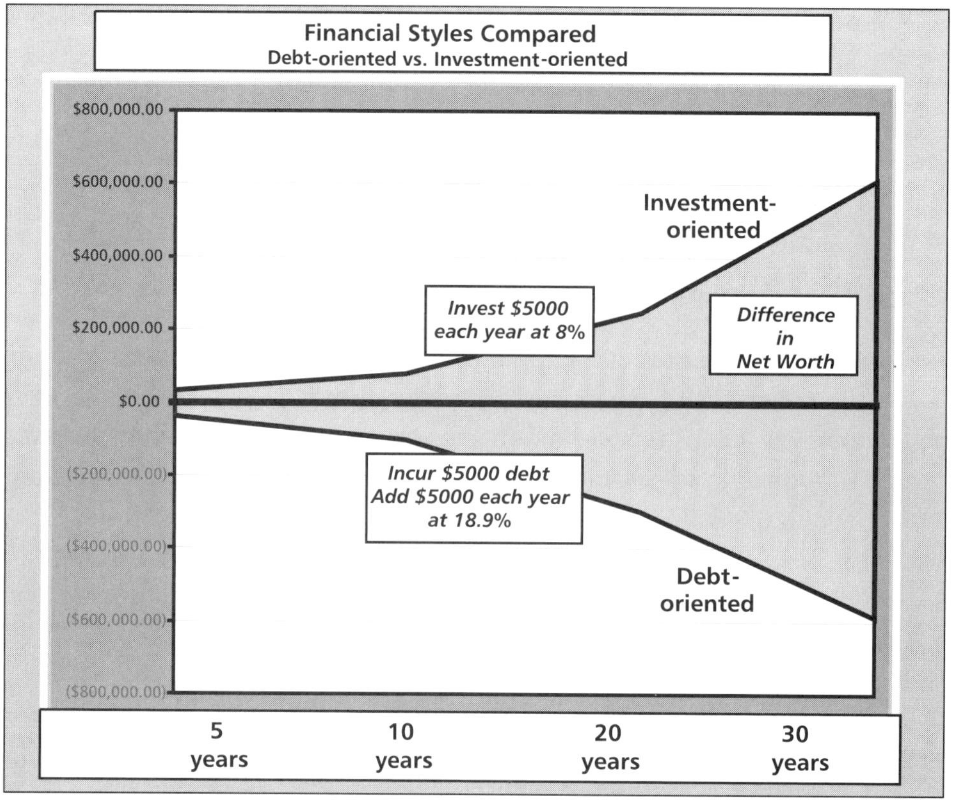

▲ Comparing net worth: investment- versus debt-oriented households.

Not All Debt Is Created Equal

Now that you've got a warning on the kinds of dangers posed by debt, it's time to remind you that not all debt is bad debt. You do need a mortgage to buy your home—your family can't be expected to live in an old trailer or at your parents' house until you save enough money. And sometimes it's useful to rely on a credit card to pay for a necessity, if you know that you will be able to pay off the debt in the near future. So, there is good debt out there. In fact, there are several kinds of good debt that you need to be aware of.

Debt on Buying Long-Term Appreciating Assets

Going into debt to purchase a long-term asset that appreciates in value over time, particularly if the purchase is a necessity, is a sound financial decision. The best example of such debt is taking out a mortgage to purchase a home. Houses generally appreciate in value, and even if they don't, they serve a vital function in your life. However, you should still make sure that the size and cost of the mortgage is reasonable—good debt means finding a home that fits your family's needs, not purchasing the neighborhood mansion. Another example of this type of debt is an educational loan; because education will improve your career options and result in a higher salary, think of your educational debt as an investment in your financial future.

As you can see, good debt is an investment in the future. Although you are in debt now, once you pay it off you will be in a better financial position than you were when you started. People get into trouble with debt when they use it to buy assets that depreciate in value or that don't last as long as the debt does. Borrow $10,000 to buy a speedboat, and the minute you drive it off the lot, you have already lost a percentage of its value. In three years, that speedboat is only worth $5,000. Unless you have already paid off $5,000 of that debt, you are in trouble. (The same is true for buying a new car—although for many people a car is a necessity, not a luxury.)

Timing May Be Everything

If you need something, and it is sold only at certain times of the year (or is sold at a significantly lower price at certain times of the year), you may be justified in going into debt to take advantage of the sales opportunity. Let's say you need a set of patio furniture. Most stores only sell it in the springtime, and you would get the best selection as well as sales incentives. If you know you will be able to pay off this purchase in the upcoming season, it may make sense to go ahead and charge this on your credit card. However, the decision must be made strategically—that is, you must know that now is the best time to buy and that the debt incurred is manageable. If the debt will still be around next spring, your "strategy" probably isn't working.

Secrets to Getting out of Debt

You now know about good debt and bad debt, and you know how much debt can cost. But before building a strategy to stay out of debt, you need to get rid of any existing debt load. There are several commonly used methods to get out of debt. But remember, your strategy for becoming debt-free depends on your particular situation.

ESSENTIAL

Nearly everything goes on sale if you wait long enough. If you need something, and suddenly that 20-percent-off sale comes along, it may be okay to go ahead and purchase it on credit. If you will save more money than you will spend on paying off the debt, getting into debt is reasonable.

Keep Track of Your Cash Flow

The first step to getting out of debt is to know where it comes from in the first place. For a period of time, try to keep track of all expenses and purchases. Each day, write down what you spend and on what. Sooner or later, patterns will emerge. For instance, you might realize that you go to the supermarket for a big shopping trip once a week, but you also drop by the local (more expensive) grocery store three or four times a week for additional food items. Each time you do that, you pay a higher price and probably add an impulse buy or two to the pile.

Think of Money as Money

It's easy to spend, especially if you keep charging expenses and lose track of how much you've actually spent. You don't see the cash, and you don't visualize the wealth it represents. Three hundred dollars seems like more in the form of crisp tens and twenties than it does on a credit card statement. The advice here: Think of every expense as though it were made with cash—and try using cash as much as possible. The next time you want to buy that kitchen gadget, you might decide it's not worth breaking a $100 bill to pay for it.

Don't Borrow to Get Out of Debt

It won't work. It's tempting to consolidate your bills and get a single "low interest" loan to pay them off. Does the debt go away? No. In fact, it usually creeps back and becomes bigger than ever. Those credit cards, now with clean balances, are ripe for new spending. You end up with old debt *plus* new debt.

Build a Budget

Ultimately, in order to combat your debt, you need to have a well-thought-out and accepted budget. A budget can help you put a lid on expenses and allocate income to gradually reduce debt by helping you take control of your finances. Once you succeed in reducing debt, you can continue with your budget plan to grow your savings. Some of the best personal-savings programs emerge from a completed debt reduction strategy.

Living on a Budget

A budget is basically a financial plan to manage incoming funds and outgoing expenses developed and agreed to as a household. Budgets are usually constructed for each month, but they can be set up for longer time periods. A good budget won't necessarily solve all your problems, but it can put you in the position to solve them.

The concept and process of budgeting is often misperceived. Many people think that budgeting means sitting down and planning—and tracking—every expense to the penny. Nothing comes in or goes out without writing something down in a little notebook (or PDA, these days). If you go out with your work friends for Friday afternoon refreshments, you need to go home and transcribe that expense into your budget worksheet. Well, that's not exactly budgeting.

Budgeting, per se, is not an exercise in green-eyeshade personal accounting. It helps to be accurate, but that's not the point. If you had to get to that level of detail, you probably wouldn't do it anyway! That's one of the main sticking points to budgeting in most people's minds—they think it's too much work. Here, the point is to build a plan and construct the big picture—the framework. Then the real point, beyond that, is to agree to that framework, stick to it, and live it through the month. Budgeting is managed spending, not spending detail.

Budgeting 101

Now the good news—you already took the first step toward creating your budget back in Chapter 2, where you had a chance to examine your own financial situation. With that assessment, you categorized your expenses and examined your spending behavior. Now, you can make a plan for each of the following categories:

- **Income**. Your budget needs to fit your income. Make sure to properly assess income, including irregular self-employment income.
- **Obligations.** You can't change these fixed, legal or contractual expenses. But they must become part of your budget. Again, be careful about irregular obligations, like homeowner's and auto insurance.
- **Necessities**. These are the things you need in life, but have some control over their cost through careful planning and shopping.
- **Discretionary expenses**. These are your elective expenses—your "wants"—for things like travel and entertainment. In a moment, we'll break these expenses down into *family* and *personal allowances.*
- **Savings.** Yes, savings are part of a budget, too. In fact, a good budget has a commitment to take a certain amount for savings *off the top*—that is, before other expenses are addressed. It is like making a contract with yourself.
- **Debt:** Large debt balances should receive the same treatment as savings. That is, a certain amount of money is set aside each month to pay off debts. Debt reduction is usually your first priority. Once paid off, it is common to reroute those payments into your savings account.

FALs and PALs

Aside from irregular or excessive obligations and necessities, discretionary expenses are the place where most people—and especially families—get into trouble. These expenses are often impulsive and can easily get out of control. Too many trips to the movies, dinners out, weekend trips, toys for the kids, or after-work refreshments can send the best budget off-track. Unfortunately, most people have no idea how much they spend on discretionary expenses and therefore no way of budgeting for them.

Here is one simple approach that may work for you. Break down your discretionary-expenses category into two subcategories: FALs and PALs.

All in the Family: the FAL or Family Allowance

Set up a family allowance to manage all those expenses related to your family's day-to-day activities. Instead of budgeting $44 each month for movie tickets, $123 for meals out, $15 for kids' toys, $11 for snacks and sodas during road trips, and $1.50 to buy a new box of ping-pong balls, just take care of the whole thing by budgeting, say, $400 a month toward these and similar expenses. Then keep track of how much you as a family have already spent towards this total.

PALs and Other Friends: The Personal Allowance

In addition to a family allowance, each family member should budget for his or her own personal expenses. Each gets his or her own "PAL"—a personal allowance. Basically, this is your "ATM" money, your own petty cash account, covering meals at work, snacks, magazines, newspapers, drinks after work, and other incidentals. Again, the detail isn't important—just set aside $50 each month and stick with it.

ESSENTIAL

One good way to separate "FAL" and "PAL" expenses is to keep two credit cards, one for each allowance. At the end of each month, you can then see how much you spent. If excessive, you can review your plan to avoid making the same mistakes again. (Checking your balance during the course of the month can also be a good idea!)

Sticking to Your Budget

Budgeting isn't simple. Inevitably, there are additional expenses to deal with, extra bills to pay that don't fit into the budget, and many other issues that come up as you first introduce a budget into your life. But budgeting is an ongoing process. You may have to go back and forth through the budget to see what can be "pushed around" to make ends meet. You may have to negotiate and change timing on certain expenses to arrive at a balanced plan with the right amounts in all categories—savings, debt reduction, obligations, necessities, PALs, and FALs. At the end of that exercise, you'll have a better understanding of your financial position, and a plan your household can work with.

In order for your budget to work, it's critical that your entire family agrees with it and helps you keep track of all the major expenses. Once you are used to how your budget works, it is unlikely you'll have to do much sit-down work at the beginning and end of every month. You'll be following your plan by rote, and keeping your expenses under control will require little effort.

As you establish a budgeting contract with your family, here's an idea that may help make it all actually work: A little incentive or payback goes a long way. Good performance should be rewarded! A special gift for each family member, a nice dinner out, a short trip, or a generous holiday gift can all be good rewards for a job well done meeting expense and savings goals.

Chapter 6

How to—and How Not to—Spend

It's been proven over and over: The best way to save is to avoid spending. Read on for some favorite tools to control spending and to spend wisely. If you learn how to manage spending money wisely, you will not only stay out of debt and accumulate wealth, but will also feel better about yourself.

What Are Your Spending Habits?

If there's one thing you take away from this chapter, it should be this idea: It's not what you make, it's what you spend. Your personal financial success—and wealth accumulation—has more to do with how you spend your money than how much you earn. Of course, you're more likely to achieve wealth if you earn $100,000 a year than if you earn $25,000. But the person who earns $100,000 and spends $100,000 is in no better position, financially, than the one who earns and spends $25,000. At the end of the day, success depends on how much of your money you keep (and on how well you grow the money that you keep, as will be discussed in Chapter 9). How much you keep depends on how much you spend. And how much you spend depends on your spending habits: how you decide what you need, how you prioritize these needs, and how you control impulses. Remember that what you don't spend is just as important as what you *do*.

A Few Tenets to Control Spending

The philosophy and practice of spending covers a lot of ground. Before advancing into specifics, here are a few concepts that lead to good spending habits:

- **Spending is about value.** Smart consumers know that focusing on value and quality is more important than worrying about the cost. Long-term thinking is important—you need to be aware that today's bargain could lead to more expenses in the near future.
- **Not spending feels better.** Restraint in spending should make you feel good about yourself. So-called "retail therapy" won't make your problems go away. Only you and your self-control can make a difference in your financial and emotional well-being.
- **Show wisdom, not wealth.** If you want to show off, show off your wisdom, not your wealth. (Remember those old Honda commercials?) Millionaires don't need to prove they are rich—they *are* rich, and they got to where they are through sound financial decisions, not showing off by throwing money away on expensive items.

- **Don't respond to advertising.** Advertising is designed to get you to spend money, and it's your job to be aware of that and not fall prey to its messages. If you're already in the market for a car, by all means, pay attention to ads and look for a good deal. But if a car is not your first priority, there's no reason to visit the dealership, no matter how attractive that car looked or how great the deal sounded.

ESSENTIAL

The truth about luxuries: Small luxuries are okay, particularly if they keep you away from the big ones! Most budgeting books go on and on about that daily cup of coffee, but if that coffee provides you with the social interaction of spending time with your friends at a coffee shop and reduces the urge to go out for lunch or dinner every day, so much the better.

A Rational Approach to Spending

Becoming a total tightwad is not the goal. The idea is not to starve yourself or live in a freezing cold house all winter. Most of your expenses are a normal part of daily living and cannot be avoided. The point is to do a good job managing your expenses, which requires the following essential steps:

1. **Planning your expenses.** Plan your budget, and make sure your expenses don't break your budget's limits.
2. **Developing a buying process.** Figure out the best way of making purchasing decisions that help you acquire the most value for the least cost.
3. **Learning what you can do without.** Also figure out what expenses are unnecessary, and avoid spending money on things you don't really need.

You have already learned about planning your expenses in the section on budgeting in Chapter 5. Here are some suggestions on two other steps toward taking control of your spending.

Where to Shop

Part of developing a buying process is to figure out the best places for making particular purchases. Don't just head to the nearest mall any time you need something. Instead, consider where you could get the same item (or one of equal quality and value) at a lower price.

One such place is a warehouse club (such as Costco or Sam's Club), where you can save money by buying in bulk. But approach warehouse clubs with extreme financial discipline. Make sure you buy only what you need. If you are buying perishable items, make sure that you will use them before the expiration date. Otherwise, consider finding friends or family members to buy items with you and then split them up.

Another option is to make your purchases online. If you get a better discount even after you add on the shipping costs, go ahead and place your order. However, it's no longer wise to assume that products sold online are cheapest—it depends on the situation and supplier. In fact, smart shoppers often use the "bricks and clicks" model—they research products on the Internet and then head to the store to purchase what they've chosen. This model works particularly well when you are purchasing items that would be difficult to return on your own.

Also consider buying used. Internet auction sites—notably eBay.com—have created a marketplace for almost any product you can imagine. And don't forget local consignment shops. They are still around to offer some good old-fashioned bargains.

FACT

Smart buyers learn when they can buy things cheap. Lawnmowers are cheaper in the fall. Gardening supplies get cheaper after the spring planting season. Firewood and heating oil are cheaper in the summer. This applies to services and entertainment as well. If you are planning a family trip to the movies, remember that matinee prices can save a bundle.

The most effective way to shop for the everyday items you generally need (like groceries and bathroom products) is to create a routine. Do a weekly trip to the supermarket in your area that has the best prices, and purchase items you know you will need throughout the week. Make a monthly trip to the warehouse club for supplies you can purchase in bulk, and so forth. Routines help because they get you to the best suppliers available and help you avoid impulse purchases, which almost always happen on "impulse" trips to the store.

Buy Only What You Need

This brings us to another tenet of shopping—buying only what you need. Although this point sounds obvious, buying unnecessary goods is actually a big problem for the average consumer. This point is not limited to buying groceries you will never eat and clothes you won't wear more than once or twice. What about leaving the air conditioner on in your house while you go away for a weekend trip? Or using a full cup of concentrated laundry detergent, even though the whole point of concentrated detergent is that a much smaller quantity will do the same job? And how many people fret and fume about the high price of gas and yet refuse to think for a moment about how to cut down on their mileage and avoid excessive commutes?

The point is not that you should never use your air conditioning or that you must avoid driving at all costs. It's up to you to examine your behaviors and then decide what you really do need and what you can do without. And the need to make these considerations is even greater when it comes to larger purchases. Do you really need to hire a professional landscaper to work on your lawn? Do you really need to renovate your entire house? These are all legitimate questions you need to ask yourself—you may in fact need to hire a professional landscaper if it will save you time that you can use more profitably or if you are planning to sell the house and want it to appear in the best condition possible for prospective buyers. If, on the other hand, you are merely playing catch-up with your neighbors, perhaps that money would be better spent on something else, like paying off your debt or investing in your retirement fund.

To Buy or Not to Buy

You're having a party tomorrow night. Time to clean up the house, the back yard, the patio, the deck—wherever it is you are planning to host the party. You are not looking forward to the cleanup, but then you get a bright idea: Wouldn't it be nice to have one of those pressure washers to blast away the loose dirt and give everything a clean look?

An excellent idea, you think, and drive down to your local home improvement store. It turns out they carry five different models, priced from $400 to $1,300. The little one does five gallons per minute at 1200 psi. The big one does thirteen gallons a minute at 3000 psi. You are bent on buying one of these gizmos, but you can't decide which one you need. And then you remember that splurging on a pressure washer would dry up your family allowance until the end of the month.

When you find yourself in a similar situation, stop and think about your alternatives. What are you really trying to accomplish? If you purchase the pressure washer, how many times will you actually use it? Is the expense worth it? Maybe the best idea is to rent one from a local cleaning company or an equipment-rental supplier. That way you can still clean your house or patio but won't actually have to worry about purchasing a major piece of cleaning equipment, finding a place to store it, or figuring out how to fix it if it breaks down. With most big purchases, you can almost always find a suitable and less expensive alternative—you can fix it, clean it, rent it, do it yourself, or do without it altogether!

Fix It, Clean It, or Rent It

Most obviously, the option to clean applies to cars; you should also consider it when it comes to computers, refrigerators, dishwashers, and other appliances. It hurts to put out $600 to fix that car, but be aware of the alternative: shelling out perhaps $1,500 or $2,000 in sales tax and $500 a year more in insurance costs. When you need to decide whether to fix or replace, evaluate the total costs of each option. Generally, if the repair price for something is less than 40 percent of the replacement cost, it makes sense to fix it, unless other factors dictate otherwise (for instance, technology obsolescence in computers). It usually doesn't make sense to fix a toaster.

Another option is to get a good professional cleaning. Again, cars are the prime example—a good $20 hand wash will make you feel much better about your car. For furniture, appliances, clothes, and even your home, a good professional cleaning job is invariably an excellent investment.

Finally, you have the option of renting, and the pressure washer scenario is an excellent example. Every financially conscious person should make a trip to the local rental yard to see what's available. You'll be amazed at what you can get—and what you can save.

Do It Yourself

Not everyone has the skills and time to build furniture or remodel a house, but whenever you can do something on your own or even work with a professional cooperatively, you can certainly save yourself a bundle. If you can rebuild an engine, reface or refinish kitchen cabinets, install your own lawn irrigation system, build your own patio or deck, or make your own clothes, you can come out light years ahead, both financially and motivationally. It's amazing how, if you do your own home improvements, the house starts to look like it's really yours, and you're less likely to pick up and move.

ESSENTIAL

> Ask yourself: Can I do without it altogether? It may be hard to admit, but there are many things you don't actually need. Maybe last year's dress or suit will do just fine for the upcoming business conference. Maybe you don't need a car because you live near public transportation. These decisions need to be made every day in light of your financial situation and objectives.

Six Things You Should Never Buy

There are situations where you can justify buying almost anything—and really, if all your financial objectives are met with certainty, why not? But this isn't the case with most people. The items in the following list should be prohibitive to all but those who are most successful with their personal finances. These items are expensive and have considerable maintenance and upkeep costs that consumers often ignore.

1. **Pleasure boats.** Boaters joke that the happiest two days in owning a boat are the day you buy it and the day you sell it. True, boats can be a lot of fun and a great way to entertain friends and family. But they are expensive, they retain little of their value, and they require lots of spending—you need to consider upkeep costs, storage fees, dock fees, fuel costs, insurance, licenses, and the cost of providing entertainment for your friends, who will all want to visit you on your boat. A boat is a "hole in the water into which you pour money." It will almost invariably destroy a good financial plan.
2. **RVs.** Although it makes a little more sense to purchase an RV than it does to purchase a boat—they can save on travel costs—it is nevertheless an unwise investment. If you think about it, you could stay in first-class hotels every vacation day for the rest of your life on what it would cost you to purchase and maintain an RV.
3. **Vacation homes.** Again, purchasing a vacation home makes no financial sense—you can use that money to stay at resort hotels of your choice, and you don't need to go to the same place every time. The only exception is to think of your vacation home as a real estate investment. The key to making this decision is to know why you're buying and what the costs and benefits are.
4. **Timeshare units.** It is never a good idea to buy a timeshare. Again, it's better to stay in a hotel. Timeshares are a very expensive way of subdividing a fixed property by time. Suppose you buy one week of a "one-bedroom timeshare" (usually a remodeled motel room) for $10,000. Sounds like a bargain—you take title to property, and you have a place to stay one week each year. But the reality is that you have paid the equivalent of $520,000 for that little room ($10,000 per week multiplied by fifty-two weeks per year), and they'll probably add on a few hundred dollars a year of maintenance costs to boot. On top of that, selling timeshare properties is difficult—the secondary market is very weak for all but the best units.
5. **Sports cars.** Although good sports cars do hold their value relatively well, most sports cars are an unnecessary luxury that come with high

upkeep, maintenance, storage, and insurance costs. Evaluate whether you would really get much use out of a sports car. The same also goes for off-road vehicles. Think "rental."

6. **Swimming pools.** It's 95 degrees, and boy, would it be nice to have a pool to take a dip in. Or a pool for next Saturday's party. But here's the trouble: It isn't 95 degrees that often, and you can only have pool parties a couple of times a year. The pool's needs, on the other hand, never stop—chemicals, cleaning, repairs, and maintenance. Owning a swimming pool is costly and time-consuming.

When It's Time to Buy

When you have decided that your best option is to make a purchase, be sure that you choose wisely. Don't be fooled by the latest sales pitch or a popular fad. Your first step should be basic research. Informed buyers are invariably better buyers. Know the choices, manufacturers, and prices. Check consumer reports and information available online, and do some comparison shopping. And use the Web—the jury's still out on whether it's a good place to buy, but it certainly is a good place to shop.

E FACT

For online research, visit Sears at *www.sears.com* to learn about appliances; Autobytel at *www.autobytel.com* to learn about cars; or CNET at *www.cnet.com* to get information on electronics and computers. These sites list products and their features, specifications, prices, feature comparisons, and customer commentary.

Buy Exactly What You Need

In an economy and market where most major products are becoming commodities, manufacturers struggle to set themselves apart by adding features to their products. Refrigerators may now come with water filtration, digital readouts, icemakers, lights, and fancy shelving. VCRs and camcorders come with special features most of us are unlikely to even understand, let alone use. Most of those extra features are there to make the product different—and to jack up the price. The point is this: Don't get talked into those "nice-to-have" features. Know what the extras are and what they cost, figure out which of them you actually need, and stick with your decision.

Along the same lines, it makes no sense to buy *less* than what you need, so don't try to save a few bucks when it means you're getting an item of lesser quality. Quality refers to the enduring functionality of the product itself and your overall satisfaction with it—when you are more satisfied with something, you keep it longer, thus saving on replacement costs. However, sometimes the premium for quality is simply too high. It doesn't make sense to spend six times as much for a Mercedes sedan as for a one-year-out-of-lease Ford Taurus, and it doesn't make sense to spend four times as much for a fancy SubZero refrigerator as for the Sears equivalent—but it may make sense to spend 20 percent more for the Maytag model.

ALERT!

If at all possible, try it out before you buy it. It's hard to bring home that refrigerator and "take it for a spin," but you can certainly rent a car or a pressure washer with similar features and characteristics, or try to borrow one from a friend. There is no substitute for experience.

Extended Warranties

Think twice about extended warranties. Many products sold today generate little profit for their sellers. How do they make their money? By selling extended warranties. Extended warranties "protect" you beyond the manufacturer's warranty period. But do you need this protection? Not if you have to pay as much as a third of the product price for it. For any product under $1,000, it is better to self-insure rather than pay $60 or more against the slim chance that the product might break, in which case the warranty would cover the costs of fixing or replacement without a hassle. A better approach is to buy quality items and skip the extended warranty altogether.

Chapter 7

Bank on Your Advantage

Banks. Are they big and scary institutions full of stuffy employees trying to cheat you out of your money, or are they tools to achieve your financial objectives? In this day and age, it's probably the latter. It is almost essential to use a bank for day-to-day personal finances. With some basic knowledge, you can work your relationship with banks to your advantage.

An Introduction to Banking

A bank is a financial institution that handles money for its customers, whether as savings, a checking account, bank loans, or a variety of other financial services. Banks are money stores; they deal with money, buying it from willing sellers and selling it to willing buyers at a certain price. In order to attract customers to deposit their money, banks offer an assortment of services that are not only essential—they provide great convenience to managing household finances. As part of your financial plan and process, it is important to understand banks, how they do business, what services they have to offer, how to choose a bank, and how to transact business effectively with them.

How Banks Work

How do banks make money? Banks have two sources of income: First, they lend money to individual and business customers, and they charge interest on that; second, they charge fees for many of their services. They also borrow money from the central bank—the Federal Reserve—at discounted rates. Their profits depend on how many customers, both depositors and borrowers, they serve, as well as prevailing interest rates. The banking industry has evolved rapidly in the past twenty years. Driven by deregulation and "economies of scale" (greater efficiency brought on by size), banks have grown, merged, and stepped into each other's markets and services. That said, there are still three main "forms" of banking institutions that you, as a consumer, will encounter:

1. **Full-service banks:** Full-service banks usually have "bank" in their name—Wells Fargo Bank, Bank of America, Citibank. Some of them are huge corporations; others may be niche players in local markets or even local industries, such as farming. Full-service banks offer a large array of savings-and-loan services like checking, savings, loan, and credit, and they are expanding into financial services, such as insurance and investments.
2. **Savings and loans (S&Ls):** Savings-and-loan banks offer fewer services and operate with lower costs and longer-term commitments

from borrowers and depositors. As a result, they can afford to pay higher rates on deposits and charge lower rates on mortgages and other loans. Although this branch of the industry was hurt by the savings-and-loan scandal of the 1980s, stronger players have survived the crisis. If you want slightly better interest rates and a little more personalized service, and you are willing to forgo some fancier bank services, using an S&L may be a good choice for you.

3. **Credit unions:** Credit unions are popular for long-term savings and lending needs. Part of the reason is that they are nonprofit and don't charge a 1–2 percent markup to provide a profit margin. It was once difficult to join a credit union—their membership charters allowed only employees of specific businesses or government units. But the number of credit unions has grown, and so has the breadth of their charters. Today, not everyone can join, but opportunities have expanded. Credit unions have "crossed over" to offer more banklike services, including checking and ATM services.

FACT

Collectively, the package of services offered by the bank makes up its product, and should be evaluated accordingly. When shopping for a bank, it is good to know what services you need, how much they cost, and which bank provides the best total package of services for you.

Banking Services

Banks provide a safe, convenient way to store and transact your short and long-term money. Banks provide checking accounts, essential in the economy of today that runs on commercial instruments such as checks instead of cash. Without a bank, you would have difficulty cashing your paycheck. You would have to store the proceeds in a mattress and hand-carry cash to your debtors.

Banks are also good places to keep your current savings. The Federal Depositor's Insurance Corporation (FDIC) insures money deposited at a bank from loss of up to $100,000. Finally, money can be borrowed from banks for any purpose—either in the form of credit cards and other "revolving" credit or as fixed-value "installment" loans. In today's world, an economy without banks would barely function. Households that don't use banking services regularly are really behind in the way they manage their finances.

Nearly all full-service banks—and nowadays most savings-and-loans and credit unions—provide the following services:

- **Checking accounts:** Checking accounts allow you to deposit short-term funds and write unlimited checks against those funds. Most don't pay interest—in return for the service the bank provides for you, they get to use your average balance (or "float") for free. In addition, most checking accounts have monthly, per-check, and check-printing service charges, but you may be able to waive those fees with a minimum balance of as low as $1,000.
- **Savings accounts:** Savings accounts pay low rates (especially at full-service banks), but they offer flexibility to withdraw your money at any time and protection through FDIC insurance. Different types of savings accounts are emerging, including money market accounts (MMAs), in which funds are invested in large corporate debt instruments. Although you might gain 1 or 2 percent more in interest from funds deposited in MMAs, you would no longer have the FDIC protection in case of the bank's bankruptcy.
- **Certificates of deposit (CDs):** A CD acts like a contractual savings account. It has a fixed period, allows no withdrawals during that period, and typically pays a higher rate than an MMA. CDs allow you to "lock in" an interest rate, and the longer you lock it in, the higher it typically is; furthermore, CDs are insured from loss. CDs are a good bet for conservative savings and true emergency money. (If you need that money, you can withdraw it earlier than planned, but you will have to pay the penalty fees for early termination.)
- **Installment loans:** Lending money is a "bread-and-butter" bank business. For most banks, the majority of their loans are made to businesses and business owners, but a sizable portion is lent to ordinary individuals in the form of auto and other loans with a fixed

payment period, interest rate, and monthly payment. The installment loan business, however, has been declining as more customers use credit unions, dealer financing, and so forth. Generally, if you're in the market for a consumer loan, credit unions are cheaper than banks. If you have a business, a bank is usually your first stop.

- **Credit cards:** If banks are lending less in installment loans, they are making up that shortfall in credit cards and other revolving forms of credit. Most major banks have VISA and MasterCard products, and most are also aggressively pursuing home-equity and other forms of revolving credit lines. These products have higher margins and less risk to the bank than most installment loans.
- **Cash access:** If you put money in a bank, you want to be able to take it out! And the ease, convenience, and time flexibility in doing so are important. Fortunately, computer and networking technology have provided ATMs, or automated teller machines, to convert cash access and many other banking transactions into a do-it-yourself affair. Some banks have ATMs installed everywhere, while S&Ls and credit unions may have only a few or none at all. ATM transactions at your own bank are usually free, while transactions through another firm's ATM often result in service charges from both banks, which might mean you have to pay a total of $3.50 or $4 just to withdraw a $20 bill.
- **Debit cards:** Debit cards are a useful cash-access tool and close cousin of the credit card provided by most banks. Debit cards work like electronic checks—just swipe it through at the grocery, and your account (usually a checking account) is automatically debited—that is, the funds are removed and transferred on the spot. Debit cards can double as ATM cards, and they usually have a major credit card imprint and network behind them.

ALERT!

Know the limitations of debit cards. Because they have no credit resource standing behind them, they are good only up to what you have in your account, and no more, so if you lose track of how much you have "charged" on them, you might overdraw your account and end up paying a hefty overdraft fee!

"Feature" Services

In addition to basic services, banks offer a number of specialized "feature" services designed to build a more complete financial management product for you and earn more money in fees for themselves. For good personal financial management, the following feature services can be very helpful:

- **Direct deposit:** You can have your paycheck deposited directly into your checking, savings, or loan account (or a combination of any of the above).
- **Direct loan payments:** You can set up direct loan payments out of your accounts or as a deduction from a direct deposit. Direct loan payments are a good way to make sure you don't get behind; some banks and credit unions even offer slightly lower interest rates on loans serviced by direct deposit.
- **Automated bill payment:** Many banks allow you to pay bills and loans online, without writing checks and paying expensive postage. You can pay all bills quickly in one sitting, or you can even set them up to pay automatically. However, most banks still charge fees for automated payment exceeding the cost of normal postage and check fees. This will probably change over time.
- **Automated account inquiry:** Through the Internet or with automated voice (phone) systems, banks can inform you of your balances and recent transactions.
- **Overdraft protection:** By connecting your checking and savings account, you can avoid overdrawing your accounts because the overdrawn amount will be transferred automatically from the backup account. The fees may be steep, but they are a lot cheaper than returned check charges and the inconvenience of "bouncing" a check. Know the fees, and don't overrely on this feature.
- **Safe-deposit boxes:** Banks have long provided safe vaulted repositories for valuables and important documents. For peace of mind, most people should have a safe deposit box.
- **Financial services:** Banks may provide the following financial services to its customers: financial planning, securities brokerage, insurance, trust management, and other services.

Beware of Service Fees

Banks make a lot of money "buying" money at wholesale and lending it at retail prices. But with lower interest rates and a wider variety of lending sources (credit unions, online lenders, etc.) it has become more difficult for banks to make money this way. As a result, banks are becoming more aggressive in charging fees for the services they provide. Every bank has a different fee schedule, and it is hard to generalize, but the smart home financier should be aware of the following fees:

- **Checking account fees:** Banks may charge you a monthly checking fee, a small fee for every check that you write, and a fee for supplying you with the checks. These fees may be waived if you maintain a minimum balance (as set by your bank).
- **Overdraft charges:** Whether or not you have overdraft protection, your bank might charge you for overdrawing your account.
- **"Stop payment" fees:** It may be necessary to stop a payment on a check—say, if goods and services promised aren't delivered. Banks may charge $10 or $15 for this service.
- **ATM charges:** Banks may charge you for using their ATMs; more often, however, these charges will only apply if you use ATMs sponsored by other banks.
- **Savings withdrawals:** Banks may charge a small fee for every savings withdrawal in excess of three (or however many) per month.
- **Balance inquiries:** Some banks may charge a dollar or more to do a detailed balance inquiry through an ATM or through an automated customer interface.

How Many Accounts Do You Need?

If you are dealing with your personal finances as a family, you may wonder how many bank accounts (and what types) you actually need. Should there be a "household" checking account to pay the bills and handle "family allowance" items? Do you need separate checking accounts for each spouse (and child) for personal allowances? And how about savings accounts? Making these decisions is tough because people's emotions will certainly be involved.

ESSENTIAL

While everyone needs to keep the family's best interests and its household budget in mind, each member may also want control of their own account to handle personal expenses and build their own savings reserve.

Your family will need to find an approach that balances individual trust and the need for independence with the cost of doing business with the bank. It's generally a good idea to have a single household checking account with a household savings reserve behind it to keep funds for annual bills and expenses, vacations, and so forth, as well as to provide an overdraft reserve. Individual earners may have their own savings account as a personal reserve, and can direct deposit a certain amount of their salary to their personal savings account before depositing the rest of their funds in the household checking account.

Banking Online

What's nice about online banking is that you can do what you like. It's not an "all or nothing" proposition. You can use as much or as little as you want, depending on your needs and preferences for doing things with a computer. You may choose a mix of ways to deal with your bank–write paper checks, deposit money and negotiate loans in person, withdraw cash by ATM, and use your computer to track balances and transfer money between savings and checking. The evolution of online banking is still in its early stages. Like the computer itself, however, sooner or later you're likely to use online banking to some degree, so it's a good idea to start learning some of the capabilities, advantages, and shortcomings of cyberbanking.

Online Banking Services

Online banking services exist primarily as Web-based extensions of existing major banks. To do basic online banking, usually you just call your bank's customer service center and ask for a PIN (personal identification number) to get online access to your existing accounts. You do not normally need to set up new accounts.

There are a few online-only banks as well. The biggest is NetBank; some of the Web-based financial service firms like E-trade have banking arms as well. With these banks everything occurs online. Although they do have a toll-free number that you can call for customer support, there is little "physical" infrastructure. (However, E-Trade is building its own network of ATM machines, and NetBank and others have partner agreements with major ATM owners.)

E ALERT!

Little could be more damaging than a hacker gaining illicit access to your online banking platform! Online bank players clearly recognize this, and they go to great lengths to protect your transactions with passwords and encryption. If you use the latest Internet browsers, safeguard your passwords, and avoid sites without a clear information-sharing policy, you should be safe.

It's worth exploring some of the features of online banking and their advantages and disadvantages:

- **Around-the-clock access:** A great advantage of online banking–it is never closed! Busy people can bank at two in the morning just as easily as they can in the middle of the working day. And they can do it from anywhere–which is handy for people who travel a lot. If incoming funds are set up for direct deposit and outgoing expenses are for electronic or automated payment, and there is a cash access vehicle (like access to ATMs) for pocket cash, there is little need for a physical bank.
- **Higher interest rates:** Because of reduced overhead, true online banks like NetBank can offer slightly higher interest rates on deposits and lower rates on loans. Some major banks follow suit, offering slight advantages or specials to online customers, usually amounting to a quarter of 1 percent or less. Changing over to online banking won't make you rich, but it may give you better control of your money and fewer fees and penalties for mistakes.

- **Keeping your balance:** Another major online-banking feature is "real time" tracking of account balances. You can see the whole picture—deposits, payments, and withdrawals. Account aggregation, a more advanced feature on the drawing board but still only in limited service, allows you to have one screen that shows all your accounts—not just those from a single institution.
- **Paying the bills:** With most online banking services, you can do bill payment online. Although you generally have to pay a fee, it may help you avoid late charges that you might accumulate if you tend to be late on mailing your bill payments.
- **Expense management:** With some online services, you can get a complete breakdown of your expenses by category, with neat graphs showing trends and composition. Expense-management tools can be especially powerful if they're linked to software packages, such as Intuit's Quicken and Microsoft Money, but it may take a while to learn to use these tools effectively.
- **Pay "P2P":** P2P stands for direct person-to-person payment that enables people to buy from each other with immediate payment and without risk of bounced checks or high credit card fees.

FACT

One of the biggest P2P providers is PayPal; it offers free services in exchange for the brief period of time that they hold your money as they are processing the payment transaction.

Internet banking is still a new concept. It is experiencing growing pains as banks experiment with what works best for them and their consumers. While it's certainly a good idea to gradually make yourself familiar with your current bank's online banking options, don't give up on a "bricks-and-mortar" bank altogether unless online banking offers you all the services you need from your bank.

Secrets to Getting Along with Your Bank

Whatever type of bank you choose and whatever services you sign up for, it may be helpful for you to know a few tried-and-true ways to get more for your money from your bank:

- **Be a long-term customer.** While there may not be any specific benefits, you'll usually get greater cooperation from personnel, and disputed charges are more likely to be waived.
- **Be a profitable customer.** The more money you keep at your bank, the better treatment you are likely to receive. Likewise, the more services you use, the better. Many banks recognize their valuable customers with better service.
- **Know the key personnel at your bank** (or the local branch of your bank). Being on a first-name basis can help resolve problems and get you linked to the right set of services.
- **Beware of sales pitches.** Banks do try to sell products—whether it's their latest money market account or insurance products. (Careful! These insurance products probably aren't theirs, but they're paid handsomely to market them as if they were).
- **Avoid unnecessary charges.** If your bank charges you a fee for using another bank's ATMs, be prepared in advance. Try to plan ahead. Withdraw money from your bank, or use a debit card that gives you the option to receive cash back when you make purchases at the supermarket or other stores.
- **Be aware of which bank services cost you money** and which are offered free of charge. Remember that if you manage your finances well and keep enough money in the bank to make it successful, your overall cost of banking will be lower.
- **Check your balances regularly** and reconcile them with your own records. It is usually a good idea to reconcile balances at least once a month.
- **Build your savings.** Use direct deposit, direct loan payments, and direct balance transfers to build your savings and reduce your debts by having your salary go directly to your savings account and to pay off your debts before you actually touch your money. Ⓔ

Chapter 8

Getting Credit Where Credit Is Due

Credit is the actual and potential level of borrowing and purchasing power granted by a financial institution. When used correctly, credit is a tool for achieving financial objectives; when used unwisely, it becomes dangerous to one's financial health. It's important to understand the role of credit in your personal finances. This chapter covers concepts, details, and wise use of this all-important financial tool.

Understanding the Concept of Credit

The idea of credit goes back to the beginning of the history of commerce—government and business institutions have used credit widely for years to finance their activities. However, the introduction of widespread consumer credit is a fairly recent phenomenon; credit as we know it did not really exist just a century ago. Today, credit has evolved into an all-powerful engine of the modern economy, but for the individual user the power must be used carefully. As you continue learning about credit, keep in mind that it is a way to pay, a means to buy something, not an expense in and of itself.

Credit Isn't the Same as Debt

When expenses exceed income, the resulting negative balance is debt. How do most of us deal with debt? We either earn more money to pay off the debt, or we use credit to push that payoff out into the future. Credit is a tool for financing debt. Is it a bad thing? No, actually it is a good thing. The more credit you have, the more lenders are willing to lend you, and the less purchasing power has already been consumed. Having credit and no debt is a good thing. Having debt with no credit is a very bad thing.

ALERT!

When you rely too much on credit, your debt increases (because credit costs money), which makes you a riskier debtor and raises the cost of your credit. And, of course, the more credit you use up, the less credit is available.

Common Credit Varieties

There is more than one way of getting credit. Although the most common—and most dangerous one—is the credit card, there are other forms as well. Before exploring credit cards in further detail, the following are brief descriptions of the types of credit.

- **Mortgage loans:** Mortgages are long-term loans, usually for real estate, where the purchased asset secures the loan. If payments stop and the loan is foreclosed, the property itself may be repossessed by the lender and sold for cash to settle the loan. The security to the lender provided by such an agreement permits the lender to lend more money at a lower rate. Since it's difficult to purchase a home without use of a mortgage, mortgage debt is usually considered "good" debt. (Chapter 15 covers mortgages in more detail.)
- **Installment loans:** These loans are set for a fixed amount and must be paid back over a fixed period of time using a fixed monthly payment. A car loan is a good example of an installment loan.
- **Revolving credit:** This allows you to borrow up to a credit limit, for an undefined period of time, with an undefined (but exceeding minimum) payment. As payments are made and more purchases are made, the balance revolves, with old debt being replaced by new debt. Credit cards are the most popular form of revolving credit.
- **Equity lines:** These combine features of mortgage and revolving credit. They allow you to secure a loan, which helps lower interest rates. But they also allow you to add more to that balance and pay it off as you please. Equity lines can cost as much as 15 percent less than unsecured revolving credit, and they have the additional advantage of tax-deductible interest.

FACT

You may think it's been around since the beginning of time, but the availability of revolving credit is a comparatively recent phenomenon. In 1916, Arthur Morris, a retailer, made the first revolving credit plan available; it was known as the Morris plan. The use of credit cards started with department stores, with "bank cards" such as VISA and MasterCard not hitting the scene until the late 1950s.

The Power of a Credit Card

Credit cards are quickly replacing cash as a means of purchasing everything from household goods and gasoline to electronics and dinners out—and online sales depend on them. Cash has become the exception, not the rule, in a great part of today's economy.

Credit cards also happen to be one of the most profitable businesses for lenders. High-interest markups and exorbitant fees have created a race to issue cards to anybody breathing—and it's not uncommon for dead people to get credit cards, too. Many of these cards come with so many features that they require a small booklet to explain all the services they offer.

Major Credit Cards

Major credit cards include the familiar VISA, MasterCard, and Discover. "VISA" and "MasterCard" are franchise brand names. The companies who own these names set the standards and do heavy brand-name marketing. Banks and other companies license the names and set up credit card accounts using the brand name with their name ("Wells Fargo VISA" or "Bank One MasterCard"). A recent trend is for nonbank companies to partner with banks and VISA/MC to issue affiliate cards—"Sears MasterCard" and "L.L. Bean VISA" are just a few examples. These cards have special purchase features involving the nonbank company. Discover does not franchise but runs as one central card and offers an important special feature (to be discussed along with other "reward" cards).

The major credit cards are all revolving cards. They allow you to charge and pay as you please, as long as you comply with the credit maximums and payment minimums. They have very high interest rates—usually more than 10 percent and often approaching 20 percent or more. Although they charge substantial fees to merchants accepting the cards (up to 3 percent of purchase value) and a variety of fees to unsuspecting customers, they make most of their money on interest. Low minimum payments and high interest-rate markups result in a profitable interest business. Repeat: *The major credit-card companies make their money on interest*. Their profits are derived from credit-card holders who tend to carry a balance (as opposed to paying off the balance at the end of the month).

Charge Cards

Not all credit cards are charge cards. Technically speaking, charge cards require balances to be paid in full each month. Charge cards are a convenient way to pay for things. They make their money not from interest but from high annual fees, higher merchant fees, and direct marketing. The basic American Express and its "Gold" and "Platinum" versions are the most popular examples. These cards are more suited to travelers and business customers, and make less sense for the average consumer.

Department Store and Other Specialty Cards

Credit cards originated with department stores, and most still offer their own credit products. They make money on interest, and–although less true today, since most stores also accept major credit cards–they direct traffic to their stores. Some stores, like Target and Home Depot, actively seek customers and use the cards to build customer loyalty. Others are moving away from specialty cards and towards affiliation with a major credit card (as in the case of Sears, which offers the Sears MasterCard). Either way, you'll pay high interest rates, but having these cards will entitle you to special sales and promotions.

ALERT!

Don't sign up for too many cards! While most department store and specialty cards cost nothing to own—and you may get a tempting "10 percent off" discount when you sign up—too many cards can compromise your financial control and lower your credit rating, which is affected by the amount of outstanding credit you already have.

How Credit Cards Work

It's a good idea to know how credit cards work. Each card, and each issuer, will have slight variations to the general principles. Here are some things to know.

Interest Rates

Credit-card companies set their own interest rates. With the exception of a few states, there are no usury laws governing how the rates are set or how they change. Most credit-card interest rates are 5–15 percent higher than preferred business ("prime") lending rates. These rates are annual, but they are compounded daily. For example, an 18 percent APR (annualized percentage rate) becomes 19.65 percent with daily compounding.

Some credit-card companies like to attract new customers by offering an introductory (teaser) rate. If you sign up, make sure you know how long the introductory rate will last and what it will eventually revert to. In general, you should avoid paying interest by paying off your balance each month.

Balance Calculations

Most credit cards calculate interest on the "average daily balance" during the credit period. If you buy something on May 1 for $50, and something on May 15 for $100, your average daily balance (assuming a May 30 period end) will be $125 ($50 for fifteen days and $200 for fifteen days), and interest will be assessed on this amount.

If you do carry a balance, don't wait until the next billing period to pay. Send in payment as soon as possible because interest accrues daily. Watch out for credit cards that charge interest on the highest balance or period-end balance, or use "two-cycle billing" where charges are assessed on the previous and current cycle if you carry a balance for the first time.

Grace Period

The grace period is the time from the statement date to the due date. Recently, aggressive companies have been cutting this time to the bone. Some cards only allow fifteen days, which compels you to pretty much pay the bill the day you get it (and not be out of town when it arrives). Why are companies getting aggressive? Because they make a lot of money charging fees for late payments. To minimize problems, make sure that your credit-card company is not located at the other end of the country—this should decrease the amount of time your bill and payment are in the mail—and shop around for longer grace periods.

Credit Limit

The credit limit is the maximum amount you can charge on a credit card. Generally, credit-card companies have no problem raising your credit limit at your request. The danger, however, is that the higher the limit, the more you are likely to spend.

Cash Advances

You *can* get cash advances on most major credit cards, but in a word, *don't*. Cash advances come with high cash-advance fees, higher-than-normal interest rates, and will immediately start the interest rate "clock" on an otherwise-paid-up account—the entire balance of it, not just the cash advance! Ignore cash advance offers—including those checks that come from your statements. Cash advances are trouble—and if you're using them, it's a sure sign *you're* in trouble.

Endless Fees and Charges

As a wise consumer, you should be aware of how credit-card companies catch you with high interest rates. Additionally, you need to be aware of the fees and charges that your credit-card company may be charging you for services. Here are a few:

- **Annual fees:** These fees are charged for major credit and charge cards, but they should not be seen on department store or specialty cards. Lately, many issuers have dropped annual fees as a competitive move. One type of credit card that retains annual fees is the "reward" card that rewards you with "cash back," frequent flyer miles, and so forth for the amount of money you charge on the card. These cards make sense if you really plan to take advantage of the rewards—for instance, if you are a frequent traveler.
- **Late fees:** These are the result of missing your payment deadline. They may be steep, so consider paying off your card with a direct-deposit program. Some companies also allow you to make your payment online or by phone.
- **Cash advance fees:** These are the fees for borrowing cash from your credit-card company (as opposed to charging purchases on their card).
- **Over-limit fees:** Issuers may charge $15, $20, or more for going over the credit limit—then turn around and raise your limit!

QUESTION?

Can I get a late fee reversed?
It's certainly worth a try. If you have a consistently good history with the issuer and you charge enough or pay enough interest to be profitable to them, they will often waive the fee. Take ten minutes to save $30 and improve your credit rating—and to let your issuer know you're watching.

Credit Card Features

As mentioned above, credit cards are coming with an ever-greater assortment of features. Here is what you should know about:

- **Gold and Platinum cards**: Once reserved for the rich and famous, these cards are now available to almost everyone, but they come with higher fees and an assortment of other services you're unlikely to actually ever use.
- **Reward cards:** These reward users for the money charged on the card. Airline mileage cards–where you accrue a mile for every dollar purchased–make sense for frequent business travelers. Other cards (like Discover) reward customers with cash–for example, a 1 percent cash rebate on all purchases made during the year.
- **Affiliate cards:** As mentioned above, affiliates allow retailers to partner with major credit-card brand names. As a result, you get credit from VISA or MasterCard *plus* discounts on merchandise at the retail partner's store. Some cards also offer rewards, like a percentage off on your next new purchase.
- **Insurance protection:** This will protect your finances by paying off your credit-card balance in case of death or disability. It is expensive and unnecessary if you have other insurance and don't tend to carry a large balance. There is also theft and loss insurance for the credit card itself, but current laws make this largely unnecessary.
- **Purchase protection:** Some cards, particularly the gold and platinum variety, offer merchandise guarantees on purchases made with that card. If something breaks in, say, a year, the credit-card company will reimburse full value for the product purchased.

ESSENTIAL

You are not responsible for illegal purchases charged to your credit card if you report your card stolen before a fraudulent purchase was made. If your card was used before you reported it stolen, your maximum liability is $50 for each credit-card account. And if the purchase was done through the Internet, your liability is zero. By the way, since you are already protected, don't bother buying credit-card insurance.

Good Credit, and How to Get It

You may or may not use a lot of credit in your daily finances. While most homeowners have a mortgage, the use of other forms of credit depends a lot on your spending habits and the lifestyle choices you make. Good credit habits entail reasonable levels of debt, reasonable use of credit, and highly consistent and timely payments on outstanding debt.

Good credit provides potential buying power and indicates good financial habits. Good credit means that you've kept reasonable debt levels for your income and lifestyle profile, and you have a solid personal financial system to manage the debts you have. Your credit can be objectively measured, and credit scores will be explored—but first let's review the factors that lead to good and bad credit.

Good Credit Ratings

What makes you have good credit? From a credit-quality standpoint, lenders look at your dependability in making payments and keeping debt levels below certain thresholds. Some lenders, however, might evaluate you based on your potential profitability—so it is not only whether you pay bills on time, but also if you leave large balances—debt—on the cards at high interest rates. Pay off your balance monthly, and credit-card companies will gripe that you're unprofitable.

You should, as a consumer, strive to achieve the highest possible quality of credit rating. But there's no compelling reason for you to be highly profitable to credit-card companies, and for the most part you should avoid habits that make lots of money for them. Credit quality is a function of your "ability and willingness" to pay—whether you can pay your debts and whether you actually do, reliably and dependably.

FACT

> Lenders don't have any good way to track your assets, so asset-rich income-poor retirees may have trouble getting credit. But they do look at credit limits and lines and the percentage of those limits tapped—not just the amount of debt carried.

Here are some of the factors widely recognized as responsible for determining good credit:

- **Employment:** Having a job—especially over a long period of time—helps. Steady professions are better than those with less consistent income, such as farming or self-employment.
- **Home ownership:** Ownership and length of home ownership indicate stability. Stability also helps those who rent. Living in one place over a long period of time is a good indicator of stability.
- **Having few credit cards:** Too many credit cards (more than ten or fifteen) on your hands shows that you are exposed to excessive debt. This is especially true if you have too many "major" credit cards (you should have no more than three per individual or five as a family).
- **A long credit history:** An extensive record of your credit history can certainly help in establishing your credit rating.
- **Paying on time:** It doesn't matter if you choose to pay just the minimum—you should always pay on time. Even one or two missed deadlines can lower a lender's perception of your dependability. Late payments should be discussed with lenders by phone and removed from your record, if possible.
- **Paying in full:** Pay balances in full, and your rating will go up.
- **Carrying reasonable amounts of debt:** Balances or debt that is reasonable for your level of income is important. Lenders look for total debt payments including mortgages to equal less than 38 percent of your income and for mortgages by themselves to represent 28 percent. That leaves 10 percent of your income for servicing debt.

- **A small number of recent credit applications:** If you've applied for a lot of credit recently, that's considered unfavorable.
- **No delinquencies, writeoffs, liens, collections, or bankruptcies:** If any of these actions have been taken by your creditors, your score will suffer. Bankruptcies stay with your record for as long as ten years. Some bankruptcies are looked at less favorably than others—an entrepreneurial flop isn't regarded as badly as an out-of-control case of middle-class overspending.

Even a Little Snag Can Hurt

Here is a story to illustrate how even a small mistake can hurt your credit rating. A customer who had a pretty good track record bought an $11.95 clock from an insert in a department-store credit-card bill. The clock broke two days after arrival. The customer called the toll-free number provided, but he could not reach anyone. He then figured—quite wrongly—that the department store would take some responsibility for products sold through their own billings and didn't pay the bill.

As a result, the department store promptly slapped a $29 late fee on the account and reported it to the credit bureaus. Ensuing phone inquiries with the department store revealed that the account was managed by an entirely different company, which had no interest in satisfying the department store's customers or giving them the benefit of the doubt.

ESSENTIAL

Late fees show up on your credit record. To protect yourself, pay your bills on time, and if there's a glitch or misunderstanding, pull out the stops and get it cleared up as soon as possible.

What's Your Credit Rating?

Now it's time to see how well you are doing. Public credit-management services such as Fair, Isaac, and Company (FICO) provide highly specific credit quality measures to lenders to help them evaluate you as a borrower. In fact, FICO scores have become the *de facto* standard for appraising your credit and credit worthiness. These scores are not only used by countless lenders and financial institutions, they are now being employed in the form of what amounts to a character test by employers, insurance companies, and other organizations. You should become familiar with FICO and your FICO score, because the business world is using it to monitor your financial performance—even if you aren't! Fortunately, FICO has made it easy for you to access—and interpret—your score.

Whether you know it or not—and whether you like it or not—national data-service bureaus like Equifax and InfoUSA collect vast amounts of data about you, your demographics, and your commercial and credit history. Facts like where you live, how much you earn, where you bank, your age, marital status, and how many kids you have are commonly known and shared with creditors and marketers. All types of credit information are also captured and shared—what credit you have received from whom, how much was available, how much you used, and your payment history. Using this data, FICO has built an analytical model to predict your credit worthiness. By applying algorithms that this company has developed and to which it holds proprietary rights—and by drawing on vast experience with people who have similar financial status—FICO can predict the likelihood of any person experiencing delinquency and credit problems.

The FICO scoring model is based on a 350 to 850 scale, with 850 being the highest possible score. The table below explains the meanings behind each score.

FICO Scores and Their Meaning

Score range	Percentile ranking	Delinquency rate
up to 499	lowest 1 percent	87 percent
500 to 549	next 5 percent	71 percent
550 to 599	next 7 percent	51 percent
600 to 649	next 11 percent	31 percent
650 to 699	next 16 percent	15 percent
700 to 749	next 20 percent	5 percent
750 to 799	next 29 percent	2 percent
800 and above	next 11 percent	1 percent

Here's how you can use this information. If your FICO score is 485, you're in the worst 1 percent of all borrowers. Out of 100 borrowers like you, 87 are likely to be delinquent in payment. That's not a good score—not by any means. On the other hand, if your score is 760, you're in the top 40 percent of all borrowers, and your delinquency rate is estimated at only 2 percent. Simply put, the FICO score tells how lenders look at your finances and your credit to see how well (or poorly) you're doing.

FACT

To get your own FICO score, all you need to do is go to *www.myfico.com,* enter your information, and pay $13.95 with a major credit card. The FICO report is extremely informative, providing detailed credit history and summary of positive and negative factors influencing the score. It gives guidance to improve the score and even a simulator to show how certain actions will improve it.

Using Credit Wisely

Credit is a powerful and complex tool, and you should have a personal and family strategy for using credit. First off, you need to remember that credit is a way to pay, not money that you wouldn't otherwise have. If you won't have the money to pay for something, you generally shouldn't charge it. Here are some good reasons for using credit:

- **As a convenience:** It's easier than cash, especially when buying durable household merchandise and other items for which carrying sufficient cash would be risky. Credit cards have become almost indispensable for travel.
- **To capture good deals:** If it's on sale today, but outside this month's budget, using credit to capture the better price is valid—but only if you need to make that purchase in the first place.
- **To handle emergencies:** If your car needs a new water pump, don't drive it busted into the next month just because a water pump isn't in this month's budget. If you have an emergency fund, that's better, but

use of credit in lieu of the fund can be okay–with the right adjustments to lead to a quick payoff.

Once you charge something to a credit card, you need to make sure that you pay off the balance at the end of the month to avoid those high-interest costs and to protect yourself from falling into debt. Remember: An unpaid May balance just gets added to June charges, and now you have two months' worth of purchases to pay off.

ALERT!

> Here is one strategy that may work for families. Each family member gets one bank card to manage their "PAL" or personal allowance. The entire family then shares an additional card for household purchases and family travel—their "FAL" or family allowance.

Other dos and don'ts include the following:

- Don't focus on interest rates–focus on balances.
- Don't borrow to get out of debt.
- Never take cash advances–they are not worth the fees and high interest rates.

Perhaps the most important piece of advice, though, is to avoid overusing your credit cards. Don't go crazy signing up for yet another credit card because you get a free mug or because the card looks appealing to you. There should be a good reason why you are signing up for it.

Chapter 9

What to Expect When You're Investing

You manage your daily finances pretty well—so well that now you're able to save some of your income. Now what? Once you begin to accumulate assets, you need to think about growing them. This chapter will give you an introduction to the investment options that are available.

Put Your Money to Work!

Ever heard people say that money breeds more money? Despite its negative connotations of filthy-rich people becoming ever wealthier, the concept is valid—and important—for all of us. Just as you can invest your labor to produce income, you can invest your cash assets as capital to produce a return. You can do so in two ways:

1. You can invest your capital directly in businesses that produce a return.
2. You can lend your money to those businesses.

Either way, your surplus or reserve funds should be put to work. Put another way, why should you have to do all the work to achieve wealth when your money can do some of it for you?

Make It, Keep It, Grow It

You earned money through hard work. Through awareness, control, and commitment, you kept some of it. Now, you need to get it out there to pull part of the sled. How does this work? You invest it. For some, investing is a sport or hobby, and if they're good, it becomes material for water-cooler bragging rights. For the rest of us, investing is a way to increase our financial assets.

The two objectives of investing your capital (savings) are the following:

1. **Asset protection:** Preserving your hard-earned savings.
2. **Asset growth:** Growing your savings base.

The simplest way to invest is to put your money in the bank that offers you a modest rate of return. Does it require much thought? Hardly. Just deposit it and leave it.

Putting money into an ordinary savings bank account achieves the first objective—asset protection. Remember: FDIC insurance protects up to $100,000 of savings invested in the bank. But what about growth? With ordinary bank savings you achieve very low yields. Because they are safe, and because banks take a high "cut" on redeploying those assets into profitable businesses or ventures, you don't get much. In fact, if you take into account the loss of value due to inflation, you may actually lose purchasing power with bank savings, particularly after the interest you make on your income is taxed.

ALERT!

When it comes to investing your savings, beware of the "inflation tax," which can do damage to your purchasing power. Look at it this way: If your fixed savings balance earns 2 percent interest, and the inflation rate is 3 percent, you're losing 1 percent even before paying taxes on that 2 percent interest. As you define your investment strategy, make sure your assets are beating—or at least keeping up with—inflation.

Risks and Rewards

The tradeoff in investing is simple and makes sense: the higher the risk, the higher the (potential) payoff. You can keep your money in a savings account and rest assured that it'll still be there (even if it depreciates a little), or you can invest it in a more aggressive venture that may grow your capital but may also lead to high losses. So what should you choose–safety or growth?

The reality is, people pay you to take risks. The more risky a business is, the more it will be forced to pay investors for their capital. Why? Because the investors face a greater chance of losing it. With that risk in mind, the price of the capital goes up. Look at it this way–if Business A had a 2 percent chance of failure and Business B had a 20 percent chance of not making it, would you charge a higher interest to commit your investment capital to Business B? You bet.

FACT

The risk/reward tradeoff is a central principle in modern capitalism. If you want to increase the return, or asset growth, you will have to sacrifice protection. If you want more protection, you'll have to sacrifice some growth. In the short term, this tradeoff is sometimes distorted by market perceptions, but in the long run it always holds true.

Different types of investments have different risk/reward profiles. The bank account has a risk/reward profile biased towards protection, while soybean futures, oil-drilling projects, and dot.com stocks promise greater growth potential with little-to-no protection. Every type of investment has its own risk/reward profile; they will be examined shortly.

Investing Objectives

At the end of the day, your investing objective is to achieve the greatest possible growth for the given level of risk that you're willing (or should be willing) to take. Get the best gain without too much pain, as they might say. Beyond growth and risk, here are a few other investing objectives to keep in mind as you develop your investment strategy.

Tame the Inflation Tiger

Your assets should at least keep up with the inflation rate; otherwise, your purchasing power erodes over time. Taken over a thirty-year period with even a modest 3 percent inflation rate, a $100,000 asset will depreciate to about $40,000 in equivalent purchasing power: $\$100{,}000 \times (1 - .03)^{30} = \$41{,}198$ (for those who like formulas). At minimum, your investments should keep up with inflation, otherwise you might be better off spending the money today, particularly on something that doesn't depreciate! If you don't keep up with inflation, you will not be able to meet your goals, and your long-term financial results will be disappointing.

Grow with the Flow

You and your assets are both part of the economy. You work to provide something for someone else, and in return you receive a financial reward. Your assets do the same—they are put to work by you or someone else to achieve a reward. As the economy grows, so should your assets. If your assets aren't growing in lockstep with the economy, then they are not being invested as well as the assets in the economy as a whole. And how much does the economy as a whole grow? This is where the widely known indicator called GDP (Gross Domestic Product) comes into play.

GDP is the total measure of all goods and services produced in the economy, and it happens to be an important benchmark for economic performance. A growing economy will show a positive GDP growth rate that averages 2–3 percent and often up to 4–5 percent in boom years while turning towards 0 or dipping into the negatives during recessions.

Of course, you can't invest your money in "the Economy." You must direct your investment dollars to individual components of the economy to reap the returns it affords. Certain investments—mainly stocks, or equities—participate in economic growth, while other investments, like bonds, don't—they generate a return as compensation for use of your capital. Since their returns are more predictable, and you are not counting on a possible share of economic growth, there is less risk in these investments. (Again, you need to keep in mind that risk and reward are closely tied.)

ESSENTIAL

To participate in economic growth you will have to, in most cases, invest in businesses. If the companies you choose to invest in perform as well or better than the economy as a whole, you will do well. But if you invest in entities or businesses that are getting left out of the economic expansion, you will "underperform" the economy.

As an investor, you have two goals:

1. To avoid the underperformers.
2. To choose investments that at the very least represent the economy as a whole, and, if possible, that are likely to outperform it.

Unfortunately, it's almost always impossible to predict with certainty which businesses will be underperformers and which will grow your capital for you. As a result, the best strategy is to pick a "basketful" of entities that best represents economic performance and eases the negative effects of individual bad performers. This approach is called diversification; you will learn more about diversification shortly.

Take the Compounding Train

Deposit a sum of money, let it earn a return, and keep both the original sum and all of its returns invested. The original sum keeps earning, and the returns that are earned along the way earn, too! That $100,000 you deposited for thirty years, this time, say, at 7 percent, grows to $797,661: $100{,}000 \times (1 + .07)^{30} = 797{,}661$. And you don't have to do a thing, except keep your mitts off and leave that money alone. Can you earn this much extra money in thirty years by working? Well, let's see. By investing $100,000, you will get $797,661 after thirty years, which means you earn $697,661 in compounded interest. To get that same amount by saving, you would have to put away $23,255 of your income every year.

Even better, if you invest $100,000 and are also able to add money to grow your asset base, you get an accumulation annuity. (See Chapter 4 to review how accumulation annuities work.) If you're able to add $5,000 each year for thirty years, at the end you'll have a nest egg over $1.2 million.

Even if you earn a more modest return rate of 4 percent—keeping up but not beating the economy at large—you'll still end up with $345,000 at the end of thirty years and $616,000 if you go the $5,000 accumulation annuity route.

ESSENTIAL

Building an asset base allows you to take advantage of the power of compounding—which in turn builds the asset base faster. Money does indeed breed more money!

Take the Express

Not only should you think about boarding the compounding train as soon as possible, but you'll find out that the "express" train gets you there much faster. In the previous example, did you notice the difference between the 7 percent return and the 4 percent return? That difference illustrates an important point: The power of compounding is far, far greater at higher rates of return and over longer time periods. If you beat the average market rate of return on an investment even by a small amount, the effects are magnified, particularly over a sustained period of time.

FIGURE 9-1

	Number of Years: 1	2	5	10	15	20	30	40
6% Market Return	$ 1,060	$ 1,124	$ 1,338	$ 1,791	$ 2,397	$ 3,207	$ 5,743	$ 10,286
BEAT the market by 2.0%	$ 1,080	$ 1,166	$ 1,469	$ 2,159	$ 3,172	$ 4,661	$ 10,063	$ 21,725
4.0%	$ 1,100	$ 1,210	$ 1,611	$ 2,594	$ 4,177	$ 6,727	$ 17,449	$ 45,259
6.0%	$ 1,120	$ 1,254	$ 1,762	$ 3,106	$ 5,474	$ 9,646	$ 29,960	$ 93,051
8.0%	$ 1,140	$ 1,300	$ 1,925	$ 3,707	$ 7,138	$ 13,743	$ 50,950	$ 188,884
10.0%	$ 1,160	$ 1,346	$ 2,100	$ 4,411	$ 9,266	$ 19,461	$ 85,850	$ 378,721

▲ Beating the market.

The table in **FIGURE 9-1** illustrates what happens to $1,000 when it's invested over a course of anywhere from one to forty years. The top line shows what happens to this sum of money invested at a 6 percent return, which is assumed to be the market return rate. And as you can see, even with this return rate you will have $10,286 (over ten times the original investment) in forty years. But if you were to "beat the market" and produce returns at even a modest 2 percent premium (that is, 2 percent higher than the market rate, for an 8 percent total), at the end of forty years you can make $21,725—double the amount of the 6 percent return. Double the rate of return to 12 percent (6 percent over the market rate), and your forty-year return is nine times what it would be with the base 6 percent.

ALERT!

There is additional risk involved in going for high returns. But if you're aware of the potential gains and can accept the risk for a part of your portfolio, you're much more likely to come out ahead.

Getting Left Behind

It's also important to keep in mind what happens if you underperform the market (or the economy). The same principles are involved—only now you're taking a few percentage points away from the market return. If you earn 2 percent less than the market, in forty years your $1,000 investment will only get to $4,801 (see **FIGURE 9-2**)! And if you lose money on your investments, your original principal declines, making your earnings even lower than expected.

FIGURE 9-2

Number of Years		1	2	5	10	15	20	30	40
6% Market Return		$1,060	$1,124	$1,338	$1,791	$2,397	$3,207	$5,743	$10,286
UNDERPERFORM the market by	2.0%	$ 1,040	$ 1,082	$ 1,217	$ 1,480	$ 1,801	$ 2,191	$ 3,243	$ 4,801
	4.0%	$ 1,020	$ 1,040	$ 1,104	$ 1,219	$ 1,346	$ 1,486	$ 1,811	$ 2,208
	6.0%	$ 1,000	$ 1,000	$ 1,000	$ 1,000	$ 1,000	$ 1,000	$ 1,000	$ 1,000
	8.0%	$ 980	$ 960	$ 904	$ 817	$ 739	$ 668	$ 545	$ 446
	10.0%	$ 960	$ 922	$ 815	$ 665	$ 542	$ 442	$ 294	$ 195

▲ Underperforming the market.

Beating the market is no easy feat; most individual investors do a little worse than the market. There isn't one perfect investing formula or strategy that works for everybody all of the time. You will need to learn what your options are and what the current financial climate is before you can make the investment decision for your own finances.

The Choice Is Yours

Investing is a game of choices—there are literally tens of thousands of ways to invest your assets. These choices cover the spectrum from high-growth/high-risk at one end to low-growth/no-risk at the low end. Specific investing choices you make depend on two factors:

1. Your investment goals (and where they are on the growth/risk spectrum).
2. How well any particular investment option matches your goals.

First, you need to decide how much risk you are willing to take in order to maximize your return, and then you need to look for investment opportunities that can help you achieve these results. If you decide that you have $10,000 to invest in a high-risk/high-growth investment and another $20,000 to invest safely, then you need to look for a combination of aggressive and cautious investment opportunities.

No matter what your goals are, you don't have to put all your eggs in one basket. A good investment strategy takes advantage of different investment opportunities, including some aggressive and some comfortable options. You don't want all your assets invested in high-growth/high-risk investments, and you don't want all your high-growth/high-risk investments to be in one business or entity. This strategy, known as diversification, will be discussed in greater detail once you have had the opportunity to learn what types of investment are available to you.

Buying Stocks

The most obvious form of investment is in the stock market. Everyone has heard of stocks. But does everyone know what exactly stocks are? Without getting too technical, stocks are "owner" investments in a business. That is, business ownership is divided into shares, and as an investor, you buy a few shares to represent your ownership, or equity, in the business. When you purchase a company's shares (stocks), your money goes into the company. If all goes according to plan, this company uses your capital to earn money (generate profits), and you as an owner are entitled to a share of that profit. Profit on a per-share basis is described as earnings per share; this money may be paid back to you in the form of dividends, or it may be reinvested in the business with the idea of growing the business and producing even greater profits.

You may be interested to know that if you are investing in the stock market, you are not investing money in the business *directly*. Instead, investors buy and sell shares to each other, often through stock dealers who act as intermediaries. For instance, if you buy 100 shares of XYZ Corporation, your money likely goes to someone else who already committed capital to that business. You may be buying shares secondhand, thirdhand, or hundredthhand, not from the company itself. An IPO (initial public offering), where new shares are sold for the first time, is the only situation where your money goes directly to the company in which you are investing.

Stock Performance

To get a clear picture of how stock investments fit into your own personal investment picture, it is important to consider historic performance. To get right to the point, stocks have outperformed all other forms of investments over time. As a whole, stocks and corporate growth have averaged an 11 percent return over time (since the 1920s). Why? Because they participate in the growth both of the business you invest in and of the economy as a whole.

FACT

If you analyze the long-term stock growth rate of 11 percent, you'll find that over time, 3–4 percent is owed to true economic growth, another 3–4 percent is due to inflation, and 1–2 percent is the result of productivity gains in the economy (the ability to generate more profit with fewer resources). There is also a factor of increased corporate market-share of economic activity. (A good example is Wal-Mart, a big corporation that has captured a lot of business from local merchants.)

However, it's critical to understand that the rule specifies that stocks are more successful than other forms of investment *over time*. Stock-owners of a business are obligated to share its losses as well as to share its profits. Many companies—even the most successful ones—experience lean years. Sometimes, companies lose money; when a company faces losses, its value as a business drops, and its shares are devalued as well (that is, each share is worth less than before). Company profits are subject to the volatility of the economy at large, the volatility of the business or market they serve, and to the steps (and missteps) the company takes and the decisions its leaders make. As a result, returns for an individual company—and stocks in general—are more volatile in the short run. For more on investing in stocks, see Chapter 11.

Investing in Bonds

A less obvious and somewhat less glamorous way to invest in the stock market is to purchase bonds. As a stock investor, you invest in a business as an owner, looking for a share of profits. As a bond investor, you invest as a lender, looking for a fixed rate of return, or interest, on your assets committed. When you purchase bonds, you make a contractual commitment with the bond seller (the company that is borrowing your money) over the bond "security" (the money that you lend).

At the end of the lending term, you receive the money you invested, plus the money earned from interest at the interest rate you had agreed upon. Beyond that, you are not entitled to any profits the bond seller made on your money. On the other hand, you will not be subject to the profit losses the bond seller may have faced. As a result, bonds offer safer but less spectacular returns of, on average, about 6 percent. For a detailed look at bond investments, see Chapter 12.

Mutual-Fund Investments

Mutual funds are professionally managed portfolios of stocks and/or bonds constructed to meet a variety of investing objectives and risk profiles. Mutual funds are a favorite choice among investors who don't have the time or the skills to pick out individual companies. For a modest fee (usually at a half to two percent per year) fund managers do it for you. Selecting a mutual-funds portfolio can be an art and science in and of itself, and there are many, many types of funds to choose from. Chapter 13 explores the mechanics and evaluation of mutual funds.

Real Estate

The term "real estate" refers to developed or undeveloped land and structures built on that land. Real estate can be commercial (used for business) or residential (for individuals to live in). There are many ways to invest in real estate. You can either buy properties directly as an owner, or you can buy into limited partnerships and trusts that own property portfolios.

Property investments don't all work out. But because of favorable supply and demand—growing demand with a relatively fixed supply—property values over time have generally risen. Like other investments, some properties are better than others, but as a whole, the category has had good returns with relatively low risk. Favorable tax treatment, especially for residential property, and the ability to borrow large amounts of relatively inexpensive money to purchase it (secured mortgages) have worked in favor of real estate investments. However, long-term value can be hard to predict. (Where will that next chemical spill or forest fire occur, and where will the local government decide to build a landfill or a new airport?) For more on investing in real estate, see Chapter 14.

ALERT!

When it comes to direct ownership of real estate property, keep in mind that dealing with the issues and responsibilities of a real estate owner is a time-consuming and often stressful job, especially when you own property that you lease or rent.

Derivative Securities

A derivative is any security (that is, an investment instrument such as a bond or a stock) whose performance is "derived" from, or determined by, how another instrument or asset performs. Two examples of derivatives are futures contracts and options. For instance, you can buy a futures contract for delivery of 100,000 barrels of oil at a set date at a set price. You aren't actually buying the oil, you are buying the *right* to buy the oil at a specific price–so you don't have to pay the full price. If the price of oil goes above the target (or strike) price before the delivery date, you make a profit either by selling the security or by taking delivery of the oil at the set, lower price. (Private investors would of course opt to sell the security–what would you do with 100,000 barrels of oil?)

Derivatives are essentially a mechanism to transfer price and time risk from one party to another. Buying derivatives is a very high-risk proposition because you are gambling on what the price of a particular commodity will be some time from now. But selling derivatives on owned assets can actually be a good income-producing strategy, because you collect the money for transferring the right (instead of paying for it), and if the right thing doesn't happen, you profit. You become the dealer at the blackjack table.

Chapter 10

Investment Tools You Can Use

You have already started thinking about how you will invest your assets. Before you go on to learn about stocks, bonds, and mutual funds in greater detail (see Chapters 11, 12, and 13), you will need to know how to manage your investments and where to get the information and help you will need.

Managing Your Investments

As an investor, you have many choices. You can't possibly predict the future and know everything about the businesses you invest in. You can only do the best that you can. Because of the nature of the risk/reward tradeoff, financial professionals create blended portfolios of investments to achieve goals and manage risks. They adjust these portfolios over time as growth and protection needs change.

When in Doubt—Diversify

Diversify! This command is probably the most frequent advice you'll get as an investor. Instead of betting your life's savings on one company that might go under tomorrow, you spread your money over various companies in different markets *and* save some money to invest in bonds and keep as savings. That way, if the stocks fail you, you can fall back on the money made on bonds.

Here are some guidelines that may help you diversify your investments to your best advantage:

- **Spread your assets across the major classes.** It's best to have at least some investments in stocks, bonds, mutual funds, real estate, and cash. (It's okay not to have derivatives—they are too risky for personal investors.) Asset allocation models (described in the next section) provide guidance for doing this.
- **Have several investments within each investment class.** For stocks and bonds, consider spreading out your investments over five to ten companies each. If you're investing in mutual funds, you're already getting diversification, so getting two to four fund portfolios makes sense.
- **Don't overdiversify.** If you spread yourself too thin, you risk missing out on the best companies and putting a lot of money in the mediocre investment options that won't get you very good results. If you own thirty stocks and only one or two double, your total portfolio won't be much to get excited about. Likewise, more than one or two of the same type of mutual funds doesn't make sense—they are probably investing in the same stocks!

E ALERT!

Don't diversify just because you don't know what you're doing. Spread your investments around to reduce the risk of any one investment, but don't diversify so much that you dilute the winners! Diversification is not a substitute for investing knowledge and rationale. Find good businesses and investments—and know what you're doing when you invest in them.

Asset Allocation

Asset allocation is a tool created and advocated in the investment industry as a way to methodically spread your assets across different classes of investments. Asset allocation answers the following question: "How much should I have in stocks, bonds, cash, and other investments?" The idea is that allocation between these asset classes varies depending on each investor's level of risk tolerance and situation in life.

Allocation models look at potential gain and loss for each of the different classes and create investment options that provide different combinations of gain and risk potential; you can choose your blend depending on your risk tolerance and age. Sample investment options and their risk/reward profiles are listed in the following table.

Asset Allocation Options and Respective Risks and Rewards

investment	average return (%)	largest gain per year (%)	largest loss per year (%)
stocks	12.8	52.6	–26.5
80 percent stocks; 20 percent bonds	12.6	41.3	–20.5
60 percent stocks; 30 percent bonds; 10 percent cash	10.2	30.5	–14.1
40 percent stocks; 40 percent bonds; 20 percent cash	8.8	22.5	–7.5

(continued on the following page)

Asset Allocation Options and Respective Risks and Rewards *(continued)*

investment	average return (%)	largest gain per year (%)	largest loss per year (%)
25 percent stocks; 40 percent bonds; 35 percent cash	7.6	20.8	–2.1
cash	6.9	14.7	0.9

Source: Jane Bryant Quinn/Ibbotson Associates

Note that the values in this table cover the period from 1950 to 1996 and do not include the off-the-chart returns investors got in 1998, 1999, and 2000 (during the dot.com boom).

ESSENTIAL

Brokerage houses make big headlines recommending and publicly announcing changes to their recommended asset allocation models. Where would Abby Joseph Cohen of Goldman Sachs be without these high-profile announcements? If you work with financial professionals, you'll get a lot of advice about asset allocation. Be aware that sometimes too much is made of this concept.

In addition to risk/reward considerations, you have to take your age and general standing in life into account. When it comes to investing long-term, it makes a big difference whether you are ten years away from retirement or ten years into your working career. Generally, the common wisdom is that when you're younger, you should invest more heavily in stocks; while they are more volatile, the growth potential is there, and if they have a bad year or two, there is plenty of time for them to recover. As you get older, you shift to more conservative "protection" assets, such as bonds and cash. A simple formula for the percentile of your assets allocated to stocks is $100 - a$ (where a = your age). For instance, if you are thirty years old, allocate 70 percent of your investments to stocks (or stock mutual funds). If you are fifty, you should have 50 percent of your money in stocks. If you are seventy years old, avoid putting more than 30 percent in stocks (unless you have some funds that you are willing to gamble with).

Now, combine the numbers based on your age with the ones based on your risk/reward goals. As you can see, a thirty-year-old with high-risk/high-return goals may wish to invest as much as 90 percent of investment assets in stocks. For an older person with a less aggressive approach, the asset-allocation ratio will be very different.

As you take the time to consider your own assets and to turn to professionals for advice, don't let anyone overwhelm you with lots of information about asset allocation. Some investment professionals make such a big deal about asset allocation models. They insist on generating elaborate statistical models that optimize risk/reward tradeoffs based on precise measures of risk, risk tolerance, and growth forecasts. At the level of individual investors such as yourself, precise modeling makes less sense. If the model said to switch from 60 percent stocks/40 percent bonds to 55 percent stocks/45 percent bonds, it wouldn't make too much difference for a $50,000 portfolio. But the switch would generate commissions for your investment broker.

Volatility Is the Spice of (Investing) Life

By their very nature, some investments fluctuate in value more than others. Stock returns vary according to company profits, which in turn are affected by a long list of factors, including the following:

- Strength of the economy
- Growth and size of the markets they serve
- Success of products in their market(s)
- Presence and actions of competitors
- Good operational and financial management

ALERT!

Markets are vast, stormy seas of conflicting opinions and emotions. The best you can do as a stock investor is set your course straight ahead, close the windows, and keep going ahead. If you get seasick easily, safer investments like bonds or managed investments like mutual funds are probably better for your investing ship.

Although you can make educated guesses about these factors and how they will affect a company's performance, there is no way of knowing for certain how a company will perform. In general, these factors may be divided in two categories: external factors (that is, external influences such as the general health of the economy, over which the company has no control) and internal factors (that is, factors that are in the company's control, such as the financial decisions made by its leaders). The variability of these factors determines the unpredictability of a company's financial performance.

But what about the volatility of the company's stock—that is, your investment in that company? Since stocks are traded on markets, they are only worth what others will pay. This is, in turn, determined by what investors think these stocks are worth.

That "what investors think" is an important phrase. Different people perceive company worth differently, based on their own assessment of company performance, the advice of the stock-market experts, the general health of the economy, and so forth. So when you are deciding what stocks to invest in, you have to look at the company *and* the market. Unstable perception, or investor sentiment, will make your investments more volatile.

FIGURE 10-1

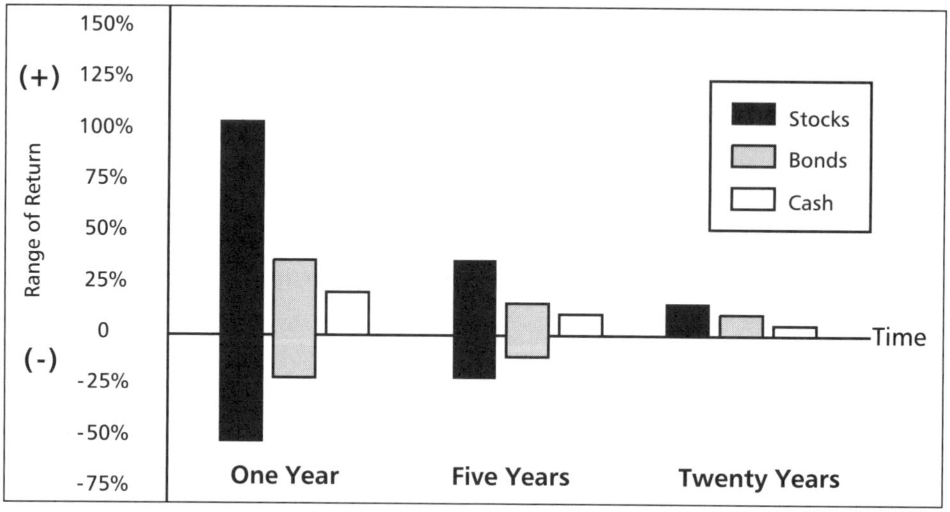

▲ Performance comparison over time.

To illustrate the volatile nature of stocks versus other investments (bonds and cash), particularly in the short run, consider the chart in **FIGURE 10-1**. The chart reflects data collected over most of the twentieth century. One-year performance for stocks as an investment class has varied from 100 percent positive (the late 1990s NASDAQ) to about 50 percent negative ("lemon" years 1929, 1974, and now 2001). But as the horizon extends out five and especially twenty years, the range diminishes and performance becomes consistently positive. Over any twenty-year period since the 1920s, stock returns have been consistent and positive—if you can tolerate the turbulence along the way.

Note that bond performance is less volatile, but also less profitable. Inflation is the mortal enemy of bonds, since payments of interest or principal down the road can't be adjusted for inflation. If inflation grows, the value of bonds declines. However, bonds pay more than cash investments (like savings) and do fluctuate with prevailing interest rates, so performance is a little more volatile and the good years are better.

Seven Habits of a Successful Investor

To conclude this chapter, here are the seven habits of the highly successful investor that you should learn and practice in your own personal finance planning:

1. **Think long-term.** Don't react to market gyrations, particularly as a stock investor. As you've seen, long-term growth is fairly certain.
2. **Invest, don't gamble.** Know what you're doing, and don't react to ideas or tips from your friends. Remember, as an investor, you are allocating capital to someone else in order to generate a return for you. If you have a concern about letting the CEO of Net.Com, Inc., have your money to do as they please, don't invest there.
3. **Invest and reinvest continuously.** Invest over time, and keep that asset base growing as an accumulation annuity. Also, by investing over time, you'll "dollar cost average" your investments, buying more when prices are down. (You will learn about dollar cost averages in Chapter 11.)

4. **Keep track.** Know how your investments are performing versus the market and your objectives. Keep in mind how overachieving investments help you and underachieving ones hurt your potential—don't be afraid to prune dead branches. Keep your assets in play in the best investments possible—don't let parts of your portfolio languish in bad investments for years.
5. **Don't overreact to short-term fluctuations.** Look at business fundamentals, not investment prices. Watch the papers—if not every day, at least weekly or a few times a month.
6. **Keep it simple.** Invest in things you know and understand, in businesses that make sense to you and look good from personal experience. If you don't understand the business or product produced by the company, you're asking for trouble.
6. **Be patient.** Despite what you might have heard, most investments don't double overnight—or even in a year. You have to be willing to give the businesses you invest in time to work with your money.

An Introduction to Investment Firms

Regardless of how you decide to invest, you will need investment services to handle your transactions, provide information, and maybe even offer advice. The industry provides an array of different financial services to individual and institutional clients. They make your money by "dealing" securities, handling your money, providing information, and by charging commission on securities transactions. Many of the larger firms also earn money by helping companies find capital by selling securities (stocks, bonds) to willing investors like you. In essence, brokers are dealers, matching buyers and sellers of investment products. There are three types of brokers to choose from: full-service brokers, discount brokers, and Internet brokers.

Full-Service Brokers

Full-service brokers execute transactions and provide personal investment, coaching, and professional analysis. Household names such as Merrill Lynch and UBS Paine Webber, as well as regional names like Edward Jones, are examples. They usually have professional analysts on staff and publish detailed company or industry reports. To get their services, investors have to pay high commissions—ten times or more the rate of the discount brokers.

FACT

Full-service brokerage firms are moving towards a "fee based" asset management model, where the commissions are lower but an annual fee of ½ to 1½ percent of account value is charged. Fee-based plans reduce the incentive for brokers to "churn"—over-trade—your account, but 1 percent each year can be a hefty sum.

Many full-service brokers offer more comprehensive financial planning services and products like insurance and retirement planning, and most provide a "one account"—unlimited checking, a debit card, and comprehensive monthly account statements. If you want dedicated professional advice and are willing to pay for it, full-service firms are an option. However, be aware that most full-service brokers have a minimum-investment policy, so you have to invest a certain sum of money in order to be eligible for their services.

Discount Brokers

Charles Schwab & Company started the discount broker niche the very day that brokerage commissions were deregulated in 1975. Schwab provided minimal services for the do-it-yourself investors who did not need the services of a personal advisor and were not interested in paying for in-house research.

Other discount brokerage firms such as Fidelity and Waterhouse Securities (now TD Waterhouse) soon began to offer services as well. Originally, stock transactions were handled by phone; now they can be done through the Internet or a "telebroker"—a touchtone telephone system.

Recently, many discount brokers have begun to offer a limited amount of advice and support through their offices. They generally post a good set of investment tools on their Web sites. They also provide basic financial planning services; "one accounts" are a standard feature. For the knowledgeable investors who want low costs but do require help from time to time, the discount model works well.

Internet Brokers

Like everything else, it looked for a while like the entire stock market industry was about to move into cyberspace. Although this never happened, several new brokerage firms have modestly succeeded in offering financial services online. E-Trade, Ameritrade, and TD Waterhouse are a few names in what was once a longer list.

These firms offer rock-bottom commissions (as low as $5 or $10 per trade), real-time quotes, portfolio management, and varying levels of investor education and analysis tools. A few of these firms are moving to a total financial services model, providing banking and financial planning advice, along with Internet-based trading. For the total do-it-yourselfer, these services are good, but if you need any help—even someone to talk to over the phone about a particular transaction—be careful.

All the Resources You Will Need

Even if you choose to work with a full-service broker, it's still a good idea to get additional information. And if you are an active, do-it-yourself investor, obviously you'll have to do lots of exploring on your own. Whether you need a once-a-month mutual fund price check in a newspaper, or real-time stock quotes and up-to-the-minute news flashes, or detailed professional security analysis and reports, the following sources of information can tell you all you need to know.

Newspapers and Magazines

When it comes to financial information, good old newspapers are, for many, the best information source. Traditional city dailies usually have decent stock quotes and summaries of daily stock-market activity. For the involved investor, the *Wall Street Journal* is an excellent investing source that goes beyond the numbers to cover the businesses behind the investments. *Investor's Business Daily* is a more numbers-intensive publication targeted for the more sophisticated investor. Premier city papers like the *New York Times* and *Los Angeles Times* have excellent business and investing sections.

ESSENTIAL

You can read magazines like *Forbes, Fortune,* and *Smart Money* for more general information on the economy, specific companies, and financial trends. Plus, they have good supporting Web sites with more current information. *BusinessWeek* is also a pretty good (and more timely) investing information source.

Online Resources

The Web has made access to investment information easier, and you can get that information fast. No longer do you have to drive to your local brokerage office or library, or wait for dated information to show up by mail. The latest—and often most complete—information is available from your desktop. You can get basic information for free—and upgrade from there if you're willing to pay. There are three basic types of financial information sources online:

- **Finance portals:** These contain quotes, data, and broad sources of investment information. They also post links to more specific information sources. Yahoo!Finance *(http://finance.yahoo.com)* is probably the best, and it is free. It provides excellent quotes, charts, news, and summarized company profiles. You can also register for a modest dollar fee and get published investment analysis and reports.
- **Online financial services:** These services are offered by companies such as Bloomberg *(www.bloomberg.com),* Kiplinger finance *(www.kiplinger.com),* CNBC *(www.cnbc.com),* and CNN/money *(www.cnnfn.com),* which are essentially online periodicals with investing information and real-time news and articles about business and the industry.
- **Internet-based brokerage services:** Traditional and discount brokers are making more and more information available on their Web sites. Furthermore, online-only brokers such as E-Trade and Ameritrade are putting ever more complete information resources on the Web to differentiate their products. Most of these sites have published investment reports, "in-house" analysis, and real-time stock quotes. Be aware that online broker offerings change frequently and should be checked out before using them.

Do you want real-time stock quotes? In the 1920s, to keep up to the minute, you went to the corner broker and watched the ticker tape. Now most of this information is at your fingertips. But many online quote services show only "delayed" quotes. Usually NASDAQ has a fifteen-minute delay and the NYSE a twenty-minute delay. Why? Does stock quote data travel at less than the speed of light? No—instead, major exchanges publish "delayed" information for free and make real-time data available for a fee. So if your online broker or Web site serves up delayed quotes, they are trying to save money.

Special Services

For the individual investor, there are comprehensive information services that digest and analyze company information and publish regular reports based on their analyses. Some are "consumer friendly"; others are meant more for investing professionals. They all charge a fee, and some are pretty expensive. Here's a sampling:

- *Morningstar (✎ www.morningstar.com)* emerged mainly as a mutual fund investing source (more in Chapter 13) but has expanded to provide excellent coverage for individual companies. You can subscribe to Morningstar for $11.95 a month.
- *Value Line* has been around for years. It publishes the *Value Line Investment Survey,* a complete evaluation of about 1700 companies rotated through once-a-week analysis by sector. *Value Line* packs a tremendous amount of data and analysis into a well-organized one-page summary that costs about $570 each year ($65 trial subscriptions are available). *Value Line* publishes reports for specialized securities such as convertible bonds, and is expanding their online presence.
- *Hoover's Online (✎ www.hoovers.com)* is a more sophisticated and professionally oriented information source with complete company information, news releases, and analysis. A subscription costs $1,000/year and up, depending on the service you want. Rather than pay that kind of money for a newsletter, it may be better to work with a broker or investment advisor who has access to Hoover's! Ⓔ

Chapter 11

Investing in Stocks

This chapter expands on the whys of stock investing (covered in Chapter 10) to offer a broad survey of techniques, styles, strategies, and a few tools. However, be aware that if you're planning to manage your own stock investments, you should probably get more detailed information before jumping in to play in the stock market.

Making Money in Stocks

By purchasing stock from a particular company, shareholders invest in that company as its owners. As a shareholder, you allocate capital—your assets—for use in a firm's business (usually indirectly—not paid directly to the firm). In return, you expect a share of that firm's profits, or earnings. Those earnings are either paid back to you in the form of dividends or retained for use in the firm's business to grow the business and generate still more earnings in the future. Many profitable companies pay a portion of their earnings as dividends and keep the rest in the business as retained earnings. And if the company isn't profitable—if it is losing money—a portion of that loss also belongs to you. It is usually represented in the long run by a decrease in the stock price and in the value of your invested capital.

E FACT

Know the tax rules. Dividends and short-term capital gains are taxed at your ordinary "marginal" income tax rates. Thus, if you are in the 27 percent bracket, dividends and short term gains (gains on stocks held less than one year) are taxed at 27 percent. On the other hand, long-term capital gains (held more than one year) are taxed at a maximum rate of 20 percent, and the rate may be lower depending on your tax bracket.

Cashing In

Dividends are most commonly paid to shareholders as cash (actually a check or automatic transfer to a brokerage account). Retained earnings are reinvested in the business. You receive no cash, but growth in the size and profitability of the business is ultimately translated to a growth in the share price. Thus, your investment grows and turns into cash only if and when you decide to sell. The distinction between the two methods for getting paid is important:

- Dividends are taxable as current income (just like your wages or any other earned income). Unless you reinvest this current income, you give away the power of compounding.

- Stock price gains that build up over time are called "capital gains" when the stock is sold. As capital gains, they receive favorable tax treatment—that is, they are taxed at lower rates. If you don't sell, there is no tax hit—and even more importantly, the earnings are left "on the table" to continue compounding.

These tax deferral and compounding features are a primary pillar in the long-term "buy and hold" strategy of stock investing. But you must stay on top to ensure that the company is still using and investing retained earnings wisely.

Regardless of the investing climate, making money in stocks still boils down to current cash income (dividends) paid by the company and long-term appreciation in the value of your "capital" investment. Your investing strategy will be governed by how much you want now versus later and by how much risk you want to take in the accumulation of long-term capital growth.

The Stock Market

Does it seem to you that you hear more talk about stock markets than about individual companies and their stocks? Most news and business reports talk about "the market" and how it performed on a given day. Stock markets are forums in which buyers and sellers of company shares are linked together—mainly by brokers and dealers acting as shareowner representatives. As a stock investor, you should know a little about stock markets and how they really work.

The Major Players

In the United States, three major stock markets dominate the playing field: the New York Stock Exchange (NYSE), the American Stock Exchange (AMEX), and the NASDAQ system or stock market (NASDAQ stands for "National Association of Securities Dealers Automated Quotation"). NYSE and AMEX have traditional trading floors where buyers and sellers are linked together through dealer and broker representatives dealing in person. These exchanges are known as "auction" markets, because a specialist brings buyer and seller together.

Each company stock has a specialist. Buy and sell orders are routed electronically or brought in person to that specialist on the exchange floor. The specialist matches buy and sell orders, thus executing stock trades. The specialist may also act as buyer or seller for him or herself—and is supposed to do so in troubled times to help preserve an orderly market. When you see a stock price for an NYSE or AMEX stock, it is the last price at which stock changed hands.

FACT

At the time of this writing, there were about 3,500 listed NYSE stocks, 4,000 NASDAQ stocks, and about 1,000 AMEX stocks. Each exchange has minimum qualifications for a listing.

The NASDAQ is an entirely different type of market. There is no trading floor; it operates entirely through a massive computer network. Essentially, it is an immense electronic dealer quote board. While NYSE and AMEX have a single specialist to match and execute trades for a stock, NASDAQ is an open market, with multiple dealers making a market for a given stock. Each stock has one or (usually) many dealers, or market makers. Each dealer posts a bid price—a price they are willing to pay you as a holder to buy your shares, and an offer (or "ask") price—the price at which they would sell you shares. Each dealer is required to post a bid and an offer price, but they can be at any price level. Naturally, if you're selling stock, you look for the market maker making the highest bid, and if you're buying, you're looking for the dealer posting the lowest offer. The current price for a stock is essentially the best bid and lowest offer available among all dealers. Unless you're doing high-performance direct access trading (or "day trading"), your broker routs orders to the dealer with the best price. Stocks will be quoted at the last traded price and at the best quoted current bid and offer.

The NYSE is the most stringent, requiring market cap (total market value, which is calculated by multiplying the share price by the number of shares outstanding) in excess of $100 million. Traditionally, NYSE stocks were the more established, steadier "blue chip" corporations; the new or more speculative companies tended to trade on the NASDAQ. That line has blurred during the past twenty years, with mainstays such as Microsoft and Intel choosing to remain on the NASDAQ, even though they'd easily qualify as NYSE stocks.

QUESTION?

What's a "market cap"?
It's the total capitalization of a company—the price of its shares multiplied by the number of shares outstanding. For example: a company with 500 million shares outstanding at $5 each has a market cap of $2.5 billion. Companies with total capitalization of over $5 billion are called "large cap"; companies with $1 billion to $5 billion are "medium cap"; and those with less than $1 billion in total capitalization are "small cap" companies.

In addition to the "big three," there are several smaller or more specialized markets and exchanges. NASDAQ has a "small cap" market for smaller, emerging companies. There are regional exchanges, such as Boston, Cincinnati, and the Pacific Stock Exchange (investors generally rely on these for additional trading coverage at lower fees). There are also specialized exchanges to handle futures and option contracts. You won't encounter these exchanges very often.

What Makes Stock Prices Move?

Stock prices move according to supply and demand. If there are more buyers than sellers, the price goes up; if there are more sellers than buyers, the price comes down until either more buyers come into the market and/or more sellers leave the market.

Can you influence stock prices, or are you just along for the ride? It's hard to say. On one hand, you are in the market with many other investors just like you. But there are also large institutional investors that carry more influence than individuals. Institutional investors include the following.

- **Mutual funds:** Professionally managed funds that use money collected from individual investors like you to buy large quantities of stock.
- **Pension and retirement funds:** Trust funds from large and small corporations that invest retirement savings assets.
- **Financial services companies:** Insurance companies and others who invest collected premiums and fees as a reserve against future losses and expenses.

It isn't so important that you understand institutions per se as to understand their effect on the market. Obviously, institutions buy and sell a lot more stock than you can, and as such, they have a lot to do with which way prices are heading. If the "market" as a whole is going up or down, chances are this mainly reflects institutional activity. So the answer is, you are mostly along for the ride.

Taking the Market's Pulse

Most individuals and families should not be too concerned about the inner workings and day-to-day pulse of the markets. It's fun to watch what is happening to your stocks—especially when they are gaining value. But it can be equally painful to watch the downward movements and daily fluctuations. Patient long-term investors learn not to get too excited on the "upticks" or too alarmed on the "downticks." Determining the difference between "noise" fluctuations and true business changes is one of the major challenges in investing.

E ALERT!

It's usually a good idea to at least glance occasionally at prices for stocks you own. You should also track a few important "aggregate" indicators of what's going on in the markets.

Individual stock prices are quoted every day, and many Web sites offer "real time" quotes during trading days (Monday through Friday, 9:30 A.M. to 4 P.M., EST) online. Daily quotes in the newspaper usually include the company name, the previous day's trading volume, opening price, highest price, lowest price, closing price, and the net change for the day. More generous listings will include fifty-two-week highs and lows, so you can see how the stock's prices have changed over time. Some also include key evaluation data, such as dividend payout and the P/E (price-to-earnings) ratio—more about P/E in a minute.

Watching the Major Market Indices

To follow the market's performance, you can follow the major market indices, such as the Dow Jones Industrial Average, the NASDAQ Composite, and the S&P 500. These indices are designed to represent the markets as a whole, so by watching one number (or all three), you can get a sense for overall market performance.

Each index is a representative "basket" of stocks, a mathematical representation of the sum of price movements in the constituent stocks that make up the index. So, depending on how many stocks are up or down and what their "weight" is in the index, the index itself will move one way or another. Although some companies will have more weight than others due to the size of their "market capitalization" (total value of all shares in the market), there are enough stocks in each index to minimize random events or fluctuations for any one company.

Dow Jones Industrial Average, or the "Dow," was created back in the late nineteenth century to measure performance of the railroad stocks. The Dow tracks performance of thirty U.S. companies in different sectors of the economy. Today, it is a good indicator of how the economy performs in every major sector (except perhaps transportation and utilities). Over time, the companies that make up the chosen thirty change—some companies are dropped and are replaced by others. Today, the thirty include such big names as General Electric, Procter & Gamble, and 3M.

FACT

The "industrials" once had a stronger "smokestack" flavor, including companies like U.S. Steel. As the economy has evolved towards services and technology, companies like Intel, Microsoft, Home Depot, McDonalds, and JP Morgan Chase are now considered "industrials."

The NASDAQ Composite index reflects the price movements of all NASDAQ stocks. There is also the "NASDAQ 100" index; it shows the movements of the largest 100 stocks on NASDAQ (this index seldom reaches the general news). Both NASDAQ indexes are highly influenced by technology companies, which tend to list on the NASDAQ. The NASDAQ Composite Index moved from 1000 to above 5000 in the late 1990s, then back to 1100–1200 as the stock market bubble—which was greatly driven by technology stocks—burst.

The Standard & Poor's (S&P) 500 index, created and maintained by investment service firm Standard & Poor, is widely considered the broadest and most reliable indicator of market performance. As the name implies, the S&P index tracks 500 firms. Companies in the S&P are generally the largest traded; they represent a range of industries and sizes and can be traded on any exchange. The S&P 500 has a couple of first cousins: the somewhat narrower, larger-capitalization S&P 100, and the S&P "Midcap" 400. You won't hear much about the latter two on the news, however.

ESSENTIAL

While highly diversified in a range of industries, even the S&P 500 was considered technology-oriented in the late 1990s, as the "market cap" on big technology companies carried greater and greater weight in the index.

Other Market Indicators

Beyond the major market indices, there are a considerable number of other general and specialized indices and market indicators, such as the following:

- In addition to the Dow Jones Industrial Average, the Dow Jones also publishes the "20 Transportation," the "15 Utilities," and the broader "65 Stocks" indices. Additionally, you can take a look at their large-cap, mid-cap, and small-cap indices, "growth" and "value" stock indices (more on these terms later), and a few indexes that reflect foreign stocks.
- Standard & Poor's publishes the lesser-known 600 small-cap stock index.

- NASDAQ offers a Biotech, a Computer, and a Telecommunications index.
- For the very broadest market coverage, there are "Wilshire 5000" and "Wilshire 2000" indexes.

Where can you find and track these indicators? Most major financial publications and Web sites have at least a few of them. The *Wall Street Journal* has an excellent summary of all of them in their newly formatted "Markets Lineup" page in their Money and Investing section.

Markets by the Slice

Stock markets are divided into sectors that represent major industries or groups of companies. Different investment services have a different approach to separating the market into sectors. Most often, you'll see ten to twelve sectors. The *Wall Street Journal,* for example, divides U.S. economic sectors into the following nine categories:

1. Telecommunications
2. Technology
3. Energy
4. Health care
5. Basic materials
6. Industrial
7. Consumer cyclical
8. Consumer noncyclical
9. Utilities

Each of these sectors has subsectors—technology comprises computer, semiconductor, and software groupings, while basic materials would have mining, forest products, and steel.

QUESTION?

Why is it important to look at sectors?
Because certain sectors may be performing well in an otherwise weak market, and vice versa. You certainly want to look at individual companies when committing your investment dollars, but it's good to understand what is happening with the overall industry or "macro" environment in which the company does business.

Value Stocks Are on the Third Floor

Like any market, the stock market is a department store with many different kinds of things for sale. You should understand the different stock types to focus on what makes sense for your portfolio. There are many classification schemes; here are some basics presented as dichotomies or opposites.

Growth versus Income

Some businesses are new, emerging, high-growth organizations with most of their growth ahead of them. Most technology companies, particularly those creating and marketing new technologies, are in this category. However, high growth is associated with a high degree of risk.

Other businesses are steady, low- to no-growth, cash-generating businesses. Their markets are steady, there is little-to-no innovation, and there is little-to-no risk. Electric utilities exemplify this type of business. Returns are very steady and predictable—but not as high as from emerging-growth companies. Most profits are paid to investors as dividends instead of being retained in the business.

Growth versus Value

This distinction is harder to capture because different investors have a different idea of what value really is. Growth stocks represent emerging or maturing companies with high business growth potential. Rapid-growth companies serve emerging markets with a lot of innovation. These companies may also be capturing market share with a better product or service. Whatever the reason, these businesses are expected to grow, usually in the range of about 10–20 percent or more per year. With that expectation in place, their stocks are usually priced ahead of growth—that is, investors assume profits will eventually grow to support the stock price. Naturally, with this assumption, there is more risk—if the companies don't, in fact, gain revenues down the road, investors will decide that the stocks are overvalued and prices will drop.

Value stocks, on the other hand, usually represent solid, steady businesses with good products, command of their market, and solid management. Because of their strengths, they often have a growth story to go with their "excellence" story. The key is this: Value stocks are considered undervalued by the market. That is, the market price underestimates the value of the steady business, the growth potential, or both. Risk is usually low, but it is still higher than a pure income stock.

Blue Chip, Glamour, and Penny Stocks

Blue chip stocks are those issued by large, solid companies with established reputations, dominant market positions, and relatively few risk factors. Stocks of big consumer and industrial "staple" companies like Procter & Gamble and General Electric are considered blue chips. With these stocks, you're most likely to grow at the pace of the economy, with less risk than most stocks.

Glamour stocks are for companies with popular names; these stocks often fit into the high-growth category. Most recently, Internet stocks like Amazon.com and Yahoo! fit this category—investors fell in love with them as a concept without much regard to their underlying business models.

And what about penny stocks? Well, the name says it all. These are cheap stocks, under $5 per share, often selling literally for just pennies a share. Almost without exception, these are high-risk crapshoots.

Defensive and Cyclical Stocks

Defensive stocks do well in economic downturns. The underlying businesses of food stocks, many retailers, publishers, utilities, and some energy companies hold up relatively well as the overall level of business slows down. The reason defensive stocks are "defensive" is that demand for their products is relatively inelastic—that is, regardless of what is happening with the economy, consumers will continue to buy a relatively unchanged amount of their product.

ESSENTIAL

People need food, electricity, and other basic necessities regardless of whether they are making lots of money. The nature of defensive stocks is to provide relatively small gains at low risk because these stocks are less likely to be driven down by a sour economy.

Cyclical stocks move with the economy. That is, when the economy is doing well, these companies—usually manufacturing companies that produce chemicals, paper, and other basic materials—keep up as well. When the economy slows, these businesses slow too. Investors could play this cycle, but in recent years, the cyclical nature of these businesses has been recognized, and the stocks are less likely to rise during significant economic booms.

Preferred and Common Stocks

What is a preferred stock? A stock that you would prefer? Or is it preferred by the investment community? No—a preferred stock represents a different form of business ownership. Normal stock ownership commits capital to a company in return for a share of profits and voting power. This is called common stock. Preferred stock owners also invest as owners, but they opt for a fixed return rather than a share of profits or voting power. Preferred shares get a piece of the profits first (hence the term) but their share is fixed. If the company does really well, they don't share in the success, nor do they share in a loss if there is one. Preferred shares are really a cross between ownership and a loan to the company. Most companies do not have preferred shares.

What Color Is Your Investing Parachute?

No two people are alike and no two companies are alike, and so it follows that no two investors are alike. There are indeed different styles and strategies for investing. Investing styles are determined by your situation and investing personality. Here are important factors influencing your investing strategy:

1. **Personal time:** You can know every stock price movement and almost everything about a company—if you have the time and patience to dig in. Most people don't have this kind of time—they have other priorities and responsibilities. They prefer steady investments requiring little minute-by-minute attention.

2. **Detail tolerance:** Likewise, many people just don't want to watch the detailed numbers and fluctuation of the markets.
3. **Risk tolerance:** This is perhaps the most significant factor. People have different perceptions of how much they're willing to risk in order to achieve a gain. Some people like to take chances; others stick to more predictable outcomes while forgoing large "home run" returns.

FACT

Speculators buy on the chance that something good might happen. If it does, they are rewarded; if it doesn't, they lose the investment. Oil, gold, and many tech stocks are speculations, bought when the investor thinks the possibility of reward is worth the risk.

As a result, investors may be grouped into the following categories, each one pursuing a unique investing style:

- **Fundamental investors:** These are the investors who look at the numbers to learn about a specific company and its performance. Their belief is that good financials (key financial measures that indicate the financial health and success of a business) and strong profits support a stock price. They buy a stock because they believe the financials will improve.
- **Technical investors:** These investors make their decisions based on price and price patterns—not the fundamental financial performance of the company itself. They look at chart patterns and overall market psychology, and they buy or sell when the right mathematical signals occur. (The technical approach isn't popular with most investors.)
- **Story investors:** Story investors are drawn to "story" companies and industries, and to some extent, market psychology. The Amazon.com story a few years back was hard to resist. Other companies come into favor depending on economic conditions and, simply, if they are "hot" on any particular day. Timeliness is the key to this type of investing.
- **Momentum investors:** These investors draw on a combination of story and technical patterns. They look for good stories and strong price movements—signs that investor demand simply exceeds supply.

Many Internet stocks fell into this category—stocks were up two, three, four dollars a day and people simply had to be on for the ride. Needless to say, this is a dangerous form of investing, particularly for those investors who are uninformed or who lack experience.

- **Value investors:** Value investing is a combination of fundamental and growth investing, with the added stipulation of a reasonable or undervalued stock price. Value investors closely examine the company's business—its markets, management, and financial fundamentals—to determine its true value as a business. If the stock price is less than current and/or future value, they deem it a "buy." For more on value investing, you can read *Value Investing for Dummies* (Wiley, 2002) by this author.
- **Buy-and-hold investors:** These investors evaluate carefully, then buy and hold for the long term, believing that in the long run, the company will grow and prosper. They deliberately ignore intermediate bad news and price swings. For the most part this strategy has worked—especially with diversification and "dollar cost averaging"—to produce good returns.

QUESTION?

What is "dollar cost averaging" (DCA)?

Dollar cost averaging means making consistent periodic investments in a stock over time. It expands the "accumulation annuity" idea (Chapter 4), which says that adding consistently to an investment enhances the benefits of compounding. With this approach, you buy proportionately more shares on price dips and fewer on price spikes, resulting in a lower overall average stock price for your shares. Many long-term investors use DCA for both stocks and mutual funds—but it takes some nerve to buy more during the dips.

Evaluating Stock Investments

So when it comes to actually following through with your strategy and purchasing stocks, how do you pick the good ones? If this were an exact science, everybody would buy the same things and there would be no "market" per se. Many diverse factors and formulas are considered important in evaluating companies and their stocks. The most rational approach is to first evaluate the company, then take a look at the stock price.

Evaluating the Company

First and foremost, a company worthy of your hard-earned money should be a good business. Note that this is mainly a value-investing approach, advisable for most individual investors. What is a good business? A good business has a good market position, good management, and a good financial record.

- **Good market position** means a good brand reputation, substantial and growing market share, customer loyalty, and the command over prices and profits. You as an investor may not be a "marketeer," but you know a strong brand and market position when you see it. Good examples include Starbucks, Dell, Southwest Airlines, and Coca-Cola.
- **Good management** means that the company is led by respected, candid, honest people who are more interested in the good of the business than their own good. One way of establishing whether a company is well managed is by looking at the way it makes its decisions. Good management often goes hand in hand with good marketing and a good understanding of the company's customers.
- **Good financial records** show success through strong profit margins, earnings, balance sheets, and "cash flow." It makes sense to invest in a profitable company that is growing ever more profitable, isn't overburdened with debt, and creates more capital than it consumes.

Evaluating the Stock Price

Once you find a good company, the next question is whether it offers good stock prices. Investors evaluate price using many familiar and not-so-familiar measures. Here are the factors that they may look at:

- **Price-to-earnings ratio (P/E):** This number is derived from the current stock price divided by (usually) the last twelve months' actual earnings per share. The best way to understand P/E is to invert it, that is, to look at annual earnings as a percentage of price. In a nutshell, that is your rate of return on the investment. P/E ratios will be higher for growth companies, as future growth is projected into the earnings streams. Most P/E ratios range between 10 and 20, but they do vary from time to time and industry to industry.

- **Price-to-sales ratio (P/S):** Another good price indicator is the ratio of price to sales per share—really, the ratio of the company's "market cap" to its annual sales. A P/S ratio of 1 or less is good, and 3 or more is bad.
- **Price-to-cash ratio:** This ratio determines how much cash there is on hand per share. Look at the cash on hand (sometimes shown as "cash and cash equivalents" or "cash and investments"). Divide that figure by the number of shares outstanding (usually found at the bottom of the income statement and sometimes on the balance sheet) to get the amount of cash on hand per share. The price-to-cash ratio is the ratio of the current share price to the per-share cash figure, which can of course be inverted to get a percentage of the share price represented by cash.
- **Price to cash flow:** Instead of looking at cash on hand, you can also look at cash flow—how much real cash is being generated by the business. Earnings should go in hand with cash flow but often don't—accounting and timing issues like asset depreciation get in the way. Cash flow is a truer (and more honest) indicator of business performance, but make sure to consider capital requirements—equipment, machines, and so forth—in the cash flow equation.

Obviously, experienced investors and professional advisors look beyond these factors, but these will give you a start and at least a basis for sifting through investment information and advice.

Chapter 12

Investing in Bonds

You have a choice of how to participate in the American economy: as an owner or as a lender. Owners accept more downside risk but also share more in rewards, while lenders achieve a relatively fixed and safe return on their investments. Buy bonds, and you are a lender—either to the private sector or to public agencies like the U.S. government. This chapter will give you an introduction to investing in bonds.

Bond Basics

Bonds are a relatively steady, safe way to invest money, typically for the long term. Yet most individual investors know little about them. Whereas stocks represent owner, or equity, investments in a business, bonds allow you to act as a lender to that business. A bond is essentially a contract specifying that (1) you will be paid back at a specified maturity date, and (2) you will be paid a specified percentage in interest for the use of your money during that term. Once a bond is issued and purchased, it may be bought and sold by investors on the bonds market.

Here's how bonds work. Let's say you buy a $1,000 bond from a company or government agency specifying a thirty-year term and a 6-percent interest rate. You write a check to that entity (or a broker, who then passes on your money to that account) for $1,000. Every year, you will receive $60 of interest for that $1,000. And at the end of thirty years, you will receive your $1,000 back. Note that this is a very basic model of how bonds work. Each particular contract may have additional provisions. As with stocks, there are many different types of bonds, and many different types of organizations issue them. Moreover, very few bonds are held by the original purchaser until they mature (that is, when it's time for the company that issued it to return the original sum invested). Bonds can be bought and sold on the open market for profit or loss. This chapter shows how that works.

Although they are generally safer and more secure than stocks, bond investing has been more of a professional domain. Bonds are less glamorous, and they are more of a place to park large sums of money for a long-term investment. Some government savings bond programs are an exception to this rule. You may choose to employ these government savings programs or let professionals do the driving with bond funds, but it is still important to understand basic principles and terminology of bonds.

Face Value and Current Yield

The $1,000 mentioned in our example is known as the face value—that is, the value that you pay as your principal and that you will get back at the end of the lending term. The 6-percent interest rate is known as the *current yield,* or *coupon.* The coupon value on bonds varies depending on when it was issued.

Throughout the time you have your bond, its purchasing price (that is, how much you can sell it for) will not necessarily remain at $1,000. Most bond prices fluctuate, driven by a combination of prevailing interest rates, the term to maturity, inflation, and credit risk of the issuer. (The forces that drive bond prices will be examined in a minute.)

FACT

Interest for most bonds is paid semiannually. The 6 percent bond mentioned earlier would pay $30 twice a year. Prices will adjust slightly to accommodate the timing difference—if you buy a bond just before a June 1 interest payment, you'll pay a little more to cover the seller's earned interest for holding the bond up to (almost) the payment date.

Premium and Discount Values

Interest rates on new bonds fluctuate from year to year, affecting the purchase price of the bonds already in the market. Let's say you've had your 6-percent bond for two years. This year, the prevailing interest rate for bonds and credit of similar risk and maturity is 8 percent.

That means that people who buy bonds issued this year earn a higher current return than people who own bonds issued two years ago. You will be getting your $60 in interest from $1,000, while those who bought bonds at 8 percent interest will be getting $80 from a $1,000 face value. Basically, this means that your bond (if you were to sell it) is worth $750. At that price, your current return ($60/750) is equivalent to today's bond investor receiving $80 on an investment of $1,000. The difference between $1,000 and $750 is known as a *discount*.

Likewise, if the current interest rate were 5 percent, the $60 interest payment would equalize to the 5 percent going rate at bond price of $1,200 ($60 ÷ $1,200 = 0.05, or 5 percent). The $200 difference is known as a *premium*.

ESSENTIAL

Always remember that bond prices move opposite to interest rates. If interest rates move up, bond prices move down to adjust the fixed coupon to market rates. If interest rates move down, bond prices move up. That's because a $1,000 bond paying greater than a market return is worth more than $1,000. When you hear about the bond market going up, that means interest rates are coming down.

Yield to Maturity

Yield to maturity, or YTM, is an important gauge of total return from your bond investments. Essentially, YTM measures the total return on a bond, from the present time to the maturity date.

Recall that the 6 percent $1,000 face-value bond used in the example pays a $60 current yield, or coupon. But suppose today's prevailing interest rates are indeed 8 percent, and you go to the bond market. Will you really pay $750 for that bond? No, because if you buy that bond, you will get paid the face value of $1,000 when it matures. So you not only get the $60 current yield, but the value of the bond itself will grow as it approaches maturity, because at that time it is worth $1,000 (assuming the issuer is still in business). Thus, over time, there is a gain in the value of the bond, which must be included in the total return. Each year, you get the "current" return of $60, plus a portion of the increase in value from today's purchase price to the $1,000 face amount. This extra return is an important part of the total "yield-to-maturity" (YTM), which in turn affects bond value and pricing.

So back to the original question: Will you pay $750? No, you'll pay a little more to account for the growth potential. The price paid reflects the YTM, not the current yield. Note that the price will also reflect the risk inherent in the bond—to the extent that the issuer may fail and never pay you back, that risk is also incorporated into the bond price. Also incorporated is the potential for changes in interest rates ("interest rate risk"), which directly impacts the value of bonds. The price really paid reflects YTM plus market perception of interest rate and default risk. But for most bonds, YTM has the greatest influence on price.

Why is yield-to-maturity important? Because it is the standard by which bonds are really priced. Price takes total yield into account—all the way to maturity. If today's prevailing interest rate is 8 percent and you buy a 6 percent ten-year bond, you'll pay more than $750 because otherwise, you'd really be getting a 10.92 percent bond due to the $1,000 future payback. Figuring out the exact price is a tricky backwards calculation, but it works out to about $885. The growth from $885 to $1,000 over ten years would be worth 1.23 percent compounded, giving a total YTM just north of 8 percent. You don't need to do these calculations by hand—bond tools and price listings usually do it for you. The concept, however, is important.

ALERT!

Different calculators may calculate YTM differently because some may compound interest at different intervals—semiannually, monthly, or daily instead of annually. Some will make different assumptions about the timing of interest payments—whether at the end of the year, beginning of the year, or at different times of the year. These assumptions will change the results a little.

What Makes Bond Prices Move

Because of their "fixed income" nature, bonds tend to have steady prices and are relatively less risky than stocks. Bondholders are entitled to receive their interest before any returns are paid to stockholders, and they have first rights to assets if the company is liquidated. But bonds do fluctuate in price. Three factors influence how bond prices fluctuate: credit risk, current interest rates, and time to maturity.

Credit Risk

A bond issued by a strong, stable company has less risk than a bond issued by a company in financial trouble. The latter type of bond, known as a "junk" bond, pays higher interest rates because bond buyers (creditors) demand more compensation for the risk.

Current Interest Rates

As we have seen, a bond is originally sold at a par value with an interest rate tied to that value. Bonds adjust to market interest rates by taking on a discount or premium, resulting in a yield-to-maturity equal to current rates.

Time to Maturity

All bonds are paid back eventually. A thirty-year bond is paid back to the bondholder thirty years from issuance. A six-month bond (or note) is paid back to the lender in six months. A long-term bond will usually pay higher interest (or adjust to a lower price) than a short-term bond. Why? There are three reasons:

1. **Credit risk.** There is more time over which business conditions—and therefore credit quality—could deteriorate.
2. **Interest-rate risk.** The bondholder takes the risk that interest rates could rise, causing the bond value and price to deteriorate or discount to match the market.
3. **Inflation risk.** There is also the risk that inflation could rise and further deteriorate the buying power of returned principal years down the road.

Investors demand greater compensation for greater risk, so interest rates usually rise with the length of the term to maturity.

FACT

Generally, bonds maturing in one to five years are considered short-term bonds; those that mature over five to fifteen years are intermediate-term bonds; and bonds that mature over a period longer than fifteen years are known as long-term bonds.

Bond Ratings

Let's talk some more about credit risk. Credit risk is the risk that the company or entity won't pay you back at the bond's maturity. This doesn't happen very often, but some businesses (or governmental agencies) do fail to honor the bonds. The reason that this is rare is because bondholders are higher on the "food chain" of creditors than shareholders—that is, every last penny of shareholder equity will be exhausted to meet a bond obligation. That said, companies do go bankrupt, destroying both shareholder and bondholder values.

Credit risk can vary from low to very high, and interest rates vary accordingly. Credit risk is assessed and published by three major rating agencies: Standard & Poor's, Moody's, and Fitch. Each recognizes investment-grade and noninvestment-grade bonds. As you might guess, investment-grade bonds carry less risk—and lower interest rates. Noninvestment-grade, or "junk," bonds are issued by entities perceived to have higher credit risk, and they will carry interest rates two percent or higher than the going rate.

The rating system used for corporate bonds is illustrated in the following table. Municipal and agency rating systems use different codes but have the same flavor.

Standard Credit Rating System

Investment grade	**Standard & Poor's**	**Moody's**
High grade	AAA-AA	Aaa-Aa
Medium grade	A-BBB	A-Baa
Noninvestment grade	**Standard & Poor's**	**Moody's**
Speculative	BB-B	Ba-B
Default	CCC-D	Caa-C

Each bond issue is assigned a credit rating by the major credit agencies. Typically, the financial health and business prospects of a bond issuing company are analyzed, and a rating is assigned to the debt securities issued. In the wake of 2001 bankruptcies and accounting scandals, rating agencies are keeping a closer eye on credit quality and are making more frequent rating changes or assigning "credit watches" to companies with changing financial pictures.

Four Major Types of Bonds

There are four major kinds of bonds: corporate, government, municipal, and agency bonds. They differ based on the nature of issuer. Corporate bonds, naturally, are issued by private businesses (corporations), while government and municipal bonds are issued by entities in the public sector. Agency bonds are either issued or backed by public agencies. Among other differences, these bond types have different risk profiles and tax characteristics and are traded in different markets.

Corporate Bonds

Corporate bonds are sold and repaid by private business corporations. These bonds are the major source of corporate long-term borrowing. They are traded in ordinary bond markets and "over the counter"—through networks of securities dealers similar to the NASDAQ dealer network. There are different flavors of corporate bonds. Some bonds are "asset backed," secured by certain assets or covenants in the corporation; others are "debentures," bonds backed by the general creditworthiness of the corporation.

Corporate bonds, in general, bear higher risk than government bonds since payback depends on the continued success of the corporation. As a result, they typically offer higher interest rates. As just seen, there are many different risk/reward profiles within the corporate bond world as indicated by the rating system—you can buy "junk" bonds to get a higher yield or stay with the safer "blue chip" companies, sacrificing a few percentage points of yield for safety and security. Corporate bond prices do fluctuate freely based on the forces highlighted earlier in this chapter.

Government Bonds

Government bonds are issued and backed by the U.S. government. As a practical matter, this eliminates credit risk, because the government can always print more money! As a result, they pay lower interest rates, but a big risk factor is eliminated. (Prices can still fluctuate with interest rates, however.)

There are three different flavors of government bonds sold and traded in securities markets (or available directly from the U.S. Treasury):

- **Treasury bills** are short-term and mature in one year or less.
- **Treasury notes** mature in two to ten years.
- **Treasury bonds**, or "long bonds," mature in ten years or longer.

In most cases, interest rates are higher for longer-term contracts.

ESSENTIAL

Treasury bonds and savings bonds have tax advantages. While corporate bond interest is fully taxable, U.S. Treasury obligations are (by Constitutional mandate!) not taxable at the state and local level. Interest can be taxed as income at the federal level. However, they aren't taxable until maturity and, in the case of some salvation bonds, are not taxable *at all* if used for college expenses for eligible family members (if originally issued in 1990 or after).

In addition to these traded securities, the U.S. government also issues savings bonds. These bonds are targeted at the small investor and can be bought in increments as small as $25 from your local bank, through a payroll deduction, or directly from the U.S. Treasury. Savings bonds are simple–you buy at half the face value, and at maturity, you receive the face value. There are no annual or semi-annual interest payments. The maturity periods vary and are currently seventeen years. Something that doubles in seventeen years pays a modest interest rate of 4.23 percent (recall the Rule of 72, from Chapter 4), but there are tax advantages, and unlike stocks and most other bonds, there is no commission or sales charge.

Municipal Bonds

"Munis" are actually a broad category of bonds issued by state and local governments. States, counties, cities, and districts such as sewer or school districts, can all issue bonds. Since these organizations can't print money, there is a minute amount of credit risk (as Orange County bondholders learned a few years ago) and some interest rate risk, but these securities are generally safe. There is a key to municipal bonds.

The interest received is not taxable by the federal government. This small subsidy provided by the federal government allows them to pay lower interest rates since the yield is tax-free. However, they are subject to state and local taxes.

FACT

Municipal bonds can be "revenue" bonds, with specific tax or user fees (like tolls) set aside to pay them back, or they can be "general obligation" bonds, backed by the general credit and cash flow of the entity. The latter are a little riskier and carry slightly higher rates. Credit risk can vary slightly, as some entities are more fiscally sound than others.

Agency Bonds

Government agency bonds are bonds for public or semipublic agencies created by the federal government. These agencies support projects related to public policy and programs—small businesses, first-time homebuyer loans, farming grants, and assistance with college tuition. These bonds don't carry the full U.S. Treasury guarantee but are generally considered very safe—after all, they are issued by a government agency and a default would be devastating. Typically the yields are slightly higher than straight Treasury securities. Some of the popular and familiar agencies include the following:

- Federal National Mortgage Association (Fannie Mae)
- Government National Mortgage Association (Ginnie Mae)
- Federal Home Loan Mortgage Corporation (Freddie Mac)
- Federal Agricultural Mortgage Corporation (Farmer Mac)
- Student Loan Marketing Association (Sallie Mae)
- Small Business Administration (SBA)

Most of these agencies lend money to their target constituents and issue bonds to acquire the funds to lend. You can purchase these securities through brokers, although many have high minimum denominations and are more often found in institutional or bond mutual fund portfolios.

Other Bond Features

As with most other products in the investing world, there is a tremendous assortment of variations and special features around the central theme of bonds. As each bond is a contract, it can be written in whatever way the issuing company prefers (within legal reason). It's impossible to go into all the options and special features you may encounter, but there are two important bond features that you do need to be familiar with. In the following sections, you can familiarize yourself with callable, convertible, and zero-coupon bonds.

Is This Call for You?

If a bond is callable, that means the company can pay you back earlier than the maturity date (think of it as a "recall"). This is not a good option. It means that if interest rates decline, a company can repay the bonds you hold and issue new ones at lower rates, turning your investment outcome into a lose-lose situation: If interest rates fall, your bonds get called, forcing you to redeploy your money at lower rates, and if interest rates rise—you got it—your bond value falls prior to maturity.

When you are purchasing a bond, make sure you look at call provisions—when the issuing company has the right to call the bond (often an earliest date must be specified) and at what price. Aggressive call provisions aren't as much an issue with short-term maturities.

Convertible Bonds

Way back when, someone had a great idea—in return for a lower interest rate, why not give bondholders a "piece of the action" just in case the company to which they lent money really succeeds? This idea turned into the convertible bond. Convertible bonds allow bondholders to convert their bonds into a specified number of common stock shares. Convertible bonds are usually issued at a premium—that is, if converted at issue, the number of shares times the market price would fall short of the bond value. But if the share price appreciates, suddenly, the bond price can look quite attractive.

Bonds selling at a large premium to share price conversion value are priced as bonds—that is, according to the yield-to-maturity with a slight conversion potential added in. Where the underlying common stock has appreciated, the convertible bond price starts to move in lockstep with the stock price, and the yield becomes less and less meaningful. Convertibles can be a good way to lock in an interest rate return while also participating in company growth.

ALERT!

To date, the convertible bond world is complex and mysterious, and it is not easily accessed by the individual do-it-yourself investor. You'll probably need a broker with convertible bond experience to play this one well. Still, convertibles are intriguing investments. Note also that there are convertible preferred stocks, in addition to convertible bonds.

Make Mine a Zero

Zero-coupon bonds do not offer an annual or semiannual fixed interest payment to the bondholder. Instead, they sell at a deep discount to face value, and the price gradually rises towards maturity. (In the yield-to-maturity calculation, there is no current-yield component but only a compounded gain to maturity.) Zeroes are good for people trying to pinpoint a specific maturity date at which they want to receive their return—for example, if they are planning their retirement or expect to be paying college tuition sometime in the future. Since payment is deferred, they may carry a higher implied interest rate.

One drawback to zero-coupon bonds is that the IRS will hold you liable for taxes on "imputed" interest earned by these bonds (even though you actually receive nothing). This concern goes away, however, if zeroes are used in a qualified retirement or college savings plan eliminating current taxation. Zeroes are issued both by corporate and government entities.

Bond Investment Basics

Bonds typically provide a cornerstone to the "low risk" portion of your investing portfolio. Steady, predictable interest payments and relatively modest price fluctuations (compared to most stocks) are desirable, particularly the older you get and the closer you get to needing your stash to achieve a goal. Bonds are also used as a hedge and more secure alternative to stocks in turbulent times.

Buying and Selling Bonds

Bonds are typically bought and sold on securities exchanges or on the open market. But the investing process–and information sources–are far less developed than those for stocks. As a result, you should probably work with a knowledgeable broker or advisor to build a bond portfolio–or use a specialized bond mutual fund.

ESSENTIAL

If you're lucky enough to find any bond price listing—most business periodicals, even the *Wall Street Journal*, provide only limited coverage or none at all—you'll find bonds priced in decimals just as stocks. You may see a given bond at $97.50. Does that mean it costs $97.50? No. Since the face amount for most bonds is $1,000, the actual price you pay is $975.

Purchasing U.S. Treasury bonds, bills, notes, and savings bonds is easier–you can do it on the Internet. The service is called "Treasury Direct" and can be found at *www.savingsbonds.gov*. The site also provides information on current products, interest rates, and special savings plans.

Bond Mutual Funds

Another option is to invest in a bond mutual fund, but these have had a very mixed track record over the years. While they have professional management and can buy in economically large quantities, they often get trapped by portfolio rotation and call provisions, and many have ended up offering the same "lose-lose" proposition as an individual callable bond. That is, when interest rates are falling, bonds that mature or are called out of their portfolio must be replaced at lower yields; when interest rates rise, the value of the portfolio declines. The prevailing wisdom is to avoid long-term bond funds and find funds with short- to intermediate-term maturities or with effective "laddering" to mitigate the effects of interest rate fluctuations.

Bond Laddering

One strategy frequently used by bond investors to balance risk and return is called "laddering." As the term implies, you build a ladder of maturities ranging through short-, intermediate-, and long-term bonds. Each year, the one-year term bond matures; the proceeds are reinvested at the "top" of the ladder into a ten-year bond. The maturities roll over, with an even split between one, two, three, four, and all the way to ten years. Yields on the longer-range bonds are higher, while the downside price risk due to interest-rate fluctuations is minimized in the shorter-term bonds. If you have to roll over a bond into a lower-yield ten-year bond, you'll at least be capturing price gains on the other nine years of maturity (lower interest rates means higher bond prices). At the end of the day, you get the best yield with the least risk.

ALERT!

Unless you're managing a large portfolio, individual bond investments may be spread thin to cover each year, bringing in more credit risk and transaction cost. For smaller bond portfolios, look for a fund that uses a laddering strategy.

When Not to Invest in Bonds

If you have a home mortgage, it may make sense to pay it off early instead of investing in bonds. The interest rate on the mortgage is analogous to the interest rate on purchased bonds. Paying off an 8 percent mortgage is just like buying an 8 percent bond—but you get peace of mind and the satisfaction of owning more of your castle. Your return is the savings in interest costs. There are no transaction costs. Tax effects are largely a wash. Your investment—your house—is more secure than most bonds.

Chapter 13

All About Mutual Funds

Mutual funds offer one of the most popular investment vehicles for the average family. With a mutual fund, you get diversification and professional management, but these services come at a small cost. In this chapter, you'll learn about mutual funds, how to evaluate them, and how to use them in your investment portfolio.

What Is a Mutual Fund?

A mutual fund is an investment company. Investment companies are in business to pool your assets with those of other investors and to invest those assets in securities. Mutual funds have been around since the 1930s, but they have become more prominent as more and more people have taken up investing in stocks and begun managing their own retirement plans. Mutual funds allow shareholders—even those with small investments—to participate efficiently in a larger portfolio. Particularly for beginning investors, they provide important "value add" to the investing process—and a way to get started.

FACT

There are over 8,000 mutual funds to choose from—that's more funds than listed stocks—with over $8 trillion in assets invested. It's up to you to choose the funds that are right for you.

Why Mutual Funds?

Mutual funds offer the following compelling advantages:

- **Expertise:** Every fund is managed by a single professional fund manager, who makes buy and sell decisions for all investments in the fund. Most funds also have a staff of professionally trained and qualified analysts helping that manager make choices. They have the time, knowledge, and access to information that you're unlikely to have.
- **Diversification:** Since mutual funds pool investor assets, they may have millions—or even billions—of dollars to invest. As a result, they can build and fine-tune a portfolio of several—sometimes hundreds—of individual investments at high risk and low risk, growth and income, to achieve safety and stability in numbers. Buying a mutual fund achieves more diversification than you can on your own. Translation: You may not "win" as much with a fund, but your likelihood of losing everything is almost nil.
- **Convenience:** Mutual funds are an easy way to invest. Just send a check and—presto!—you have a portfolio. You can move money

between funds with a phone call or through an online transaction, and you can easily set up monthly payroll deductions to keep building and reinvesting your wealth. Most fund "families" have toll-free phone support and helpful Web sites to quickly answer questions at any hour of the day.

- **Low cost of entry:** While small investments in individual stocks can be expensive (high commissions) and provide little diversification, many mutual funds will allow initial investments of as low as $500 or $1,000 and incremental investments as low as $25. You generally don't need to save up to invest in a mutual fund.

Of course, these advantages come with some disadvantages, which will be discussed further. Mutual funds are offered by for-profit companies that earn their living charging management fees and sales charges for their services. Furthermore, some investors may feel uncomfortable about their lack of control and the mutual funds' style of diversification.

Fund Facts

The mutual fund world brings in a whole new assortment of terms and concepts that you need to be familiar with. First and most basic: A mutual fund is a single portfolio of stocks, bonds, other securities, or cash held on behalf of a set of contributing investors. Typically a fund is constructed around a specific investing philosophy and set of investing goals. Here's a sample philosophy: "Follows a value discipline by purchasing large-cap stocks at large discounts to intrinsic value" (Legg Mason Value Trust).

ESSENTIAL

All funds hold assets, and each day, they measure the combined total value of the assets they hold. Dividing by the number of fund shares outstanding gives a net asset value, or NAV, for their holdings. Mutual fund companies are required to post their NAV every day—this is what gets printed in the paper as the fund price.

Funds often have rules and guidelines, like portfolio allocation minimums and maximums, written into their charters. A fund has a manager, who may manage more than one fund. A fund may be "standalone"; today, most funds are part of a fund family offered by a fund company.

A fund family is a coordinated assortment of funds covering a range of investment strategies or sectors with similar entry and exit criteria. For instance, Fidelity offers Freedom, Invest, Select, and Advisor families. The Select family is a set of funds, each invested in a sector of the economy—airline, biotech, computer, energy, and so forth. The Invest group has growth, income, international, domestic, small-cap, mid-cap, and large-cap funds, as well as blends of all of the above. As an investor, you can freely switch your investments (called "fund switching") between funds in a family with a simple phone call or instruction placed via the company's Web site.

A fund company is an investment company in business to manage mutual funds. There are hundreds of these companies, and some are quite large—to the degree that they may be publicly traded stock corporations themselves. Fidelity, Vanguard, Van Kampen, Franklin/Templeton, and Alliance Capital are but a few of the many household names. In addition, most large brokerage firms and some large banks run their own funds.

Open-End and Closed-End Funds

Funds can be either "open end" or "closed end." With open-end funds, every dollar added by investors becomes part of the fund. New shares are created and sold every time new investment dollars come in. When an investor wants to remove assets, shares are redeemed and converted to cash. They aren't sold to another investor. There is no "market" for these shares—the investor deals directly with the fund. The value of each share is exactly equal to its portion of the fund's asset value—there is no premium or discount.

Closed-end funds work differently. They manage a portfolio of assets for investors, but there is a fixed number of shares available because all funds are raised at once at the start of the fund. The shares are bought and sold on exchanges—not by dealing direct with the fund. Price is determined by supply and demand, and the price considers both present asset value and future expectations—therefore, closed-end fund shares will often sell at a discount and sometimes a premium to the value of underlying assets.

FACT

There are a few hundred closed-end funds. They can be a good, accessible way to play certain markets, particularly international stocks through "country" funds such as Germany Fund, Indonesia Fund, and others traded on the NYSE. Most of the rest of this chapter, however, concerns open-end funds, which are more prominent and popular.

Fund Prospectus

Every fund is required to publish and update a prospectus once a year. A prospectus describes the fund's objectives, philosophy, past performance, and major holdings. Some of these documents can be quite dry; recently, though, many mutual fund companies have been preparing prospectuses that are more lively and colorful (though still compliant with Securities and Exchange Commission, or SEC, guidelines). When evaluating funds and fund families, it's important to familiarize yourself with the prospectus; you can usually obtain them online or by mail.

ESSENTIAL

A prospectus is important, but it won't give you the whole story. Many are published only once a year and may have "summary" information—without the details—on a fund's management and holdings. If you really want to know what you're getting when you buy a fund, you will need to dig a little deeper.

Paying for Mutual Fund Services

As stated earlier, mutual funds are businesses that employ professionals and carry the overhead of buildings, management costs, marketing costs, customer service, and other costs, just like any other business. As a result, funds cover these costs (and make a profit) through a system of fees and charges, which you as an investor should understand. Why? Each fund (usually, each fund family) assesses these charges in its own way, and if you aren't aware of the fee structure, you may make investing mistakes. Some funds are simply more expensive than others.

There are two main types of charges. First, there are sales charges—the actual commission paid for the transaction where you acquire or sell fund shares. Second, there are operating expenses—marketing, management, and overhead expenses—that must be recovered. As a fund investor, you need to be aware of both, because they can affect your long-term performance and investing strategy.

Sales Charges

Funds carry sales charges because each time the broker or advisor makes a sale, he or she is paid a commission. By law, these charges cannot exceed 8.5 percent, and most are lower—in the 4–6 percent range. Sales charges, also known as loads, are assessed in any of three ways: as a front-end load at the time of purchase, as a back-end load or redemption fee at the time of redemption, or as a load spread throughout the ownership of the fund. While a back-end load seems more attractive (pay later instead of now), if the fund is successful, you'll be paying a percentage of a higher base. What about "no-load" funds? Are they a way to get around sales charges? Not really. No-load funds simply extract the sales charge from the value of your portfolio, reducing your investment returns and taking "compoundable" money off the table.

E ALERT!

No-load funds position themselves in the market as the less expensive alternative, but the reality may be different. For you, the reality is "pick your poison"—either way, somehow, you pay.

So what's better, load or no-load? Practically every personal finance newspaper column and radio talk show has taken up this debate at one time or another, and no one has won it as of yet. As already explained, if the fund is no-load, sales charges are buried by deducting from net asset value—so you pay in the form of investing performance. No load is certainly easier to understand. If you aren't quite comfortable with a fund, fund family, or mutual fund investing altogether, no-load funds might make sense because removing your assets from the fund won't be as costly. Similarly, if the assets involved may be required for something else—an emergency fund or a house down payment—no-load might be the way to go.

No-load advocates say that since costs come out of investing performance, fund managers have an interest in keeping costs low (to make performance look better). Additionally, they say that load fund results look better than they are precisely because no sales charges are deducted. But for many in the investment community, no-load is simply an advertising gimmick to make people think they're getting something for nothing—when they really aren't. Load fund advocates quip about lack of visibility to sales charges in no-load funds. Here's the bottom line: As an investor, you should look more at the fund itself—its strategy, its holdings, its performance. If it meets your needs, the load/no-load question is a secondary issue.

12b-1 Fees

The "12b-1" fee is industry jargon for "marketing and distribution expenses" for customers already in the fund base. These fees turn into trailing commissions for brokers; combined with service fees, they cover customer service costs (toll-free number information hotline, Web site management, and so forth). The maximum 12b-1 fee is 0.75 percent, with a maximum service fee of 0.25 percent optionally added. Each mutual fund company has a different term for the 12b-1 fee: Most often, it may be called the "account maintenance fee" or "distribution fee."

QUESTION?

Can a fund call itself a "no-load" fund by burying sales costs in 12b-1 fees (and thus in the expense ratio)?
No. The law says any fund with a 12b-1 greater than 0.25 percent must be considered a load fund.

Management and Operating Fees

Getting away from marketing and account maintenance costs, now comes the fee for the professional services of the fund advisors and managers. These fees run higher for actively managed portfolios that require continuous investment research and management. For funds invested in fixed baskets of stocks—as in index funds—these fees will be lower, because no active management decisions are required. Management fees are typically in the 0.5–1 percent range, but they may go from 0.10 percent for "money market" or sector portfolios (as in ETFs, which you will learn about later in this chapter) to 1.5 percent or more for international equity funds—if you see "global" in the fund name, these expenses will be higher! Operating expenses—buildings and other overhead—must also be recovered and may be included in management fees or itemized separately.

The Expense Ratio

The 12b-1, management, and operating expense fees are usually lumped together for comparison into a total expense bucket, then expressed as a percentage of the total assets of the fund. A 1 percent expense ratio means that management and operating costs are 1 percent of the total value of the fund each year. If you have $10,000 invested, your portion of this cost is $100.

ESSENTIAL

Normally, expense costs are covered in one of two ways. Many funds charge ongoing "account maintenance" fees, usually annually, which are deducted directly from your account. Or they may be tacitly removed from the fund's asset base, reducing your "gain" (if there is one) or increasing your loss in the fund. Either way, you pay.

The expense ratio is an important criterion in fund selection. If it seems like 1 percent isn't much, consider this. If you make a 7 percent profit, 1 percent of that is 15 percent of your profit! Even small differences between expense ratios can make a big difference in long-term asset performance.

All-inclusive expense ratios run from 0.10 percent for inactively managed portfolios to as high as 2.5 percent for actively managed and specialized portfolios. International funds, small-cap funds, and special objective funds such as social purpose funds tend to be on the high end. Expense ratios are required to be published in the prospectus and other fund literature. They are featured in more extensive mutual-fund price listings, such as the monthly *Wall Street Journal* mutual-fund review.

To summarize, you should be aware of sales charges and expenses—and their effects on mutual fund performance. Are you getting value for the fees you pay? A 2 percent or higher expense ratio can only be justified by performance.

The ABCDs of Fees and Charges

Let's examine how fees and charges are assessed in practice. You can pick your load or no-load poison. If you pick a mutual fund with a load, you are often faced with another choice—when you want to pay it. Fund companies know that different investors have different preferences and investing habits, and so they have created a set of share classes within their fund families—A shares, B shares, C shares, and (sometimes) D shares. These "grades" have nothing to do with investing performance or objectives—rather, they offer load assessment choices tied to the same portfolio of underlying investments. There is no "standard" classification—each fund may use its own variation. But generally speaking, the breakdown is done in a manner similar to this:

- A shares charge a front-end load with a smaller 12b-1 fee.
- B shares charge a back-end redemption fee and a higher 12b-1 fee, but no front-end load.
- C shares will have a level deferred sales charge fee, which may go away after a set number of years, in addition to a 12b-1 and other ongoing fees.

Additionally, some funds allow switching from one class to another after a certain number of years. If you stay with the fund for awhile, paying the higher 12b-1 and other expenses, the fund may allow a switch to class A or some other class of shares with lower fees, thus waiving sales and redemption charges from then forward. It can get so complex that you need a financial advisor just to explain the fee options—never mind the underlying investment strategy of the fund!

As an example, here is the class breakdown for the Merrill Lynch Select Pricing System, a four-class system Merrill Lynch uses for most of their funds, quoted directly from the fund literature. This one is more complex than most:

- **Class A** shares incur a maximum initial sales charge (front-end load) of 5.25 percent and bear no ongoing distribution or account maintenance fees; these shares are only available to eligible investors.
- **Class B** shares are subject to a maximum contingent deferred sales charge of 4 percent declining to 0 percent after six years. In addition, they are subject to a distribution fee of 0.75 percent and an account maintenance fee of 0.25 percent. These shares automatically convert to Class D shares after eight years.
- **Class C** shares are subject to a distribution fee of 0.75 percent and an account maintenance fee of 0.25 percent. In addition, they are subject to a 1 percent contingent deferred sales charge if redeemed within one year of purchase.
- **Class D** shares incur a maximum initial sales charge of 5.25 percent and an account maintenance fee of 0.25 percent.

Making the choice is difficult and depends on circumstances. If you're planning to stay with the fund family forever and you have the extra capital up front, class A shares may make sense, for the load is paid and gone and you won't incur any additional expenses. If you think you might need to recapture the money—say to buy a house, class C shares might work best. You will pay the 1 percent contingency fee if you redeem within one year, but at least you won't kiss a 4 or 5 percent sales charge goodbye. For investors making periodic—monthly or yearly—investments, class B might work. Sales charges are lower and are waived if the investment is held long enough. Note that these sales charges are not incurred if you switch between funds in a family and, with some fund companies, between families. The bottom line is to understand the facts. Don't let an advisor or broker steer you into a choice that makes more sense for them than you.

ESSENTIAL

Regardless of fund type, know your fees. All funds—load or no-load—have fees and expenses, which can vary a lot from one fund company to another. Know the fees and charges and shop comparatively. Get what you pay for.

Types of Funds to Choose From

The central theme in mutual-fund investing is diversity. There are funds set up to invest in almost any style or sector of the market you can think of. These are the broad classifications:

- **Equity funds** (investments in stocks).
- **Bond funds** (investments in bonds and other fixed income obligations).
- **Hybrid funds** (mixed investments).
- **Money market funds** (investments in short-term fixed-income securities that provide a liquid cash reserve for investors without sales charges and with extremely small management fees).

In turn, equity funds may be classified further according to the following categories:

- **Capitalization:** small cap, mid cap, and large cap.
- **Style:** growth, aggressive growth, conservative, value.
- **Managed portfolio vs. index:** index funds buy baskets of stocks to match major market indices such as S&P 500, while active portfolios pick and choose stocks based on fund objectives.

FACT

Likewise, bond funds can be classified by level of risk (investment grade, noninvestment grade, or "junk"), maturity (long-term, intermediate-term, or short-term), and type of bond (government, municipal, corporate, and so on) with blends among all of the above.

One of the more popular classifications of equity or stock funds is provided by Morningstar Investment Services. Although diversifying into other areas in the investing world, Morningstar is known as the premier mutual fund research and information service. Morningstar classifies stock funds using a classification grid, shown in **FIGURE 13-1**.

FIGURE 13-1

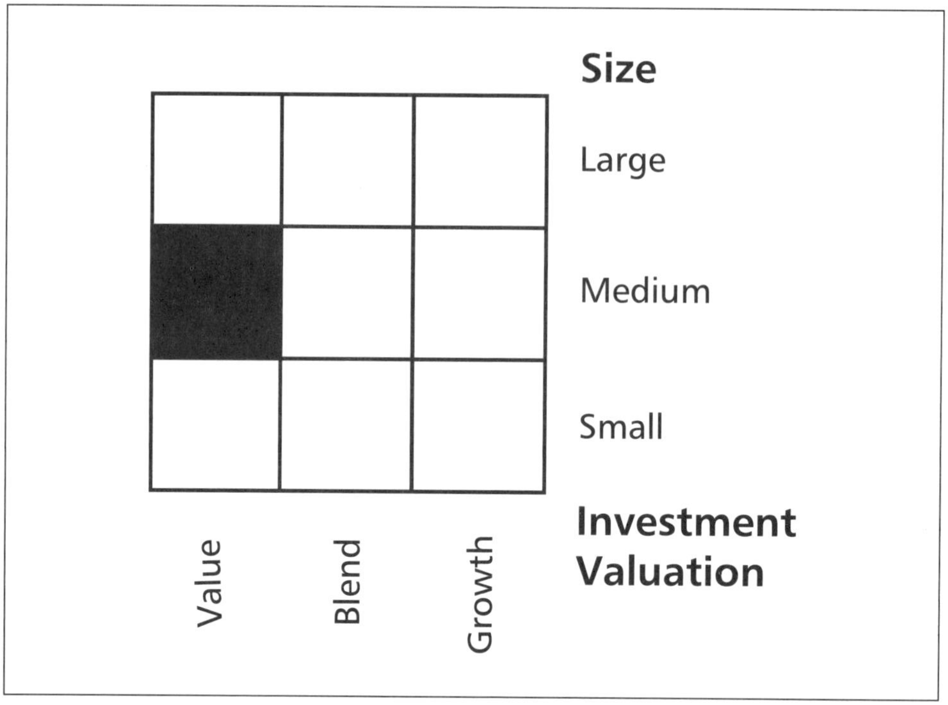

▲ Morningstar classification grid.

Each stock mutual fund is classified into one of the nine boxes. "Size" refers to market capitalization, with large-cap companies being those greater than $5 billion and small-cap companies those less than $1 billion. Investment valuation refers to the way stocks are selected. A series of ten criteria is used—looking at price compared to earnings, cash flow, book value, sales, and growth—to place funds either as "value oriented," "growth oriented," or a blend. For further details, check out *www.morningstar.com*. If you look at funds in Morningstar and in other investment services, you will often see the Morningstar classification grid.

Forty-Five Flavors

Heinz has fifty-seven varieties, and Baskin-Robbins has thirty-one flavors. The mutual fund industry and its financial reporting agencies have kept up with forty-five tiers of mutual funds. The *Wall Street Journal* and others use a two-letter classification published by Lipper, Inc. (another investment analysis firm). You will see these two-letter designations by each fund. They can be general (such as LC, which stands for "large-cap core," or funds that invest in large companies with wide latitude in the type of shares they buy) or very specific (such as NR, which stands for "natural resources," or funds that invest in natural resource stocks; PR stands for "Pacific region" stocks). In addition, there are SE (sector) funds.

The classification goes beyond stocks into taxable bond funds, municipal bond funds, and BL (balanced) funds that combine stocks and bonds. For a complete list of the forty-five types of funds, refer to Appendix C. As if it weren't obvious already, there are funds out there for virtually any investing need.

Exchange-Traded Funds

The latest "buzz" in the investment industry is about exchange-traded funds (ETFs). ETFs are trust funds that buy specific baskets of securities, mainly stocks, representing a market or portion of the market. Typically these baskets represent one of the following:

- Market indices such as NASDAQ or the S&P 500.
- Market sectors, such as technology, telecommunications, or consumer cyclicals.
- International markets—Japan, Germany, Brazil, etc.

How Do Exchange-Traded Funds (ETFs) Work?

Without going into a lot of detail, ETFs are traded on the major exchanges (particularly AMEX). You can buy or sell them just like any other stock. The price is usually tied directly to the net asset value, or NAV—the total value of the securities in the portfolio divided by the number of shares in the ETF. ETFs are assembled by large investment companies, notably Barclay's, Merrill Lynch, and Vanguard. As they represent established baskets of stocks, management costs on these ETFs are very low—perhaps only 0.25 percent of the portfolio and 1 to 2 percent for an actively managed mutual fund stock portfolio.

ETFs have been around for a while, but only recently have they come into their own as an investment vehicle. There are a large number of new offerings and an active, distinct market. "Old school" ETFs are illustrated by SPDRs (Standard & Poor's Depository Receipts), representing the S&P 500 Index, and Cubes, which represent the NASDAQ 100 and trade under the ticker symbol "QQQ" (hence the "Cubes" nickname). DIAMONDS represent the Dow Jones Industrial Average (symbol "DIA").

SPDRs and Cubes represent broad indexes, but if you want to get more specific, you could trade any one of the seventy-five or so iShare portfolios offered by Barclay's International. "iShares" are created to track stock indexes in about forty different countries and about thirty different sectors. If you think energy stocks will do well, and you want a diversified play without worrying about discounts, premiums, and costs, as well as a simple transaction, the iShare Energy ETF might be for you (symbol XLE). Ditto for technology, telecom, health, financial, utilities, consumer staples, S&P mid caps, and so forth.

QUESTION?

How do I find out more about ETFs?

ETFs are a widely marketed and popular product right now, so information isn't hard to find. The *Wall Street Journal* just started a separate listing of ETFs printed alongside the normal stock tables. Individual ETF companies have their own Web sites (Barclay's iShares site is at *www.ishares.com*). Morningstar and other major investing Web sites have separate pages covering ETFs.

Investing with ETFs

ETFs (exchange-traded funds) are often used by large and small investors to play major sectors of the market. These funds can provide a measure of safety while still concentrating assets in market sectors you think have a good potential for growth for the given risk.

Recently, "sector rotation" ETFs have come into favor. In these funds, the money is rotated from sector to sector—one week it's in energy, next it is invested in technology, and then back to energy again. An investor trimming a portfolio of NASDAQ large-cap stocks may buy a "Cube" as a hedge against an upward price movement. But more often, ETFs are used as a long-term vehicle to play the long-term success (or recovery) of a market or sector. If an investor feels that the NASDAQ in total is a good bargain today, they buy some Cubes and stash them away. The same holds true if a particular sector seems oversold. ETFs also are a good vehicle to bring international stocks into a value portfolio.

Funds That Are Right for You

Now comes the fun part. You must look at your investment objectives and the 8,000 mutual funds out there, and pick a few that make the most sense for you. Do it right, and your assets will ride a long-term horse all the way to your retirement ranch in the sky. Do it wrong, and you'll get nowhere with an underperforming fund. Like stocks and other investments, there is no one formula for success. But there are ways to make it more likely you'll find the right pasture, if not the right horse.

As a fund investor, you need a clear idea of your objectives and the amount of risk you want to take. This analysis is similar to the portfolio asset allocation discussion of Chapter 9. Do you want more aggressive funds with accompanying volatility or safer, steadier returns? It depends on your own risk profile—your financial persona and where you are in life.

From personal experience or judgment, you may think certain industries or types of companies make more sense for you. This is where your thought process should start; then, it's time to evaluate your options. Following is a discussion of important evaluation criteria.

ESSENTIAL

Expenses—fees and sales charges—have already been covered, but don't forget that looking at this criterion is very important in fund selection. Excessive fees and charges can really eat away at your returns. Look for the all-important "expense ratio" and load or sales charges, if any.

Fund Objectives

Fund objectives declare the goal or stated objective of the fund—for example, to provide a solid core holding in large-cap growth stocks with moderate risk. These objective statements may be vague or quite specific. You will find them in the prospectus as well as in company literature and on the Web site.

Fund Strategy

Fund strategy declares how the fund intends to accomplish its objective—for example, buying undervalued large-cap stocks to hold for five years or more and minimizing costs along the way. Some funds will disclose actual purchase criteria—company performance requirements and valuation ratios such as price-to-earnings, price-to-book, price-to-cash flow, and so forth. Also look for information on asset allocation within the fund.

Fund Size

Fund size is an interesting criterion. The general wisdom, subject to some debate, is that big is better—until it gets too big. A larger fund has economies-of-scale advantages to keep management fees and transaction costs at a minimum per unit invested. But when a fund gets too large, or so goes the wisdom, managers get hampered in terms of what they can do; for instance, they can't sell 50 million shares of AOL without tanking the market, even if they wanted to. Big funds can also be overdiversified, to the point that really successful investments are diluted in a sea of ordinary ones and these mediocre results are passed back to you. Some big funds have even closed their doors to new investors to prevent these things from happening. So, while there's no fast rule, you should find funds large enough to have a track record, good management, and reasonable expenses, but not so large as to be unwieldy in the marketplace.

Performance

Of course, it's important to know how the mutual fund performs (or at least how well it has performed in the past). Is the management team doing a good job? Has the fund met its stated objectives? Has it done better than the market overall? Does the management earn its fees?

Evaluating performance is tricky. Most funds publish their annualized total returns over different periods, such as year to date, one year, three years, five years, ten years, and life of fund. These return rates include change in underlying asset values, plus distributions paid to shareholders as dividends or capital gains, minus expenses absorbed by the fund (as opposed to expenses paid by investors separately).

Performance evaluations also need to account for the degree of risk the mutual fund offers investors. The subject of risk measurement is complex, but suffice it to say that mutual funds measure volatility and performance compared to the market overall. In other words, a fund that achieves 8 percent consistently with a low-volatility portfolio is a good deal. Likewise, a fund that achieves 8 percent but doesn't drop as much as the market does in a downturn (or go up as much in an upturn) is considered safer–and thus a better–return. Risk measures–because of their complexity and subjectivity–are best left to investment professionals or fund Web sites to explain. Rating services do take risk into account in determining their ratings.

Today, performance of most funds is compared not only to the markets but also to other funds that are similar. Given the fund type and approach to risk, has this fund and its management outperformed or underperformed other funds? It is getting easier to make this comparison–investment services are gearing their information more and more towards this criterion.

E ALERT!

Don't just look at the past three years. If you read too many ads, you may get caught in the trap of looking at "raw" fund performance during good market years—and projecting it into their—and your—future. You need to look at strategy, long-term performance, and performance compared to peers.

Turnover

How well does the fund manage your exposure to taxes? By the very structure of investment companies, gains from assets sold by the fund are passed on to fund holders each year as capital gains. If a fund has actively turned over its portfolio, you may end up with a big tax surprise in the form of a taxable capital gain at the end of the year. If the fund holds for the long term, you will pay taxes anyway, sooner or later, but later is better than sooner!

Beware of this tax bomb. You should be aware of how much the fund turns over or "churns" its investments, and avoid those that churn too much. Too much turnover not only invites taxes but also indicates an unclear strategy or objective on the part of the fund manager. You don't want to take money off the compounding table in the form of taxes if you don't have to—even if the taxes are paid with funds outside the mutual fund account. Note that this tax issue only applies to non-retirement assets—assets in qualified retirement plans are exempt from year-to-year capital gains taxes anyway.

Fund Strategies

To end the chapter on mutual funds, here are some good principles and strategies to keep in mind as a mutual fund investor:

- **Not too few, not too many.** It's important to have balance. Diversity is good, but overdiversifying leaves you vulnerable to higher expenses, and it doesn't accomplish anything since fund portfolios may overlap. Too little diversity leaves you too exposed to certain sectors of the market. If you're a committed fund investor, two or three, perhaps up to five funds are probably enough—more than five is probably too many.
- **Use funds as training wheels.** If you are a novice investor and aren't sure of the market and your ability to pick stocks, funds are a good way to start. Many investors have a portfolio including both individual stocks and mutual funds. Funds might be used to cover the more "mysterious" sectors, like bonds or international stocks.
- **Retire in stock.** Stock funds typically have a good, steady long-term growth track record, and in a retirement plan, there is no exposure to capital gains taxes along the way. However, unless you're getting close to retirement, it usually makes little sense to keep bond funds in a

retirement account. After-inflation, after-fee returns are dismal, you won't participate in economic growth, and you can't gain from tax-free funds, such as municipal bond funds.

- **Add monthly contributions.** Most funds make it easy to drop a direct-deposit payroll deduction right into the fund. This is an excellent, "off the top" way to save and build your accumulation annuity (described in Chapter 4). However, make sure you find out what the minimum no-charge deposit amount is to avoid paying excessive sales fees.

ESSENTIAL

Dollar cost averaging works for funds, too. Recall from Chapter 11 the principle of dollar cost averaging—making steady investments over time and driving a better average acquisition cost by buying proportionately more shares in down markets. Although the peaks and valleys aren't as steep as with stocks, this works with mutual funds too.

Novice and experienced asset investors alike should keep in mind the advantages and disadvantages of using mutual funds. On the upside, funds offer professional help, diversification, and easy market access. On the downside, all this comes at a price and may create tax problems. In conclusion, mutual funds are a solid choice for the average personal investor to achieve steady asset growth.

Chapter 14

Real Estate Investments

Some people are more comfortable if their investment is tangible—if they can see it, touch it, and step on it. For them, the obvious solution is to invest in real estate. Though it does have some pitfalls and will require your time and attention, real estate can offer good returns on your investment. This chapter covers real estate investing, including the whys and hows of selecting, buying, and selling real estate. (Chapter 15 will cover purchasing your home—the most important real estate investment you will make.)

Why Real Estate?

You can look at it, walk on it, live in it—and invest in it. Real estate is perhaps the most popular of all investments for the average and sophisticated investor alike. Real estate investments are tangible, predictable, and—for the most part—don't rely on the vagaries of the business world to make your investment grow.

What is meant by "real estate"? Real estate usually consists of land and buildings, although you can buy raw land, or, less commonly, buildings but not the land they are built on. The starting point in real estate investing, for most households, is the home—your primary residence. In fact, it is such an important component of real estate investing that it deserves its own chapter (Chapter 15). Beyond your own home, there is investment property—property acquired mainly to rent for income and hold for eventual price appreciation. Additionally, there are special vehicles that combine the virtues of real estate with those of stocks and mutual funds; these are known as REITs, or Real Estate Investment Trusts. With an REIT, you can invest in a pool of real estate assets as an alternative to owning real estate directly.

The rationale for investing in real estate is grounded in an assortment of factors, including supply and demand, tax advantages, and financing advantages.

Supply and Demand

"They ain't making any more of it" is the central credo of the dedicated real estate investor. Land is available in finite quantities. And while in theory you can keep constructing new buildings, so far the supply has not been able to keep up with demand—building restrictions and the ever-growing cost of construction tend to limit the number of new building projects.

Why does demand grow? As the U.S. population rises, so does the need for housing, shopping centers, office buildings, and so forth. The number of households is expanding at a faster rate, as people move away from home sooner, live in separate homes longer, or live greater portions of their lives single or divorced. On top of that, particularly in the last twenty-five years, waves of immigration—particularly of educated, high-income immigrants—have driven real estate prices up, especially in the larger coastal cities.

FACT

Because of the supply/demand forces, real estate investments are less subject to the effects of inflation. Other assets intrinsically valued in dollars—stocks, bonds, even money itself (cash)—depreciate in lockstep with the value of the dollar. The depreciation of bonds and cash is certain, while some stocks and the underlying businesses they represent may keep up with inflation if their business models aren't impacted by it. Real estate is a surer bet.

The persistent imbalance between supply and demand has resulted in fairly consistent and steady growth in real estate values. Taken through most of the twentieth century, real estate prices have grown on par with stocks and the economy—but have been more consistent than stocks. Simply put, there are fewer variables. This persistent growth has made real estate an excellent investing vehicle for the patient, long-term investor.

Financing Advantages

Because of the fixed, tangible nature of real estate and of government policies tilted towards getting more people into their own homes, real estate financing is considerably more flexible and accommodating than with other investment forms. Real estate loans—mortgages—are secured for the lender by the real estate itself. That means that the lender is entitled to foreclose—repossess—the property if payments aren't made. Since real estate is tangible and relatively stable in value, the lender is pretty much assured of recovering the value of the loan. That means three things:

- **Lower interest rates:** Because the risk is lower, the lender doesn't have to charge a premium interest rate to compensate for risk. A real estate loan on your personal residence (the most stable form of real estate) will probably be the lowest interest rate of any loan you can get, but loans on other types of properties are relatively inexpensive as well.

- **Longer loan terms:** Since real estate is likely to be around longer than most other assets, lenders are willing to lend for longer periods of time. Thirty years is common, with a range from ten to as much as forty years. Longer loan periods reduce the size of payments, but they also drastically increase the amount of interest you will have paid at the end of the loan period.
- **Larger loans:** Lenders will usually lend 80 percent of the value of what you are buying—and may go even higher than that. No form of borrowing to acquire assets allows such a great portion of value to be borrowed. Why is this a good thing? Enter the concept of leverage. When applied effectively, leverage significantly expands your power to grow your invested assets.

What is leverage, and how does it work for you? Leverage allows you to control larger assets with less of your own money. The result is this: Gains on that asset, which are tied to the entire value of that asset, are greatly magnified when taken against your original investment. Suppose you buy a house for $100,000 with $20,000 as a down payment (your own investment) and an $80,000 loan. If the value of that house appreciates $10,000 in two years, you have a house worth $110,000 and a nominal asset value growth of 10 percent. But since the loan remains at $80,000 (or a little less, as you have paid some principal), your original investment has grown from $20,000 to $30,000. That's an increase of 50 percent.

ALERT!

The power of leverage allows you to turn relatively modest total asset growth into much larger returns on your asset base originally invested. Of course, leverage works both ways—if the value declines by $10,000, that comes out of your original investment too (the bank still wants its $80,000 back). But the steady track record of real estate makes this scenario relatively unlikely.

Tax Advantages

Particularly since World War II, U.S. government policy has strongly favored the purchase of real estate, particularly the primary residence. The government recognizes that people in good homes are happy voters, and what's good for the housing industry is good for the country in many ways. As a result, both federal and most state governments have granted two huge tax advantages:

- **Tax-deductible interest:** Interest cost on qualified mortgage loans on a primary residence—and in most cases, one secondary residence—is fully deductible against income. If you recall the "(1 – t)" formula from Chapter 4, a 7 percent mortgage rate in a 27 percent tax bracket in reality only costs a little more than 5 percent. If, with state and local taxes, you're in a combined 50 percent bracket, the total interest cost is 3.5 percent. Tax law changes in the 1980s have made home loan interest virtually the last form of interest enjoying tax-deductible status. It's a nice subsidy enjoyed by many Americans.
- **Capital gains tax advantages:** Tax concepts, including capital gains, are examined in Chapter 17. But it's important to realize here another great tax advantage—the capital gains exclusion on owner-occupied residential property. As an individual, subject to certain limitations, you are entitled to exclude $250,000 of the gain in home value from taxation upon sale—$500,000 as a married couple. There is no other form of investment offering this kind of favorable tax treatment.

ESSENTIAL

One of the great advantages of investing in your own home is "locking in" your housing costs. Whereas rents can (and will) rise with inflation in a manner you have no control over, your mortgage commitment will be completely fixed, or it may vary within certain parameters if it is adjustable. Your housing costs are less likely to rise over time, freeing up future income increases for other things.

Credit Lines for Emergencies

Liquidity refers to the ease of converting an asset or investment into cash to meet short-term household cash needs. At one time, money tied up in real estate was pretty much "stuck" until you sold the property. With the advent of home equity credit lines, real estate asset liquidity has become less of a problem.

If you have an emergency medical expense or another sudden need for cash, you can "tap" the equity in your property (market price less loan value)—that is, you can borrow money against it. Once the home equity credit arrangement is set up with the bank or mortgage company, writing a check is all that's required.

Should you borrow money against your home in order to get cash to take a vacation, buy a boat, or go to the movies? Certainly not. But these equity lines can provide the liquidity necessary to handle emergencies or long-term asset acquisition or improvement—such as necessary home repairs or improvements destined to enhance value. An added benefit is that interest costs on home equity lines are tax deductible.

Opportunities to Buy Cheap

Stock and other investment markets are pretty liquid—buyers and sellers from all over the country (world, really) are in the market at the same time. Market prices represent the collective thoughts of many players linked together electronically, and players with inappropriately low or high prices will be quickly taken out of the market.

This is not so with real estate. Real estate markets are very local, with a lot of special situations forcing sale, and a relative handful of buyers with interest or visibility into the market for any one piece of property. As a result, it is possible to get good deals—to buy below market—more so in the real estate market than with typical securities investments.

Words of Caution

Does real estate always make sense as an investment? The answer is no. As with all investing forms, returns are not automatic, and there are situations in which investing in real estate may not be the right thing to do. You should be aware of the following situations: lack of time to devote to your properties, exorbitant prices of the real estate market, and lack of funds for more important areas of your budget, such as paying off high-interest debts or saving for retirement.

ALERT!

Real estate purchases come with fairly high transaction costs, and they can take a while to "mature." If your situation isn't clear or predictable—if you can't keep the money committed for at least three years—it may not make sense to take the plunge.

Can't Find the Time

Real estate investments will consume a lot of your time. If you own a home, you will (hopefully!) spend some time taking care of it. If you have rental real estate, you will not only take care of it, or manage others taking care of it, but you'll also have to find renters and deal with them as a landlord. If you don't have the time or patience for these things, real estate may not be for you. Other types of investments take less time. (The one exception to this is investing in REITs—the mutual fund-like investment trusts; they are more like stocks from the investing time-and-effort point of view.)

The Price Isn't Right

Real estate markets can get overcooked. A real estate boom, where demand exceeds supply, can bubble easily. First, demand exceeds supply, and prices go up. Then everyone thinks prices will rise longer and faster—and they want to get in on the action before it's too late. Particularly in areas with geographic limitations creating short supply, these price surges can be extensive and prolonged—as has happened in the San Francisco Bay Area, the New York area, and other large cities where population is increasing and land is at a premium. If the price of real estate gets out of line with value, you may want to stay away.

If the purchase price is more than 200 times the monthly rent (implying a 6 percent annual return), the property may be priced too high. Look at prices and rents for comparable properties over time in your area. It's best to do this on a per-square-foot basis for similar kinds of property.

Don't Starve Your Retirement Plan

Real estate—unlike stocks or other securities investments—requires ongoing budgetary commitments. Most of you will pay a mortgage, and there will be additional upkeep and maintenance expenses. While it's true that the mortgage payment can be looked at as a necessary housing expense, it can be so large (even after tax benefits) that it gobbles up scarce income that might otherwise achieve tax-free compounded growth in your retirement plans. Although real estate investing is a good idea, and in the case of a personal residence it also provides shelter, it shouldn't be done at the expense of retirement savings. You can borrow to buy a house later, but you can't borrow your retirement.

Investing in Rental Property

Investment real estate is not property that is intended for you to live in full time but to rent to others. There are two sources of income: the rent and the appreciation on the property. But there are also expenses and effort that go along with the income. If you are seriously interested in real estate investment, you should get more information for whatever area you choose to invest in.

First off, you need to keep in mind that investing in rental property is a business! In fact, you can turn it into a very successful, long-term enterprise. It produces income—although this is not always consistent, if you can't find tenants and your property remains vacant—and it is likely to appreciate. But it also entails expenses, management effort, and risk—just like any other business enterprise.

The compelling advantage of buying rental property is that, over time, rents will rise, while your costs will stay relatively constant. (In particular, your mortgage will remain the same.) In most cases, this means losses during initial ownership—particularly when transaction costs are counted—and profits later on. In addition, you should be able to realize asset appreciation, but you must be prepared to hold and take care of the property for a long time.

ESSENTIAL

Successful real estate investing is all about cash flow. Ask yourself: Can you afford the likely negative cash flow in the beginning? How many years will it take to become cash-flow positive?

When you are in the market for a rental property, you need to consider its location, need for upkeep and maintenance, likelihood of finding good tenants, and so forth. You also need to be prepared to work with real estate professionals like a real estate broker and an accountant. Owning rental property is a business, and it will require a lot of your time and energy—if you give it your best effort, the results will be equally profitable.

Consider the Taxes

While there are tax advantages to owning rental property, Congress has taken many of them away in recent years. It used to be possible to use early-term losses to offset income from other sources—for example, your wage and salary income. Now, "passive activity" rules only let these losses offset income from the property. (There is a limited exception that may let you deduct some of these losses against current income if your total income is below a certain level.) Passive activity rules go away if rental property is your full-time job, but you had better talk to your professional accountant (CPA) first to be sure these rules apply.

Don't fall into the depreciation trap. Enthusiastic realtors—and water-cooler colleagues—will tell you that by depreciating your property (that is, writing off property value in yearly increments) and taking the resulting tax savings, you can make the numbers come out right. But be aware that if you take depreciation deductions, they will be "recaptured" upon sale of the property unless the property is sold at its depreciated value, which is unlikely. If you go this route, you are simply deferring your taxes, not saving money on them. If you plan to never sell the property, this might work, but be aware again of the passive activity rules. If this sounds like something you need professional advice on, it probably is.

Buying a Second Home

As an investment, buying a second home (such as a vacation house) is tricky. While they may appreciate like other real estate, the tax and financing benefits aren't as clear. And they can consume a lot of effort and dictate where and how you spend your vacations! Here are a few pointers:

- **Appreciation is more speculative.** Vacation homes are located in places where people don't have to live, and in fact, they must travel to get there. In recession times or times of high travel costs (energy shortages), their value can decline, while the cost of maintaining them goes up.
- **Rental income may be spotty and unpredictable.** There may also be significant costs (agency fees) to acquire the property.
- **Tax rules don't allow for the capital gain exclusion.** This is true unless you eventually move into the property permanently (some close to retirement have enjoyed this privilege with success). If you rent it out, special tax rules apply to determine what expenses you may deduct and whether you can deduct them from ordinary income–check with an advisor.
- **Mortgage interest rates are usually slightly higher.** This is because a vacation home isn't your permanent residence.

E ALERT!

In general, vacation homes won't give you the same benefits that you would get for buying your first home. As a financial strategy, investment in a second home may be made only after you meet your financial goals.

REITs and Other Investments

Real Estate Investment Trusts are "closed-end" funds that, instead of investing in stocks, bonds, and other securities, invest in real estate. REITs pool investor money to buy commercial and/or residential real estate properties. Some REITs have general portfolios; more often, they contain portfolios of specific kinds of properties—office buildings, shopping centers, hotels, or houses—or specific geographic regions. Some REITs don't invest directly in property ownership; instead, they invest in mortgages (that is, they act as a lender by providing mortgages to other real estate buyers). REITs are bought and sold just like stocks, and just like stocks, they must be evaluated for underlying strategy, financial performance, and management quality. Just to give you an idea of what's out there, the New York Stock Exchange offers about 180 REITs that you can invest in.

REITs are a fairly quiet part of the securities market, although they have gained popularity as other types of investments have faltered. It is common to find REITs selling at a discount to portfolio value—this is often an attractive situation. To learn more about REITs, check the National Association of Real Estate Investment Trusts (NAREIT) Web site at *www.nareit.com.*

Limited Partnerships

The last option you have as a real estate investor is a limited partnership, which this author believes you would best do to avoid. Limited partnerships are a way to buy an equity share of a real property, a portfolio of properties, or some other venture like an oil drilling venture. As part owner, you would share in earnings and tax writeoffs, with limited liability exposure since you are a "limited" partner. Touted in the early 1980s as a way to own real estate and enjoy significant tax advantages (translation, tax shelter), these partnerships have poor track records and were often created as more of a tax dodge for wealthy investors than as a sound investment strategy.

Real Strategies

Real estate is a complex and engaging field of investing. For many people who are more comfortable with tangible investments that they can actively manage, investment in real estate makes sense. As a general rule, you should buy a home first, then add investment properties and REITs to your investment portfolio. Real estate is part of your asset allocation: An ideal "goal" allocation is one-third real estate, one-third retirement assets, and one-third other non-retirement assets (cash and securities), although you're unlikely to achieve this allocation for a while. Save the vacation home until other goals are met.

Chapter 15

Your Best Investment: Your Home

Your purchased home provides not only shelter and a "base" for daily living, it also represents a major investment in your asset portfolio. When you are in the market for a home, look for what you need, but also think of your purchase as a long-term investment. Buy the right property, improve it, increase your equity in it, and your home can be one of the surest paths to asset accumulation and wealth.

Your Own Castle

Owning your own home is a core real estate investment, but it's also a major convenience. Your home is your castle. There is comfort in the fact that you own it. If you don't already own a home, here is where you can get a brief introduction to purchasing your home. In a nutshell, the process is composed of the following five steps:

1. Figuring out what you can afford.
2. Selecting the right home for you and your family.
3. Making the down payment—your equity portion of the initial transaction.
4. Getting a loan, or mortgage, to make up the difference between the purchase price and the down payment.
5. Paying closing costs—costs related to the home-purchase transaction.

This is meant to be an overview. If this is the right time for you to buy a home, there are many books, Internet sites, and other resources that can help you with the details of purchasing your own home.

Figure out What You Can Afford

By now, you've developed a good idea of your economic standing—your asset base, income, expenses, and budget. Figuring out how much house you can afford is not an exact science, but you should take inventory of the following expenses:

- **Down payment:** You need to figure out how much of your assets you have available to invest as a down payment on a home. These assets will come mainly from your non-retirement savings, but there may be other sources. Not surprisingly, most financial planners advise not taking assets from retirement plans to fund home purchases.
- **Mortgage payment:** The mortgage payment should be affordable. How can you determine what exactly "affordable" is? It isn't easy to pin down. Lenders use a 28 percent guideline—that is, 28 percent of your gross monthly income before taxes can go to pay your mortgage plus

monthly home obligations (the monthly portion of property taxes and home insurance). However, if your income is on an upward path, this percentage can be higher.

- **Other obligations:** When you buy a home, you take on other obligations. Know what property taxes are and what they will become (and realize that they, too, are income-tax-deductible). Also find out what homeowner's insurance will be.
- **Other necessities:** With a house there are always other expenses—upkeep and maintenance of both the house and yard. You need to assess what changes you would like to make were you to buy a particular house and also what will need to be fixed or replaced in the near future. If you're unsure, have an experienced homeowner offer an idea of what to budget for home-improvement store purchases and other expenses.

QUESTION?

Can you afford a mortgage payment higher than your rent payment?

You bet. For one, the interest portion of a mortgage payment is income-tax deductible. If your "marginal" income tax rate is 35 percent (state plus federal), then a $1,000/month rent payment equates to a $1,538 monthly mortgage payment. ($1,538 × [1 – 0.35] = $1,000; $1,000 ÷ 0.65 = $1,538.) Note also that an accurate comparison should include tax benefits or credits for renters, if your state has any.

Essentially, you're building a home budget. When you have a monthly and annual home budget established, it is easy to work backwards into how much house you can afford. This will become clearer in the following section on mortgages.

Selecting the Right Home

Anybody who has bought a home has been through it—days, weeks, months of searching, trying to find that dream house that doesn't cost an arm and a leg. It is human nature to want more than we can afford, and the home-buying process is no exception. Managing the gap between means and desires can get downright frustrating, particularly in a hot real estate market.

Location, Location, Location

Everyone's heard of the "three Ls" of real estate. Yes, it's all about location—the value, the appreciation as an investment, the neighbors, the schools, the surrounding area. But if you can be flexible—or see a different future for certain locations than most people—you will be rewarded. It is best to buy in good or "up-and-coming" neighborhoods, and it is generally better to buy at the "low end" of that neighborhood.

Here are some of the more important factors you should consider:

- **Schools:** If you have school-age children, schools are important. Certain neighborhoods will be more expensive just because of schools. It's hard to get a true assessment of a school—its academic achievement, social quality, and so forth—but states are relying more and more on test scores to demonstrate achievement. Your best option is to talk to people whose children are attending the school and visit the school yourself to have a meeting with the principal and get a tour. Don't rely on real estate agents to assess schools for you—they will tell you what you want to hear—or what will support the high price of a home.
- **Commute:** Most of you will have to drive to work or get access to good public transportation. Don't underestimate the quality-of-life aspects of avoiding an hour-and-a-half commute. Know how far you will have to drive to get to work and how long the trip will last during commuting hours.
- **Neighbors:** Look for a neighborhood where most of the residents are in the same stage of life as you are. If you are a family with kids, you will do well if you find a neighborhood with lots of other families and children. If you are closer to retirement, look for a neighborhood that's quiet and where other older folks live. Watch the activity in the neighborhood for a period of time on a weekday and on a weekend.

Observe how people interact and how they take care of their properties. And look at how real estate prices—and rents—have fared in the neighborhood over time.

ESSENTIAL

You want to find a location that fosters increased investment value and is most likely to satisfy you over time. A home you're happy in is one that you're less likely to move away from, so your investment will appreciate. In addition, if you like your home and like to be around it, you're less likely to spend a lot of money on weekend getaways and three-day vacations.

The House Itself

It's important to take a close look at the house itself. Is it big enough now? And what about in the future? (If you are planning to start a family, will it one day be able to accommodate your kids?) Does it reflect your personality and tastes? If these factors aren't right, you're looking at another move—or substantial remodeling expenses—down the road. If you're "handy" and like doing work around the house, this may be fine, but if you are likely to call in professional help any time something breaks down or needs renovation work, you are much better off buying a house in good condition. Similarly, if you dislike gardening, don't buy a house surrounded with a garden. If that garden falls into disrepair, your home will surely depreciate in value—who wants to buy a house hidden behind weeds?

Knowing When the Price Is Right

Pricing real estate can be tricky because each piece of real estate is truly unique. Every location has its advantages and disadvantages, and almost every building is different. As stated earlier, there isn't a well-defined market for an individual piece of real estate. Particularly for homes, emotional appeal and "curb appeal"—appearance and image factors—are very important. That said, a home-investment evaluation needs to have a rational basis.

There are several approaches. Here's what works best:

- **Know the price per square foot.** In some regions of the country, pricing based on area of the house measured in square feet is the norm. Elsewhere, you have to ask about it or calculate it yourself. Look at the price and divide it by the number of square feet of livable space (excluding garages, storage, and so forth). Compare these numbers to other homes in the area, and then compare their amenities: garages, acreage, views, pools, and so forth.
- **Know the "comps" (comparable prices on like properties).** Real estate appraisers use comps to compare real estate. Property sales are public records, so it is always possible to find out what a particular property sold for and when. Look at other houses on the street or in the neighborhood with comparable size and amenities. Your realtor can help, or you can use the Web.

ESSENTIAL

You can keep up with home prices on the Web through Yahoo!Real Estate (*www.list.realestate.yahoo.com*). You can search homes for sale and get comps for everything sold in a neighborhood. Also, check out Homegain (*www.homegain.com*) for a similar service—although you'll get a little pressure to connect with someone in its realtor network. These are excellent tools to keep up with real estate values.

Should I Use a Realtor?

Realtors can help buyers and sellers who are new to the real estate market navigate property selection and transactions. They have access to more data on available properties than you do (though home locators on the Web are closing this gap). As with most professions, there are good and bad realtors.

As a potential client, you should get to know your realtor well. Make sure he or she truly understands your needs and financial situation. Check references. Be aware of potential conflicts of interest, particularly if you're a buyer. Realtors work on commission, so higher selling prices earn them more. Moreover, they are paid by the seller, so ultimately they will have the seller's best interest in mind.

However, if you are confident in your own abilities, you know something about the real estate market, and you can search for homes on sale yourself, you may not need the services of a realtor.

Determine the Down Payment

One of the toughest hurdles—particularly for the new buyer—is the down payment. You should shoot to put 20 percent down on a house, and for two good reasons:

- **Better loan terms:** Lenders are more willing to lend and offer lower rates when you have a significant stake in a property.
- **Avoiding private mortgage insurance (PMI):** PMI is an expensive insurance policy required by most lenders when loan-to-value exceeds 80 percent. Essentially, PMI is life insurance, guaranteeing mortgage repayment if something happens to you.

That said, not everyone can write a check for $50,000 on a $250,000 house! Saving for a down payment thus becomes a major "off-the-top" budget priority. If you're a first-time buyer, look for state-supported programs to get you into a house with favorable terms with less than 20 percent down. Tapping retirement assets is generally not recommended, but they can help if there's a committed strategy to replace them right away. Hard, committed saving is usually the best strategy.

ALERT!

If you decide to partner with relatives or friends to borrow some equity and share proceeds, take care to create well-defined agreements and watch out for gift taxes (see Chapter 17) if the amount is large.

The Home Mortgage

The mortgage, or loan to buy your house, may be the single biggest financial transaction most of you will make. In getting a mortgage, you are borrowing money from a bank, savings and loan, or mortgage broker and pledging your real estate as security for that loan. Mortgages come in all shapes and sizes, with different features and costs. Key features of a mortgage are the interest rate, term, and whether it is fixed or adjustable.

In Your Best Interest

Financial institutions and buyers alike closely watch mortgage interest rates. When borrowing large amounts of money, even a quarter of a percent can make a big different (actually, $35 per month in payments on a $100,000 loan). If you're in the home market, you should keep a close eye on mortgage rates and on the underlying bond market, which drives interest rates. A strong bond market indicates lower rates ahead, while a weak bond market, or inflation, indicates higher rates.

ESSENTIAL

When shopping for a mortgage, you should develop a good relationship with the mortgage provider. First, you should "prequalify" so that you're ready to move on the right house deal. Second, a good relationship will give you access to up-to-the-minute rate changes and predictions of future direction. And the lender may "lock in" rates for you to protect against last minute swings.

The Term of Your Loan

The term of your loan has a lot to do with two factors: how much interest you will end up paying over the life of the loan, and how much your equity in the asset increases over time. Mortgages are typically offered in fifteen- and thirty-year terms, but ten-, twenty-, and forty-year terms are not uncommon. To explain, numbers are much more effective than words.

Mortgage Payments for a $100,000 Loan		
Interest rate (%)	**Thirty-year term**	**Fifteen-year term**
6.0	$599.55	$843.86
6.5	$632.07	$871.11
7.0	$665.30	$898.83
7.5	$699.21	$927.01
8.0	$733.76	$955.65
8.5	$768.91	$984.74
9.0	$804.62	$1,014.27
9.5	$840.85	$1,044.22
10.0	$877.57	$1,074.61

Mortgage Payments for a $200,000 Loan		
Interest rate (%)	**Thirty-year term**	**Fifteen-year term**
6.0	$1,199.10	$1,687.71
6.5	$1,264.14	$1,742.21
7.0	$1,330.60	$1,797.66
7.5	$1,398.43	$1,854.02
8.0	$1,467.53	$1,911.30
8.5	$1,537.83	$1,969.48
9.0	$1,609.25	$2,028.45
9.5	$1,681.71	$2,088.45
10.0	$1,755.14	$2,149.21

As you can see, shortening the loan term from thirty to fifteen years does increase the payment—but *not that much*: by somewhere around 25–30 percent. The difference in equity buildup and total interest paid is eye-opening, as shown on the following page.

Cumulative Interest and Equity Buildup: $100,000 Loan, Thirty-Year Term

After *x* years	Cumulative interest	Cumulative equity
1 year	$7,468	$922
5 years	$36,750	$5,382
10 years	$70,701	$13,204
15 years	$101,285	$24,571
20 years	$126,718	$41,092
30 years	$151,721	$100,000

Cumulative Interest and Equity Buildup: $100,000 Loan, Fifteen-Year Term

After *x* years	Cumulative interest	Cumulative equity
1 year	$7,372	$3,751
5 years	$33,716	$21,903
10 years	$57,504	$53,736
15 years	$66,802	$100,000

Take a close look at these tables. After ten years, where would you rather be? Would you rather have built up $53,736 or $13,204 in asset value? That's four times the equity buildup for a mere 25 percent greater payment. And look at the total interest over the life of the loan—$66,802 for the fifteen-year loan versus $151,721 for the thirty-year loan. It makes sense for most people to shorten the loan term whenever possible (not at the cost of minimally adequate retirement savings, however).

How do you apply these tables to your situation? If you're borrowing some other amount than $100,000, what do you do? Simply "factor" everything. Divide the payment or cumulative amounts by $100,000 in either table, get a decimal factor, and multiply that by whatever amount you intend to borrow—at the matching interest rate.

Can you pay off a thirty-year loan sooner? In most cases, you can. Most loans come with no prepayment penalty, meaning you can send in an extra amount equal to the additional payment for a fifteen-year loan, or any amount you want. In fact, you can create your own fifteen-year loan but keep the flexibility of the thirty-year loan. However, be aware that interest rates might be slightly higher (0.10 to 0.25 percent) for a thirty-year loan and that most people have trouble sticking to the informal prepayment plan.

Some financial advisors advise against faster mortgage payoffs. They rationalize that it reduces your flexibility and that you can get better returns by investing the difference. Well, home equity credit lines give you back the flexibility, and particularly in recent markets, you have to be pretty good to beat return rates implied by the mortgage rate (if you save 7.5 percent, that is like earning 7.5 percent). Are these advisors looking to earn commissions by investing your money? Maybe so. As pointed out in Chapter 12, an early mortgage payoff can be thought of as a bond investment.

Adjustable-Rate Mortgages

Another popular marketing gimmick is the adjustable-rate mortgage. An adjustable rate limits some of the lender's risk, since the interest rate is not locked in at an interest rate for the full term. As a result, you can get lower up-front rates (which are often quoted below market as a teaser). Pay attention to the adjustment rules and indexes used, particularly to the maximum rate. In the low-interest-rate environment of the early 2000s, adjustables don't make much sense. But they can make sense if (1) they are the only way you can qualify *and* you expect your income to rise, *or* (2) you expect to own the home for a short time—five years or less.

Closing Costs

When you are buying a home, you also need to consider closing costs (transaction costs), which are going to vary by state and are too involved to elaborate on here.

Here is an overview of the types of fees you should expect:

- **Escrow fees:** Paid to a company to get the documents and funds together and record the transaction. Escrow officers also provide paperwork advice, useful for less savvy realtors or if you're using no realtor at all.
- **Title insurance:** Ensures the lender of the clear title—that no one else owns an interest in your property, thus compromising security.
- **Appraisal and credit report:** Professional appraisers must evaluate the

property, and credit reporting agencies must evaluate you for the benefit of the lender.

- **Loan origination fees and points:** Loan origination fees cover the lender's cost of processing the loan (usually 1 percent of loan value), and points are used to adjust the interest rate.
- **Tax and payment adjustments:** Unless you close the deal on the last day of the property tax year and on the due date of someone's mortgage, you will be required to supply funds that satisfy a prorated portion of these payments.

Home-Buying Tips

Buying a home is no easy task. For many families, it's a once-in-a-lifetime endeavor. Before you begin the process, get as much help as possible from as many sources as you can rely on. To conclude this chapter, here are three last points of advice you should keep in mind as you shop for a home:

- **Buy a little high.** Stretch your budget (though not too much) to get a home you're proud to own and will stay in for years—and on weekends. Content homeowners make more on their investments.
- **Accelerate your mortgage payoff as much as possible.** Don't compromise your retirement or getting food on the table, but even a slightly faster payoff can save a lot on interest and build asset value faster—and it feels good too! At minimum, you should plan to pay off your home before retirement.
- **Don't buy perfect.** Perfect homes are more expensive, and there is little room to personalize or add value. Converting your "sweat equity" into financial equity is a great way to build wealth.

E ALERT!

You can't avoid closing costs, but you should know what you're expected to pay—often as much as 5 percent of purchase value. Also, in negotiating the deal, have the seller pay as much as possible; it can be an effective negotiating point.

Chapter 16

All about Risk Management and Insurance

Once you create wealth, you must protect it. Life is full of risks; assets must be protected from unforeseen catastrophes. How can you protect yourself from everything? You can't—and you shouldn't. This chapter explores different kinds of risks, how to manage them, and how to use insurance to protect against the most damaging risks. It also describes the different kinds of insurance available and introduces annuities—a blended insurance/investment product offered by insurance companies.

The Risky World We Live In

According to insurance industry professionals, "risk is a condition where there's a possibility of adverse deviation from a desired outcome that is expected or hoped for." That is, there is always a chance that something unexpected might occur, and damage will result. For a forty-year-old man, to suddenly die (leaving a spouse, kids, and a mortgage payment) certainly qualifies as risk. Losing your car's muffler or having a brand-new camcorder break the minute you start using it are also risks. The point is that there are all kinds of risk. Some risks have disastrous negative consequences to your family income and wealth, while others are small perturbations that, though inconvenient, can be dealt with or even prevented. Some are more or less likely to happen. Others are extremely rare.

QUESTION?

What is the difference between risk and uncertainty?
Uncertainty reflects the random nature of possible outcomes, both positive and negative. Risk is focused specifically on the negative outcomes—the ones we need to protect against.

Every day, you are vulnerable to innumerable risks. Some of these risks are personal; others would potentially affect your property. Some must be addressed directly; others can be left to the gods—if it happens, it happens. To develop a wise risk-management strategy for you and your household, you can deal with different types of risk in four ways: you can avoid them, reduce them, retain them, or transfer them.

Avoiding Risk

There are certain risks you can avoid altogether. The risk of smashing into the ground because your parachute didn't open is pretty much eliminated if you never go skydiving. The risk of getting struck by lightning is eliminated if you don't go outside during a thunderstorm. The risk of someone drowning on your property is avoided if you don't have a swimming pool. The first and most basic form of risk management is behavioral—simply to avoid engaging in activities that invite risk.

Reducing Risk

You can also try to deal with risk by reducing it. You can go skydiving, but reduce your risk by picking a reputable skydiving instructor and checking your parachute before you jump. You can go outside in thunderstorms, but avoid trees, water, and golf courses. You can have a swimming pool, but keep it inside a fenced area with an ample supply of life jackets for everyone to use. Risk reduction is also behavioral—engaging in activities but doing so more safely.

Retaining Risk

You want to own that camcorder (so much for risk avoidance) and you already take care of it pretty well (so much for risk reduction). But it can still break, and Murphy's Law predicts that it will. An extended warranty contract (a type of insurance) costs $150 on a $600 unit, and you decide that's a waste of money. Essentially, if it breaks, you'll eat it—either you'll pay to have it fixed or buy a new one. What have you done? You have retained the risk. As a matter of fact, of the myriad risks incurred in everyday life, you probably retain—accept the responsibility and chance for—most of them.

Transferring Risk

But you aren't prepared to retain the risk of dying at the age of forty and leaving your family with financial obligations and no way of supporting themselves. You can't avoid this risk, and as much as you'd like to, you can't reduce it either (though, of course, if you exercise and eat well, you've taken a step in the right direction). The consequences are large; so what can you do? You can transfer this risk to someone else. But you can't do it for free. When you transfer risk, you must pay the transferee (the party who accepts your risk) something to take on that responsibility. This is the basis of insurance and the insurance industry—insurance companies accept money to let you transfer your risk to them.

FACT

Insurance is the contract by which this risk is transferred, in return for a premium paid. The insurance companies then put the premium into large asset pools with other transferors, so that they can absorb that risk on your behalf and compensate you for your loss.

A Logical Approach to Risk Management

FIGURE 16-1 summarizes the conventional approach to managing risks. If the cost or severity of the event to your being and finances is low, the usual approach is to reduce the risk (remove the hazard) or to retain it (be prepared to suffer the consequences). For costly high-severity risks, it is simply too expensive to transfer risks if the "casualty" occurrence is likely to be frequent. You just need to avoid skydiving through thunderstorms altogether. If the penalty is high, but the frequency of occurrence is low–just a chance–that is when you want to transfer the risk (that is, get insured).

FIGURE 16-1

		Frequency of Occurrence	
		High Frequency	*Low Frequency*
Severity of Loss	*More Severe*	**Avoid** or **Reduce**	**Transfer**
	Less Severe	**Retain** or **Reduce**	**Retain**

▲ Risk management grid.

A Brief Example

Should you buy the extended warranty agreement on that new DVD player? It's just $29.95 for what they refer to as "protection and peace of mind," and if it ever breaks, you can just return the machine to the store. Sounds like a good deal? Well, let's look at it from a risk-management perspective.

- **Severity of loss:** Low—you can probably buy a new machine for $99.
- **Frequency of occurrence:** Low—your DVD player was manufactured by an electronics company with a good record. Sure, it could still break, but the chances are small.

If you look at it this way, it should be clear that you should retain the risk rather than transferring it by purchasing the warranty. Keep the $30, and put it into your own "insurance" contingency fund. If you think it through, you'll arrive at this conclusion for almost every extended warranty or service agreement offer you confront.

How to Transfer Risk with Insurance

Insurance comes into play when we, in managing our risks, choose to pay to transfer certain risks to another party. The chances of dying, having an auto accident, a house fire, a burglary, becoming disabled, or needing major surgery are all realistic risks we face. They don't happen every day, but if they do, the consequences can be catastrophic, so we are willing to pay someone else—an insurance company—to take the risk.

FACT

Insurance companies are in the business of taking individual risks and pooling them to reduce individual exposure. They set the transfer price from experience and invest the risk transfer "premium" to further build the asset base to pay losses.

Types of Insurance

There are three main types of insurance you'll encounter and use:

- **Property and casualty insurance** covers losses in property, including homes, autos, and commercial property. These losses may be either damage to property or liability arising from property ownership. Property and casualty insurance protects your assets—both the physical asset owned and your wealth assets from liability exposure.

- **Life and disability insurance** pay off if you die or become disabled; these types of insurance protect your income.
- **Health and long-term care insurance** pay for both "acute" and long-term medical services, protecting your assets—particularly your accumulated wealth—against catastrophic medical and nursing-home bills.

Each of these types of insurance has an industry with its own practices and companies built around it. You may deal with a general agent, but you'll buy each type of insurance from a different company. As an individual risk manager, it is important to understand all three forms of insurance—you probably need to address risks in all three areas.

Insurance Concepts

Before you go on to learn about the three major areas of insurance, here are some terms you need to understand and that will help you see how insurance works:

- **Insurability:** To get insurance, you must be insurable. Insurance companies have the right to determine whether you are insurable. If you're diagnosed as having less than a year to live, insurance companies have the right to deny you life insurance. Further, you must have an insurable interest in the item being covered, so you can't buy insurance on your next-door neighbor's house, "betting" that it will burn down or get broken into.
- **Insurance premiums:** Insurance companies look at the probability of loss for the item insured using actuarial tables—statistical analysis of reams of historical data for similar customers insuring similar property against similar events. They build rates by monetizing the probability of loss and uplifting that amount to cover overhead, profit commissions, and other expenses. Investment gains are factored in, lowering the total. The result is the premium you pay.
- **Adverse selection:** People in poor health or who are aggressive drivers are more likely to buy insurance and buy more insurance. This is called adverse selection—the population of insurance buyers is not random but is biased slightly towards those who need it most.

Insurance companies are aware of adverse selection and factor it into their rating tables.

- **Deductibles and copayments:** Losses start at zero (dollars) and can go into the millions. But the vast majority of losses are small—a cracked windshield, a notebook stolen from your car. If the insurance company had to pick up all these small losses, they would have to charge a lot more. Using deductibles allows companies to avoid more frequent small losses and concentrate on the less frequent large ones. To save money on insurance, you should look for the highest per-incident deductible you think you can afford. "First dollar" coverage—coverage that pays the "first dollar" of your loss—is always more expensive. Likewise, to lower cost and reduce the effects of adverse selection, health insurers look for copayments on most policies—10 percent or 20 percent of the cost to be paid out of your pocket.
- **Standard forms:** To take the complexity out of buying insurance, the property and casualty insurance industry has gone to "standard" forms—standard contracts with standard coverage and pricing practices. This makes company and policy comparison simpler and straightforward—no apples-to-oranges discussions about one company covering roof and gutters and the other covering window glass. The contracts still aren't simple, but at least they are comparable.
- **Insurance agents:** Although the Web has made some inroads towards "do-it-yourself" purchase of insurance, it hasn't captured that much business, particularly for more complex forms of insurance. Insurance is still largely sold through agents. Agents can be independent—handling multiple lines of insurance and multiple companies—or captive—contractually obliged to handle one brand or line of insurance—for example, a State Farm or Farmer's Insurance agency.

FACT

Most insurance companies offer good educational material on their Web sites. There are also good insurance portals that provide tutorials and comparative quotes for many lines of insurance; if you are interested, they can also connect you with an agent. Insweb (*www.insweb.com*) and E-insurance (*www.e-insurance.com*) are among the many.

Buying Insurance

Buy insurance based on *need*, not based on product. Insurance agents sell product, and too often clients get caught in the trap of examining features and costs before stepping back to assess the real need. How much life insurance do you need? What kind of coverage do you need on your car? What kind of monthly expenses do you need to cover disability? Do you need full-coverage health insurance, or would "catastrophic illness" coverage do? Before signing on the dotted line, make sure you think through your needs. Your agent or planner should be able to help—if they can't, find another who can.

Property and Casualty Insurance

Property and casualty insurance protects your physical assets—houses, cars, commercial property, and so forth—against physical peril and against liability for events that may arise from the property. Auto insurance covers the car itself and the damage, injury, and loss of life that you might incur while you are driving it. Homeowner's insurance covers not only the home itself but also the contents and potential liability for injury or loss to others occurring on the property.

Automobile Insurance

The frequency and severity of the risks involved in automobile accidents suggest reducing risk (driving carefully), avoiding risk (not driving unnecessarily), and transferring the risk that remains for the driving you must do (getting auto insurance). In fact, auto insurance is required in most states.

The expense of car repair and replacement, combined with catastrophic liability exposure for a serious accident, make the transfer worthwhile, even though it seems expensive. Standard auto insurance is divided into several specific types of coverage:

- **Collision coverage** covers damage to the car itself from collisions with other vehicles or objects.

- **Comprehensive coverage** pays for noncollision expenses, including theft, vandalism, and natural disasters. It also covers other people driving your car (with your permission).
- **Liability coverage** pays for damage to the property or person of others while using the "covered" car.

Other types of coverage include uninsured motorist, medical payments, towing insurance, and a few others. Some, such as uninsured motorist coverage, are mandatory. Others are optional low-risk "bells and whistles" that you may want to retain instead of transfer—like towing coverage.

ESSENTIAL

When you buy an auto policy, initially it is for the car—and yourself and any other operator who may have permission to use it. But the coverage extends to cover you or any family member using someone else's car with permission or as a rental. Still, be careful about applying this to commercial vehicles or vehicles used in business—coverage may not apply, so know before you go.

Collision and comprehensive coverage is sold with a deductible to keep costs down, and coverage is limited to the market value of the car. Liability is typically "first dollar" coverage and is purchased to the limit you set. A "100-300-50" auto policy has liability coverage for injury up to $100,000 for one person, $300,000 for all persons involved, and $50,000 for property damage. Coverage rates usually start in the 25-50-10 range and go as high as $1 million.

How much coverage do you need? It depends on what you have to protect, but keep in mind that larger amounts of coverage (with a higher deductible) can be quite cheap. Here are some additional car-insurance buying tips:

- **Check a firm's reputation for customer service.** Does it have local claims offices and agents? What do friends, neighbors, and coworkers say about it? Contracts are fairly standard, but the way companies treat customers and pay claims does vary quite a bit.

- **Use high deductibles on collision and comprehensive.** The savings can be large, and you're usually able to self-insure (retain risk!) for these amounts. Make sure your agent offers and prices all of the options.
- **Be biased towards high-liability coverage.** If your net worth is $100,000, get the $300,000 liability policy anyway. The additional coverage is cheap, and you don't want your hard-earned assets to be exposed to the whims of a jury any more than necessary.

Homeowner's and Renter's Insurance

Homeowner's insurance policies cover your home and contents; renter's insurance policies cover only the contents. Furthermore, both cover liability for damage incurred in the home. If a guest or neighbor falls on your stairs, or if your tree falls on their house, or if you start a fire that burns down the other apartments in your building, your homeowner's or renter's liability insurance kicks in.

FACT

Homeowner's and renter's insurance comes in standard forms, with standard coverage for the dwelling, contents, outbuildings, and liability/casualty losses. And like auto insurance, the property-coverage portion comes with deductibles, and you can save a lot by retaining more risk and taking on a higher deductible.

Property and casualty insurers have been losing a lot of money lately on homeowner's insurance. Natural disasters have caused more damage to a more spread-out population, and replacement costs have gone through the roof. Today, you may have trouble getting homeowner's insurance, particularly if you don't own an auto policy with the same company; insurers try to make up the shortfall by cross-subsidizing with more profitable auto insurance. Rates are rising, and insurers are moving towards more individualized pricing, raising rates substantially to homeowners who have had claims (a long-standing practice on the auto side). Shop carefully, and develop a long-term relationship with your homeowner's insurance provider. You may be glad you did.

Get Under the Umbrella

With skyrocketing liability damage awards—and an increasingly complex world with so many ways people could cause accidents, directly or though negligence—many simply want a broad high-dollar coverage for anything that might happen. Insurance companies have responded to this need with "umbrella policies." You can extend the "top" of your auto and homeowner's/renter's liability coverage to $1 million or more to cover any kind of occurrence. The auto/homeowner's policies cover the vast majority of incidents, so the incremental "umbrella" protection is quite cheap. For peace of mind, especially if you have substantial assets, avoid the rain.

Life and Disability Insurance

Life insurance covers—well—your life, providing protection to your beneficiaries in case of your untimely death. Your beneficiaries—usually spouse and kids—would have income needs, and life insurance is designed to meet those needs. Disability insurance is similar except that it covers your ability to work and produce income, not your life in total. While disability may be permanent, it is more likely to occur than premature death.

E ALERT!

Studies show the average working-age American is more than twice as likely to have a thirty-day or greater disability during his or her work life than to die prematurely (before retirement age).

Life insurance can be simple, or it can be so complex and vexing that you can sit for hours with an agent and still not understand what you need or what you're getting. It is a product that is most often sold, not bought, because of complexity and the agent-commission system that is used to market it. It is important to understand life insurance, first by understanding your needs, then the principles and the products that are being offered.

Life insurance needs are determined mainly by the needs of your survivors. If you were providing net take-home income of $60,000 per year, and you're gone, that amount will have to be replaced somehow. Social Security and other assets may help, and your spouse may have to start working or work more. But insurance will have to make up the income gap, as well as provide for long-term goals such as college education and retirement. How much insurance do you need? It is a function of your age, income, current needs, home ownership status, kids and college education needs, and retirement goals. Most insurance Web sites (and agents) have calculators to help assess these needs.

The following is an overview of basic life insurance concepts:

- **Life expectancy:** Insurers base life insurance rates on actuarial (statistical) life expectancy for groups or classes of people. For example, eighty-year-old female smokers have a higher death rate (per 1000) than forty-year-old male nonsmokers. These tables may also include health, lifestyle, and genetic attributes such as exercise habits or the health history of the person's parents. Recently, companies have recognized that people live longer, and have adjusted their tables accordingly. Discrimination is a problem in hiring and firing, but it is fully legal in the insurance industry.
- **Insurability:** Insurance companies aren't required to write policies on you, and they may require extensive physical examinations before insuring you. Sometimes it makes sense, even though your current insurance needs are limited (if you're single, for instance) to buy a good-sized long-term policy for the future. There is always a risk you won't be able to get or increase insurance later.
- **Group and individual policies:** A group of individuals is more likely to "behave" like the norm than a particular individual. In a group, the risks are distributed among more people. Therefore, if you're eligible for group plans through your employer, you'll normally benefit from lower rates (and the employer is likely to buy some coverage as a benefit). Take advantage of group rates where you can—but beware that some insurance companies use this term as an advertising gimmick.
- **Term and permanent insurance:** Term insurance provides coverage for a specific time period, while permanent or "cash value" insurance is for

life. Term insurance is cheaper and more flexible in the early stages of life, but permanent insurance provides coverage into your eighties and nineties, which would be otherwise hard to get or expensive.

- **Tax implications:** Insurance benefits are income-tax-free (though *not* estate-tax-free) because premiums are paid with after-tax dollars.

Term Life Insurance

Term insurance is bought for a set amount of time, usually as one-year renewable and ranging up to five, ten, twenty, and even thirty years. It is the simplest and least expensive type of insurance. If you die during the term of your insurance, your beneficiary collects cash.

Term insurance gets more expensive as you get older because your risk of death increases. You can renew in one-year terms, and if you're in your twenties, your premium for a year of insurance will be very low—maybe $10 or $15 a month for $200,000 in coverage. But that same coverage may cost you $300 a month when you're in your sixties.

ESSENTIAL

Many people choose level term insurance, where the premium is fixed for a period of fifteen or twenty years. They pay more in the beginning but less in the end, when rates go up. A side benefit is that there are no renewability issues—your coverage is guaranteed through the term.

Permanent, or Cash Value, Insurance

Permanent, or cash value, insurance is for life. You pay level premiums until you are 100 years old. If you don't die, some portion of these premiums accumulates into cash value. Investment returns earned by the insurance company are added to the cash value. You own the cash value as an asset and can surrender it or borrow against it any time you want. Cash value insurance, therefore, provides both insurance coverage and a way to build asset value. Many people think of cash value insurance as a forced savings plan, adding permanent life coverage and devoid of future insurability problems.

There are three main types of cash-value life insurance:

1. **Whole life policies.** These provide lifetime protection in a specified amount. They build cash value and may pay an annual fixed dividend. Whole life is significantly more expensive than term, but the value of the policy will grow over time. Premiums may be level or graduated over the years. Dividends can be used to pay premiums or buy more insurance, or they can be paid out as cash. Critics find whole life to be a poor performer as an investment and expensive as insurance; proponents like the combined features in one package.
2. **Universal life insurance.** Universal life, a fairly recent invention, allows the policyholder to vary premium payments and coverage over time, in contrast to the fixed payments and benefits of the normal whole-life policy. You and other policyholders put money into a "bucket." The insurance company takes out necessary death benefits and administrative expenses, and your cash value is your share of what's left over (defined by your cumulative premium paid). Universal life policies directly benefit from investment performance, and you can increase or reduce your coverage according to the premiums you pay. You can even omit premiums altogether in a bad year and still retain coverage if there is sufficient cash value already in the policy. In short, universal life is like managed insurance, with you as the manager.
3. **Variable universal life.** This type of life insurance allows you an even greater degree of control over your cash value and insurance destiny. With a variable universal life policy, your cash value can be invested in different stock, bond, and real estate mutual funds—and you can pick the investment mix. You get insurance coverage and complete control over an investment asset.

Don't try buying permanent or cash value insurance without an agent. While it is easy—and probably cheaper—to buy term insurance through the Web, as of today there are no cash-value insurance offerings done this way. Products are too complex and, well, agent commissions still need protecting. Go over the options with your agent, learn about the products, and maybe someday you'll be able to "click" your way into a variable universal life policy.

QUESTION?

Should I opt for term or cash value insurance?
The prevailing wisdom dictates that if you are a good saver and investor on your own, term insurance is the simplest way to get insurance protection. Level term is a good idea—five to ten times your annual income and coverage past major obligations—college and mortgage payoff, for instance. But if managed right, permanent insurance, especially universal and variable universal life, can offer a lot of benefits, especially long term.

Disability Insurance

Disability insurance provides compensation for your inability to work or produce income. It usually covers some–but not all–of your income. Here are a few important disability concepts:

- **You need more than you think.** Temporary or permanent disability is a real risk, and Social Security coverage is very restrictive, so it's unlikely that you'll qualify. Because disabled individuals cannot work and support themselves, they need a disability insurance to help them survive.
- **Disability coverage–"own occupation" and "any occupation":** Coverage is provided–and rated–according to the degree of disability you want to cover. "Any occupation" coverage states that you must be unable to perform any reasonable income-producing work within the range of your abilities before you can collect. "Own occupation" states you can collect if you can't do your "own" occupation, regardless of what else you can do. Which is more expensive? Clearly, "own" occupation–insurance companies are much more likely to have to pay. Social Security is "any occupation" coverage, and disability must be permanent–the least likely form of disability to occur.
- **Residual or partial disability:** Insurance companies are recognizing partial disabilities. They pay on some policies in which the insured can still do the work but may not be as effective or efficient. More people collect this way, but insurers like it because total disability is avoided, so partial clauses are usually cheap to add.

- **Premium waivers:** If you become disabled and collect on a policy, that's nice, but your obligation to pay premiums goes on, and may go higher. Premium waivers—a policy "add-on"—are cheap and can come in handy.
- **Elimination periods:** Insurers want to limit exposure to adverse selection—and particularly to people who know a disabling situation is imminent—so the insured are forced to wait a certain period before their policy actually provides coverage. This term, known as the elimination period, may last between six months and three years. Longer elimination periods mean less risk for the insurer, so the premiums on these policies are more affordable.

Health Insurance

You may or may not have life insurance, but almost everyone has—or should have—some form of health coverage. Health insurance generally covers immediate medical (and sometimes dental and optical) procedures.

ESSENTIAL

If you're working for an employer, chances are you have health coverage, either as insurance or prepaid through a managed care organization (HMO or PPO). If you work but don't get this coverage as a part of your benefits, you may be able to buy it at preferred group rates.

The "true" health insurance is private health insurance, which can be purchased by individuals or as part of a group plan. With private insurance, you can get medical care where you want. There is usually a deductible and a copayment, but rates are still very high. Major medical coverage—sort of a misnomer—covers all expenses, including doctor, hospital, and drug expenses.

Managed Care

The alternatives to private health insurance are HMOs (health maintenance organizations) and PPOs (preferred provider organizations).

These organizations provide managed care through hired and contracted medical practitioners. They provide more steady income and administrative support to these practitioners in return for contracted lower rates. If you or your employer buys an HMO or PPO plan, you are essentially prepaying for your expected level of services, and the organization absorbs the risk of your "go over." HMOs require you to go to their contracted or hired staff, while PPOs allow choice but may make you pay more for certain choices.

Catastrophic Coverage

You can get full coverage, or you can elect to retain risk for modest amounts of care (up to $2,000 per year, perhaps) while transferring risk of major illness or surgery. The cost for catastrophic coverage is much lower. Combined with your own assets—or better yet, a medical savings account (or MSA)—you can make this work if you don't get coverage anywhere else.

MSAs are especially useful for those who are self-employed or work for a small business because they allow you to set aside pretax funds into an account that can be invested like a retirement account—tax deferred or tax free. You can withdraw from an MSA to pay routine medical expenses—again, the withdrawn funds are tax-free—and get catastrophic coverage to protect against major problems. The best part is that if you don't use the MSA for medical expenses, you keep it and effectively add to your retirement asset base.

Buying Health Coverage

When it's time to consider your health insurance, keep in mind the following:

- **Higher deductibles and copayments translate to lower monthly fees.**
- **Make sure your health insurance covers preventative care.** Amazingly, some insurers still won't pay for routine physicals or checkups, even though it would be in their best interest to do so.
- **Examine prescription-drug policies closely.** Providers and insurers often cut corners in the prescription drug area, providing no coverage or limited coverage on certain types of drugs. While drug costs are

seldom catastrophic and risks can be retained, they can still be significant consumers of cash.

- **Look at renewability provisions.** Make sure that your insurance company won't drop you if your health suddenly begins to fail.

In short, shop carefully. Providers—particularly managed care organizations—have a smorgasbord of products with different deductibles, maximum limits, drug-coverage options, and so forth. There is little standardization and a lot of brochures and terminology to wade through. Take your time—even with employer-provided coverage options.

Long-Term Care Insurance

Long-term care (LTC) insurance covers the eventual possibility of needing nursing-home and other types of elderly-care coverage—specifically, nursing-home stays and the fees and expenses that go along with them, as well as in-home care—a more widely used option and a practical one for most people. LTC would "kick in" when you're determined by a physician to be unable to perform a certain number of the seven "activities of daily living" (or ADLs): eating, bathing, dressing, and so on.

FACT

Today, LTC insurance is an emerging baby of the insurance industry. Most people today don't have it, but as we live longer and medical practice does more and more, especially in later years of life, LTC coverage is becoming more of an issue.

LTC coverage is relatively cheap—until you get older—but you can "level" the premiums. Expected tax rule clarifications should make it more attractive to offer LTC as an employee benefit. Inflation protection is another important optional feature of LTC policies. LTC is a long way down the road for most of us, and inflation (particularly in medical costs) can be extreme. As far as need is concerned, it is estimated that 25 percent of the population will need an average of 2.5 years of long-term care at around $150 per day in today's dollars.

Investing in Annuities

Annuities are investment vehicles developed and sold by insurance companies. Effectively, you pay a sum of money, either as a lump sum or as a series of payments over time. Those funds are invested, and at a specific maturity date, the annuitant (that is, you) can annuitize your investment—convert it into a series of payments you would receive in installments until death. As an investment, this is a time-value-of-money game. As an insurance product, annuities provide protection against outliving your assets—as the income stream goes on indefinitely.

The annuity product model incorporates the "accumulation annuity" and "distribution annuity" time value of money concepts explained in Chapter 4. You pay in a lump sum or accumulate assets until a certain date, with compounding, to achieve a certain sum. With fixed annuities, the accumulation rate is contractual; with variable annuities, it varies according to investment performance. When annuitized, the annuity pays as a distribution annuity indefinitely. Here are additional features and concepts of the annuity product:

- **Immediate and deferred annuities:** You can purchase an immediate annuity and annuitize it today, or you can buy a deferred annuity and set the time when the annuitizing will begin at a later date. With the immediate annuity, you'll get a stream of payments, but it won't be very large, as your investment won't have time to compound. (That's why deferred annuities are more popular.) Still, some people at retirement may want to "roll over" lump-sum retirement account distributions into an annuity to provide steady payments and guaranteed lifetime income.
- **Premium options:** Premiums, or the amount you pay in to the annuity, can be paid as single premium (lump sum), periodic premium (monthly payments), or flexible premium (as you wish, the value varies accordingly).
- **Lump sum or annuitizing options:** Some people may want to take their annuity value as a single lump-sum payment—that is, they close out their investment altogether and receive a single check from the insurance company. Others may want to annuitize, or convert to a

stream of payments, usually continuing until death. In making this decision, the annuity owner may consider administrative costs that may be deducted by some companies, and also alternative investments available for the lump sum. He may also consider life expectancy—if he expects to live longer than average, the annuitizing option may be more attractive. In any case, it's nice to have the flexibility to collect on these investments as the situation dictates.

- **Joint-and-survivor annuities:** J&S annuities allow payments to continue beyond your death—to provide continuing payments to a spouse or another designated survivor, so they are a good planning tool for retired couples. As the insurer's exposure to longer payment obligations necessarily increases, a J&S annuity will make smaller payments during your lifetime.
- **"Period certain" options:** You put money into an annuity all your life, then die a month after it annuitizes. What happens? The agreement is to pay until you die, so the insurance company walks away with a huge windfall. "Period certain" options promise payments for the next five, ten, or twenty years to your heirs even if you die. Although you will receive lower annuity payments, you will be ensured that your family won't lose its savings if you die.
- **Variable annuities:** As mentioned above, variable annuities grow (or don't grow) according to market performance. These are investments that are managed like mutual funds.

ALERT!

Annuities have received mixed reviews as a planning tool, particularly as an investment. The insurance company consumes a lot of the returns as operating costs. Substantial penalties can arise if you have to cash out prematurely. But they do work well as income protection and income security devices.

You should approach buying annuities with care—the complexities and choices are vast, and you'll need to work with a good insurance agent or financial advisor.

Chapter 17

An Introduction to Taxes

Every step of the way in life—and for some of us, at death—we must make involuntary contributions to our government in the form of taxes. Everyone must pay taxes, particularly the income tax, but you are not obligated to pay any more than is necessary. Although you can't eliminate taxes, you can avoid paying more than your fair share. That's why it's important that you understand the purpose of taxation and how it works.

We Can't Live Without Taxes

Civilization, as we know it, would not exist without taxes. Taxes provide for a public infrastructure in which our private lives can operate. Without taxes, we'd be living in barren cabins in a disorganized, unprotected wilderness. Governments have evolved to provide infrastructure and protection, and taxes are key to funding governments.

There are taxes on nearly all forms of economic activity related to the production of income (income taxes), the consumption of goods and services (sales, use, property, and excise taxes), and the transfer of wealth (estate and gift taxes). We all pay our fair share—or at least that's the intent of taxation. There is no legitimate way to avoid taxes; in fact, it is our civic duty to pay them.

ESSENTIAL

In managing your personal finances, you need to understand the tax system, and how taxes affect your financial situation. A clear understanding of tax implications will support sound financial decisions, and will help you pay the least amount of taxes legally necessary.

Income Taxes: A Little History

Believe it or not, income taxes first arrived on the scene during the American Civil War. The purpose, of course, was to finance the war, and it was a modest tax that was repealed in 1872. Then, in 1894, the central government grew in importance and the tax was brought back. At that time, it was 2 percent of income for those who earned $4,000 or more (a lot of money in those days).

The U.S. Supreme Court ruled the tax unconstitutional on a technicality in 1895, and the idea lay dormant until a constitutional amendment fixing the technicality was passed in 1913. Income taxes have been collected ever since.

FACT

The first income tax generated $376 million in revenue for the federal government over a ten-year period. In 1999, $879 *billion* in taxes was collected over a one-year period. In other words, the U.S. Treasury collects $100 *million* in individual income taxes every hour of every day.

Evolving Tax Legislation

About every five to ten years, a major new tax bill is passed into law. The bills usually advance an agenda—tax reduction, reducing a deficit, or rebalancing the tax burden among different groups of taxpayers. They also pay lip service to the idea of simplifying the tax code, but the end result is usually quite different—a series of "bolt on" rules and forms that effectively make things more complex. The 2001 Economic Growth and Tax Relief Reconciliation Act of 2001, known as EGTRRA, is the most recent major tax-law change. EGTRRA provides significant income tax reductions, more useful retirement and education savings provisions, and begins a phaseout of estate taxes. Beyond sweeping legislation such as EGTRRA, the tax code is constantly being modified through smaller legislation and legislative riders. It is a living "camel designed by a committee," if you will, but you, as the chief financial officer of your personal finances, should try to keep up with the big changes.

The Purpose of Taxation

The intent of taxation is, at the most basic level, to finance governments at all levels—federal, state, and local. Generating revenue is the most important goal of the system, but there are others, such as the following:

- **Economic needs:** Taxes are used as a tool to manage the economy and its growth and contraction cycles, as well as to stimulate certain economic activities, such as solar energy research.
- **Social and policy needs:** Taxes are also necessary to manage certain social issues, such as education, aging, social services, and other endeavors consistent with public policy.

- **Equality and income redistribution:** The tax system is used to "take from the rich and give to the poor" to level the playing field somewhat for disadvantaged citizens.

QUESTION?

Are Social Security taxes considered income taxes?
You pay Social Security and Medicare taxes based on your wage income. On your paycheck, these are usually called FICA (Federal Insurance Contributions Act) taxes, but technically they aren't part of the federal government income tax pool—they are additional "employment" taxes earmarked for their special purpose.

Due to the nature of our political system and the turbulent cross-currents of interests operating on the complex political playing field, the taxation system has become enormously complex—one of the most complex in the world. The Internal Revenue Code is 2,800 pages in length—but that pales in comparison to all the administrative and judicial rulings available to interpret and supplement it. Nobody—not even the IRS—completely understands the tax code.

Tax Players

IRS stands for Internal Revenue Service, the branch of the U.S. Department of the Treasury that is chartered with the proper collection of taxes and administration and enforcement of the tax law. But the IRS does not pass the tax laws. Where does tax law come from? It comes from one place, and one place only: the U.S. Congress. Congress writes the bills, the president signs them into law, the U.S. Supreme Court reviews their constitutionality, the U.S. Tax Court system and administrative law system interpret them, and the IRS administers them.

Your Responsibilities as a Taxpayer

Your most basic responsibility as a taxpayer is to pay your fair share—nothing more, nothing less. Moreover, you are trusted to determine what that fair share is. Particularly with income taxes, it's up to you to report your income and pay the correct tax on it. Unlike bridge tolls or sales taxes, you are given the responsibility to manage and interpret—within the framework of the tax law—what your fair share is.

Tax Avoidance versus Tax Evasion

Tax avoidance is legal, but tax evasion is not. What is tax avoidance? Tax avoidance is managing—within the law—the reporting of your income and expenses so as to minimize your tax liability. If you choose to sell stock next year instead of this year in order to defer the taxable capital gain until next year, that is tax avoidance, and it's perfectly legal. On the other hand, if you sell this year and deliberately fudge the numbers to reduce the gain or avoid reporting it all together, you are practicing tax evasion and are in violation of the law.

Many expenses and deductions from reported income are subject to interpretation, particularly if your situation involves a business or real estate ownership. The IRS generally supports the position that you can be aggressive in interpreting your situation, so long as your rationale makes sense and can be interpreted as being within the law. Keep good records so that you are able to justify your claims if the need should ever arise.

FACT

The renowned U.S. Federal Court Judge Learned Hand captured the essence of the government's position on taxes in a 1947 tax ruling, in which he stated the following: "Over and over again the courts have said that there is nothing sinister in so arranging one's affairs as to keep taxes as low as possible. Everybody does so, rich or poor, and all do right, for nobody owes any public duty to pay any more than the law demands: Taxes are enforced exactions, not voluntary contributions."

Always Be on Time

You're all familiar with April 15, that springtime day dreaded by most Americans. That is the day the previous year's tax returns are due to the

IRS. In reality, April 15 is more of a settlement date, to document your income tax liability for the previous year and adjust it according to what you've already paid during the year. All through the year, you pay tax as "withholding" from wages or as estimated tax payments, if you are self-employed. When April 15 comes along, you calculate whether those previous payments are sufficient. If they are more than sufficient, you get a refund; if they fall short, you owe additional tax. Your final year-end return must be postmarked by April 15, and quarterly "estimated" payments must be postmarked by April 15, June 15, September 15, and January 15, following each respective business quarter. If you're a wage earner, your withholding happens automatically with each paycheck.

QUESTION?

But can't I file an extension? My neighbor does it.
The truth is, you can put off the inevitable and file a single form (Form 4868) to get an extension of your tax-due date, from April 15 to August 15. You need not have cause—but be aware that although you will be excused from "failure to file" penalties, you will get hit with "failure to pay" penalties for taxes owed. Don't file an extension just because you owe money.

Keep Good Records

As the responsibility to calculate your tax liability rests with you, so does the responsibility to keep adequate records. You will need good records to calculate tax liability correctly in the first place, and they will support your actions if the tax returns you file are called into question. Keep all records of income, expenses, and deductions. Actual "W-2" and "1099" forms record your income; actual receipts (better than canceled checks) track your expenses and deductions.

Typically, the IRS has up to three years from the filing date of your return to question it or request substantiation of its contents. And if you are suspected of understating your income by 25 percent or more, the extension is increased to six years. Certain kinds of transactions—such as in real estate or investment—have entry and exit points that occur over periods of time well longer than an ordinary tax year. Records should be kept through that duration of time and beyond. If you want to be careful, use the suggested times below to decide how long you should keep different kinds of records.

Suggested Time Periods for Retaining Tax Records

Type of record	Period of time you should keep it
Normal income and expense records	At least three years; six or seven years are ideal
Investment records	Until sale
Real estate records	Seven years from time of sale
Tax returns	At least six years; ideally, should not be discarded

Keeping good records not only helps to support your tax decisions, it will help you prepare your returns. With a good records system, the data is there at your fingertips. For instance, many taxpayers use prior returns as useful templates for current and future returns.

FACT

Americans pay more in income taxes than in any other form of taxes. Financially conscious Americans should become familiar with income tax principles in general and with *their* taxes in particular. Consumption taxes are pretty much a given, and naturally, they are driven by your personal consumption. Transfer taxes are very specialized and only affect certain Americans at certain times, mainly at death.

The Income Tax Structure

Despite what you might think, the income tax system does have a logical structure. It starts with your total income and works through a sequence of steps to arrive at your tax payment. Understanding each section on your tax return form will help you get the big picture and help you manage your taxes. These sections all appear in logical sequence on the Form 1040—the standard U.S. Individual Tax Return form—and, in abbreviated fashion, on the "short" forms 1040A and 1040EZ. The following is a summary of what these boxes mean.

1. **Total income.** Just as the name implies, total income includes your receipts of measurable income from all sources, including wages, capital gains, alimony, and business income.
2. **Exclusions and adjustments.** Certain items are, by policy and law, excluded from income altogether—examples include most insurance proceeds and tax-free interest income. Also excluded are certain expenses you can pay with pretax dollars, such as dependent care and some medical expenses paid through flexible spending plans. Certain eligible items are then adjusted out of gross income—eligible moving expenses, alimony payments, and certain self-employment expenses, for example.
3. **Adjusted Gross Income (AGI).** Total income minus exclusions and adjustments equals your adjusted gross income, the most straightforward measure of your true income. As will be seen later, AGI is used as a basis for many important tax calculations.
4. **Exemptions.** An exemption is a device created by the government to allow tax relief for the burden of providing support to family members. Each family member (an earning taxpayer or qualified dependent) counts as one exemption. In 2002, taxable income was reduced $3,000 for each eligible exemption.
5. **Deductions.** Each filing taxpayer or household is entitled to deductions. Deductions are for items on which taxes are waived. Home mortgage interest and charitable deductions fall into this category. Deductions can be standard or itemized. Each person in a household gets an automatic "standard" deduction, an adjustment to income representing "average" deductible items; itemized deductions can be used for those with specific "items" larger than the standard allowance. Additional standard deduction amounts are available for elderly, disabled, or blind household members.
6. **Taxable income.** AGI minus exemptions and deductions gives you the number for your taxable income—the amount on which you are taxed.
7. **Calculated tax.** You can use your taxable-income number to calculate your tax (how much you owe or will get in returns) by using the tax tables provided in the booklet that came with your tax returns forms.
8. **Credit.** Policy and law allow tax liability to be reduced in certain situations. There are many different kinds of credits: dependent child

care, child credits, education, elderly, adoption, and low income are some of the more popular. Eligibility for most credits is determined by your AGI level. What's better—a credit or a deduction? Both reduce tax liability at the end of the day. But in most cases, a credit is better—it is a dollar-for-dollar reduction in your tax liability. A deduction reduces your taxable income, which is then used to calculate your taxes. The credit is actually subtracted from the amount of taxes you owe.

9. **Net tax liability.** Once you subtract your credit from your calculated tax, you arrive at your net tax liability for the tax year. Again, the Form 1040 is a reconciliation—you owe tax only if you didn't set aside enough to cover the tax liability during the year. If you set aside more than the computed tax liability, you'll be entitled to a refund.

ALERT!

Beware of the Alternative Minimum Tax, or AMT. AMT was designed to capture tax dollars escaping through loopholes. Special investment vehicles and accounting games were created to capitalize on these loopholes, and for a time, they were very attractive to wealthy investors. Now the AMT snares a lot more "ordinary" taxpayers. Beware of this tax if your AGI is over $150,000 and you have complex investment assets.

Key Terms and Concepts

Following is an overview of key terms and concepts that will help you better understand income taxes and their role in personal finances. Again, you are not being trained to become a qualified tax preparer, but it is important for you to understand how taxes work so that you can make better financial decisions throughout the year and when the time comes to prepare your tax returns.

Progressive and Regressive Taxation

Progressive taxation occurs when tax rates rise according to the taxpayer's ability to pay. Income taxation is progressive—that is, rates increase in keeping with the taxpayer's level of income.

Regressive taxes, on the other hand, are at fixed rates—that is, the same amount is paid regardless of economic resources. For example, sales taxes are the same for each consumer, regardless of his or her income.

Average and Marginal Tax Rates

The progressive nature of income taxes means that as your taxable income rises, higher rates apply. Enter the concept of the tax bracket. As your income crosses a certain level, every dollar beyond that level is taxed at the higher rate. The highest rate you're taxed at is the level at which the next incoming dollar is taxed. This is called the marginal tax rate. To illustrate, let's look at the following portion of the 2002 Tax Rate Schedule.

Sample Tax Rate Schedule: 2002 Married Filing Jointly

Taxable income:	Tax is:	On the amount over:
\$0–\$12,000	10 percent	\$0
\$12,000–\$46,700	15 percent	\$12,000
\$46,700–\$112,850	\$6,405 + 27.0 percent	\$46,700
\$112,850–\$171,950	\$24,265 + 30.0 percent	\$112,950
\$171,950–\$307,050	\$41,995 + 35.0 percent	\$171,950
\$307,0502–N/A	\$89,280 + 38.6 percent	\$307,050

You can clearly see the brackets and marginal rates. If you, as a married couple, have less than \$46,700 taxable income combined but more than \$12,000, you are in the 15 percent tax bracket, and your marginal rate, for every dollar above \$12,000 and up to \$46,700, is 15 percent. But what if you earn more than \$46,700? You will jump into the 27.0 percent bracket. Does that mean that all your taxable income is taxed at this higher rate? No. The first \$12,000 is taxed at 10 percent, the next \$46,700 is taxed at 15 percent, and then every dollar beyond \$46,700 is taxed at the higher 27.0 percent rate. Your marginal rate is 27.0 percent—and that is the rate you need to keep in mind for every additional dollar you bring in during the year (up to $112,850, where the bracket and marginal rate go up again).

Your average tax rate is the average of the dollars taxed at 10, 15, and 27 percent. If you earned $50,000 taxable income, the first $12,000 would be taxed at 10 percent ($1,200), the next $34,700 would be taxed at 15 percent ($5,205), and the final $3,300 ($50,000 – $46,700) would be taxed at 27 percent, or $891. Your total tax would be $7,296 (the total of $1,200 + $5,205 + $891). Your marginal tax rate would be 27.0 percent, and your average tax rate would be 14.6 percent ($7,296 ÷ $50,000). If you are curious about whether the 2001 EGTRRA legislation really lowered taxes, you may be interested to know that a couple with the same $50,000 income would have paid $8,100, or 16.2 percent of their income, using the 2001 income tax rates and brackets.

ESSENTIAL

Remember, moving into another tax bracket doesn't mean *all* your income moves into that next bracket—just the amount over the bracket minimum. The impact on total taxes isn't as great as you might think. Still, knowing your marginal tax rate can help you make good financial decisions. If you can easily shift income or deductions from one year to the next to keep below bracket minimums, that can help reduce your average tax rates.

Filing Status

Are you single or married? If you are married, do you file separately or jointly? Are you single and filing as a head of household with more than one dependent child living with you? Depending on your tax status, you will use different tax tables. These tables are scaled to accommodate the fact that joint or head-of-household returns count for more than one person. If you are married, there is usually no advantage to filing separately. Determining status is usually straightforward, but if your situation is particularly complex—divorced parents or a divorce in progress, or one spouse living overseas, for example—you should probably see a tax advisor.

Ordinary Income and Capital Gains

Ordinary income is earned by you as wages or as a return on an economic activity such as a business or a securities investment. Almost all income you receive is considered "ordinary" and is taxed accordingly. The lone exception is capital gains income.

A capital gain is a gain on the sale of a capital asset, in contrast to ordinary income derived from holding the asset. If you sell an asset at a higher price than what you paid (your basis), you have a capital gain. Why is the distinction important? Because if you have a long-term capital gain (defined as gain on an asset held one year or more), there is a ceiling on the tax rate, currently at 20 percent, which is preferable to the ordinary-income marginal rates of up to 38.6 percent. The lower capital gains rate is one way that the government provides incentives to invest—and to hold on to those investments.

Note that gains on assets held less than one year are considered ordinary income and that capital losses may be deducted only to a maximum ceiling of $3,000 each year.

FACT

For the purpose of most taxpayers, capital assets include securities investments (stocks, bonds, and so on) and real estate (including places of residence). Tangible personal property, such as cars and collectibles, are technically also capital assets. If you sell something at a gain, you may be liable to pay taxes on it. A happy exception, put in place in 1997, lets you exclude most of the capital gain on your primary residence, up to $500,000 for married taxpayers filing jointly.

Eligibility Limits

There is a series of eligibility limits, sometimes known as ceilings and floors, that determine maximum and minimum levels of income considered eligible for many deductions and credits. Some tax benefits may be eliminated entirely, while others may be subject to cutbacks and phaseouts. The following are a few examples.

- Ceilings come into play in testing AGI for eligibility of deductions and credits. For example, child credits have a ceiling of $75,000 AGI for a single taxpayer or "head of household," or $110,000 for a married couple filing jointly. At that level, they begin to *phase out*–that is, the credits are reduced by $50 for each $1,000 above the initial ceiling, until the final ceiling of AGI $67,000 (single) or $122,000 (joint), where they are eliminated completely.
- Floors are minimum deduction amounts considered for eligibility. You cannot deduct medical expenses unless they exceed 7.5 percent of your AGI, and you can only deduct the amount that exceeds that 7.5 percent. Similarly, you cannot deduct "miscellaneous deductions," which include a broad group of expenses like employment and personal financial expenses, unless they exceed 2 percent of your AGI.
- Cutback adjustments pose a problem for higher-income taxpayers. If your AGI exceeds certain limits, then deductions and exemptions start to get cut back. In 2002, if your AGI exceeded $68,650 (single) or $137,300 (joint), you may have had to face a 3 percent cutback on some (though not all) of your deductions. If you ran a small business in 2002, meal and entertainment expenses were cut back 50 percent.
- Phaseouts are similar to cutbacks, but instead of slapping a fixed percentage reduction on a deduction, they phase the deduction out as income grows. For example, if your 2002 AGI exceeded $137,300 (single) or $206,000 (joint), deductions tied to your personal exemptions started to disappear. Those deductions vanished completely if your AGI reached $259,800 ($328,500 joint). This is an example of a fairly gradual phaseout; other phaseouts may be steeper and more severe.

Why be concerned about these little adjustments? For most of you, they won't affect your tax liability much. The 2 percent floor on miscellaneous deductions probably hurts the most. However, as income levels rise, these items slowly creep into the picture, and what may look like a 30.0 percent or 35.0 percent marginal tax rate may in fact be several percentage points higher. What can you do to lower your tax rate and save yourself money on taxes? Find out in the next chapter.

Chapter 18
Managing Your Taxes

It isn't possible to examine every component of your taxes in detail. However, this chapter does provide an overview of key tax concepts, strategies to help you minimize your tax obligations, information on audits, and advice on how to get help with filing taxes and tax planning.

Deconstructing AGI

Of all the tax-return elements you have learned about in the previous chapter, the two key elements are the adjusted gross income (the AGI) and deductions that you are able to make.

Why is AGI important? To the federal government, AGI is the truest indicator of your income status as a taxpayer. And while AGI isn't the basis for your final tax calculation, it is used to determine cutbacks, phaseouts, and other adjustments that ultimately determine your tax rates and total tax payment.

Let's review the AGI in greater detail. You get your AGI value by adding up the following income:

- **Earned income:** Wages, salary, tips, bonuses, and commissions.
- **Unearned income:** Consists of all the following, which may be calculated with the help of relevant schedules:
    - Dividends, interest: Schedule B
    - Net business income: Schedule C
    - Net capital gains income: Schedule D
    - Net real estate and royalty income: Schedule E
    - Net farm income: Schedule F

QUESTION?

What is the difference between earned and unearned income?
For the purpose of tax returns, earned income is the income you earn from your job, as an employee, subject to payroll taxes like Social Security and Medicare taxes. Most other types of income are classified as unearned income. Alimony received is considered earned income.

Then, you subtract the following AGI adjustments (as with most other tax-related matters, this is a sample, not a complete list of adjustments):

- IRA, pension, annuity, and other retirement plan distributions.
- Unemployment compensation.

- Social security benefits.
- Moving expenses (if the move is job-related and you move more than fifty miles away from previous residence).
- Self-employment expenses (one-half of self-employment tax, the self-employed version of FICA, and a percentage of self-employed health premiums).
- Alimony you pay.

Note that Social Security benefits may be taxable above a certain AGI level, and the calculation is frightening. If your AGI is above $25,000 (single) or $32,000 (joint) excluding Social Security, up to 85 percent of your Social Security may be taxable at your effective tax rate.

Deconstructing Itemized Deductions

Deductions can be standard or itemized. If you have enough deductions, it makes sense to itemize. More specifically, "enough" is more than $4,700 (single) or $7,850 (married, filing jointly). If you have less, you are better off taking the standard deduction.

Itemized deductions should be listed in Schedule A. They include:

- Medical expense deduction. Medical and dental expenses, vision care, laser eye surgery, or health insurance premiums may all be counted up toward the deduction, but keep in mind that you can only use the amount spent *over* 7.5 percent of your AGI, which means that unless you have had unusually high medical expenses last year, you probably won't be able to rely on medical expenses for a deduction.
- Deductible taxes. State and local income taxes, property taxes, and certain others are deductible. Property taxes include real estate taxes and value-based ("*ad valorem*" is the official term) taxes on cars, intangible property, and the like. So a vehicle registration fee, by itself, isn't deductible, but a car tax, based on the value of the car, is. Gone are deductions for state sales taxes.
- Interest paid. You can deduct some forms of interest paid, for instance, mortgage interest up to $1 million on your primary and

secondary residence. You can also deduct interest on a second or revolving equity line on real estate. Finally, you can deduct investment interest—"margin" interest paid for capital borrowed from your broker—against gains realized from those investments.

- Charitable contributions can generally be deducted, with varying amounts of documentation required for gifts over $250. For small cash donations, save your receipt. For small noncash donations, the IRS leaves it pretty much up to you to value the merchandise. For higher value items—over $5,000—prepare to get a professional appraisal.
- Casualty and theft losses can be deducted as well, but these involve complex rules and a high floor at 10 percent of AGI. If you think you might qualify, some professional tax advice might be helpful.
- There is a long list of unreimbursed job search, uniform, and educational expenses related to a job that may be deducted, and another list of expenses related to your personal finances—investment advice, safe deposit boxes, tax preparation, and so forth. But the 2 percent AGI floor on the cumulative total puts this deduction out of reach for many.

Tax Strategies

Taxes are a given in your personal financial life. They cannot, by and large, be avoided. However, you need to be aware of your tax situation, and you should work to reduce tax impact where possible. On the other hand, taxes are not a reason to make foolish financial decisions. This section will review a few good tax strategies to keep in mind as you make decisions in your personal finances.

Maximize Retirement Plan Contributions

Qualified retirement plan contributions, usually done through IRAs and 401(k) plans (see Chapter 20) make a lot of sense for most taxpayers. First, the money you put away into your retirement plan is not taxed and does not count toward your AGI, so you can keep yourself in a lower tax bracket and pay less taxes. Second, the capital invested in a retirement plan will grow, and the profits you make won't be taxed until you retire and withdraw that money. Finally, in many cases, your employer will match your contributions, effectively raising your total compensation without raising your tax base.

FACT

The combined marginal tax bracket for the average wage earner approaches 40–45 percent and can go higher. Here's why: If you are in the 27.0 percent margin for federal income tax, 7.6 percent for FICA, and you pay 5 to 10 percent in state and local taxes, your incremental tax load is really 39.6–44.6 percent for every new dollar earned. This is why taking money off the top to fund retirement plans can be so attractive.

Pay in Pretax Dollars

If you are employed, many employers offer "flexible spending" or "cafeteria" plans, in which you can set aside a certain portion of your pretax income (without having taxes taken out) up to a certain limit to pay for qualified dependent care as well as for medical and certain other expenses. There is some administrative work involved in making these plans work, but they can stretch your day care or medical dollar quite a bit. Pretax medical plans can be used for copayments or to buy more insurance coverage, to pay for an eye exam, or to purchase eyeglasses. The only problem with these plans is that you have to decide how much money you are willing to set aside for this pretax account. If you don't use up the entire amount, you lose the rest.

Timing of Income and Expenses

There are situations where it makes sense to manage the timing of income and expenses. If you have an asset with a big capital gain and another with a big capital loss, and you wish to dispose of them, it makes sense to dispose of both in the same year. The loss will counterbalance the gain for tax purposes.

ESSENTIAL

If you have a big gain and it is the last week of December, you may defer selling that asset until the following year, particularly if you expect to have less income in that year (or vice versa, if you expect to have more income). Carefully plan these timing decisions (with help, if need be), but don't get carried away.

Start a Business

The IRS has strict rules about businesses. If you start a business, it must be intended to make profit and be profitable for a minimum number of years. That said, if you can create a business around an activity or service you perform, the rules for deducting expenses are usually more generous than for the typical individual taxpayer. Buy a ladder for your home, and there's no way you can write it off. But if you have a rental property, it becomes fair game—you can write it off as a valid expense against rental income. If you write books or articles, most printed matter that you buy becomes research expense.

You still must show proximate value for the business, and, again, it doesn't make sense to spend a dollar to save thirty-five cents. But if there's a business in the things you do already, you may be able to find some tax relief. To think this matter through, you may want to talk to a tax advisor.

Charitable Deductions

Giving to those in need makes most of us feel good—*and* it also helps with taxes. Here is how it works. If you are in the t tax bracket, you will be able to write off that percentage on your tax returns. If you donate $100 to your favorite charity and your t is 35 percent, you are really spending only $65.

Moreover, you can donate property—especially appreciated property, such as stocks—and get a bigger boost. You not only get to write off the appreciated value of the property, but you also avoid paying capital gains tax when you sell. If you invested $500, and your investment has grown to $1,000, you can donate the $1,000 and provide a $1,000 deduction against your current income (saving $350 in taxes at 35 percent). You would also save 20 percent (the capital gain rate) of $500, or $100, that you would have paid on the sale—so the donation would in reality cost you only $550.

ALERT!

These are only two samples of some of the key tax strategies you can employ. If you sit down for a consultation with a professional tax advisor, you can learn a whole system of tax management strategies, particularly if you own a business or have substantial investments.

A Word about Audits

An audit is simply an examination of tax computations and the data that supports them. It's the IRS's way of monitoring taxpayers and helping to assure some degree of compliance with the law. There is no need to dread and fear an audit. Just because you are being audited does not mean you are guilty—and you shouldn't act that way!

Audits are typically done in greater percentages on groups of taxpayers who have more complex tax issues or who have a history (as a group) of underpayment. Typically, business owners (especially large businesses or businesses with persistent reported losses) are the most active recipients of audits. The IRS computes an analytical score based on your characteristics and some of the numbers that you report. If you have a high score and your number comes up, you may get an audit.

There are three levels of audit:

1. **Letter or correspondence audits.** If the IRS has a question about some aspect of your return, it may detail the question in a computer-generated message. These are usually simple to resolve by letter or phone.
2. **Office audits.** These audits cover issues too complex to be handled by mail. You will have to bring your records to the IRS office and talk to an auditor.

3. **Field audits.** Dreaded by most taxpayers, these audits involve a visit from the top IRS agents, who show up at your door to conduct a full investigation of your finances and taxes.

If you are being audited, you should prepare your position as well as possible and be prepared to explain your finances to the auditor. Remember that auditors are people with jobs to do. The easier you make their job, the more favorable the outcome will be. Be easy to work with, but stand behind your position.

When It's Time to Get Help

If you are good with numbers and have lots of time, you're probably in a good position to do your own taxes and tax planning. There are many advantages to doing your own taxes: You may save a couple of hundred dollars on fees, and you will surely become familiar with the system if you learn as you go along.

However, many people just don't have the time or the skills to do their own taxes and tax planning. This is not a problem—there are a variety of tax resources available, ranging from storefront preparation services to CPAs and even tax attorneys. For most of you, it probably pays to at least sit down with a tax professional for a paid hour (the fee might range around $100–200) to review your situation and to see if you are missing anything obvious. For more complex situations involving business arrangements—especially corporations and partnerships—and complex real estate transactions (passive activity rules weren't even touched in this chapter), you'll probably want to engage a CPA or similar professional for tax advice, planning, and preparation.

Chapter 19

Planning for College

For anyone who has kids, making sure that they receive a college education is an important goal; without a college degree, your children will be unlikely to succeed in the job markets of tomorrow, which are growing more competitive each year. Yet the costs of higher education are rising as well. Meeting these costs requires careful planning—this chapter will show you how to evaluate your needs and build a savings program, and it will also teach you about the types of financial aid currently available.

The Biggest Worry

For many Americans who have children, the biggest financial worry is college. For the past twenty years, college costs have escalated at rates higher than the going inflation rate. Why? There are many reasons. Reduced state funding means that more people must rely on private institutions. Higher operating and salary costs are also a problem; colleges and universities tend to be located in high-cost areas—in cities or college towns. If you have two, three, or more college-bound kids, you may be looking at large bills to pay in the future, and the only way to be ready when the time comes is to plan in advance.

FACT

Tuition has risen 4–6 percent per year since 1985, while the rate of inflation overall hovered between 2 and 3 percent. The good news is that the difference between cost increases and inflation increases—in the 10 percent range in the late 1980s—is now decreasing.

Establishing Your Needs

How much do you really need to save for college? Like many other areas of personal finance, the amount varies according to your situation. Here are some of the specific factors that will help you establish how much money you need to save:

- **Number of children:** This point is pretty obvious. The more children you have, the more money you will need to save for their college education.
- **Children's age:** Remember the power of compounding. A kid who will start college in three years is a bigger financial problem than one starting in eighteen years, since there's plenty of time for you to enjoy the benefits of compounding.
- **Choice of college:** The college chosen—as well as its location—will have a lot to do with determining savings needs. Four years at an Ivy League school like Columbia University in New York City ($32,000 per year for tuition, room, and board), will come at a far different cost than four years at North Dakota State in Fargo ($6,100 per year for

state residents). Most importantly, you will need to consider whether your child is likely to go to a private or a state school (especially if the state school is in your home state).

ALERT!

Consider your children's intentions. Simply, not all children will attend college, and some will choose more expensive fields and kinds of education than others. You can't know this one for sure, but you should plan around a range of possibilities.

Calculating the Averages

What are the average costs, and where do you find them? An average year of education at a four-year public university costs about $10,500, of which 31 percent covers the tuition/fees, 6 percent covers books, 43 percent room and board, and 20 percent transportation and other. For private schools, the annual total swells to $22,533 with tuition and fees becoming 64 percent of the total, books 3 percent, room and board 16 percent, and other expenses 7 percent. For more accurate data, examine the annual *World Almanac* or go to the U.S. National Center for Education Statistics Web site for specific school data, at *www.ed.gov.*

However, as you know, college costs rise at a rate higher than inflation. To project forward what college costs will be, take a current year (suppose, $10,500) and apply compounding (for a refresher, see Chapter 4). For a child starting college in thirteen years and a constant 5 percent inflation assumption, the costs incurred during his or her freshman year of college would be $19,799 ($\$10{,}500 \times [1 + .05]^{13}$); during sophomore, junior, and senior year, those costs would increase to $20,789, $21,828, and $22,920, respectively, for a total of $85,336.

ESSENTIAL

In your planning, you should probably build "best-case" and "worst-case" scenarios. And each year, you should watch the costs of individual schools of interest through the National Center for Education Statistics (*www.ed.gov*).

Need Scenarios

Estimating what your college costs might be is not easy. Nobody knows whether seven-year-old Josh will turn out to be an honors student with professional aspirations, a baseball player, or a practical young man who prefers the "seat-of-the-pants" approach and gets rich on his own, without the benefits of a formal education.

Little Josh may go to school close to home or travel 3,000 miles away. He may go to college right out of high school or work for a few years. He may get an athletic or academic scholarship or he may enlist in the military and go to school on the GI Bill. The point is—you can never know for sure. Likewise, it's impossible to predict the future inflation rates, the cost of living where Josh will end up going to school, and what kind of lifestyle or interests Josh will have then.

In order to make some educated guesses, you need to develop different scenarios and figure out what the costs for each one would be. Pick different schools, try a few inflation rates, and project the cost of each scenario. At the end of this exercise, you'll have a good idea of how much you'll need in best, worst, and middle-of-the road cases. Then, try to be prepared for the worst—and if it turns out for the better, so be it. You can always use that money elsewhere, like in home renovations.

FACT

If your kids don't go to college, they'll probably live at home at least for part of that time—and possibly for many years. So some of the college costs are really just the costs of room and board that you will probably be responsible for even if your kids don't go to college.

Meeting Your Needs

Once you have established what your needs are, you need to create a plan that will help you achieve your goal. The costs may be met by a potentially large assortment of resources. Effectively, they boil down to three main groups: savings, financial aid, and tax breaks. The following is a brief overview.

- **Savings plans:** There are many savings plans geared especially toward saving money for college. The new "529" savings plans offer major tax advantages; education IRAs, once available only in trivial amounts, have expanded their limits.
- **Tax relief:** Special tax credits can help, though they start to phase out as income rises and disappear completely as Adjusted Gross Income (AGI) reaches $50,000 (single) or $100,000 (joint). You can also deduct student loan interest with an AGI ceiling of $55,000/$75,000.
- **Financial aid:** Financial aid comes in all forms. There are grants and scholarships that don't need to be repaid as well as an array of student loans—some subsidized and some unsubsidized, some based on need, some not, some direct from the government, some managed through local lenders. Loan terms are favorable, and most are designed for repayment by the student.

ALERT!

Many people don't think student loans need to be repaid, but the U.S. government has cracked down on those who default on their college loans. Those who fail to pay off their loans ruin their credit history and are often unable to receive a professional license. If your child applies for a student loan, be sure he or she is prepared to repay it.

Savings Plans

Saving money is the biggest "take-charge" action you can take towards solving the problem of paying college tuition, and there are many ways to save—in fact, some methods were designed quite specifically to achieve your college savings objectives.

It's useful to think about the fundamental savings model for college savings. The amount that you will need for a four-year college tuition is your target lump sum—how much you will need to save. So, to get back to the previous example, if Josh is going to a four-year private school starting twelve years from now, the target "future value" amount is about $175,000.

How can his parents save up this much? They have two options:

1. Deposit a lump sum into an account that will let the money grow and compound.
2. Develop a monthly or annual accumulation annuity, save a certain amount each time period, and build with compounding.

Lump Sum Deposits

Most of you probably don't have a large sum of money that you can just deposit and live without until it's time for your child to go off to college. But some of you may have other assets that could be redeployed, or there may be a family asset or inheritance to be put to good use. If such is the case, how much should you deposit?

It's an easy calculation using the Rule of 72 (see Chapter 4). As you may remember, the Rule of 72 says that if you divide the interest rate into 72, you get the number of years it takes to double a sum. Suppose you invest at an average 6 percent return—a fairly middle-of-the-road number—and Josh starts school in twelve years. So, 72 ÷ 6 = 12, which means it'll take twelve years for the sum to double. To get that $175,000 in twelve years, you will need to deposit $87,500 today.

The Monthly Savings Approach

If you don't have $87,500 lying around, the best approach is to save on a monthly or annual basis—with the accumulation annuity. The accumulation annuity assumes you deposit a certain amount each time period, and the resulting future value reflects the cumulative deposits plus returns earned on the balance as it grows. There's no shorthand calculation for this one—refer instead to **FIGURE 4-3** to find the annuity factor. Although it doesn't have a column for twelve years, if you pick something reasonable between ten and fifteen years, it will get you a close enough estimate. The factor for ten years at 6 percent is 13.2. For fifteen years, it is 23.3. Twelve is two-fifths of the way from 13.2 to 23.3 (about 4 percentage points more), so let's use 17.2 as a factor.

Now what? Divide the sum you need ($175,000) by 17.2—you get about $10,000 per year (it's an annual table), or about $833 per month. That means you should save around $833 a month in a plan with a 6 percent return in order to achieve your college-costs goal of $175,000 in twelve years.

ESSENTIAL

The calculations above assume no taxes. If your savings returns are taxed, you will need still more to achieve your goals. Fortunately, there are enough tax-free savings vehicles that you can probably avoid this problem.

Of course, you don't have to endure these college calculations yourself. There are college expense and savings calculators all over the Web and in packaged financial software like Microsoft Money and Intuit Quicken. Web sites such as Quicken (*www.quicken.com*), Morningstar (*www.morningstar.com*), and college savings portals like College Savings Plans Network (*www.collegesavings.org*) all have college savings advice and calculators.

Savings Bonds

One of the simpler and safer ways to save for college is to purchase U.S. Treasury savings bonds. Series "EE" and "I" savings bonds offer tax-free savings if issued after 1989 and if your income falls below certain AGI limits—there is a phaseout that begins at about $40,000 (single) and $80,000 (married, filing jointly). These bonds are bought at half their face value and reach their face value in seventeen years or less; there are no cash interest payments.

You can usually buy U.S. Treasury savings bonds through your local bank or through the consumer-friendly U.S. Treasury "Treasury Direct" Web site (*www.publicdebt.treas.gov*). This site allows investors to set up a monthly payment and even use major credit cards to purchase bonds.

There are several advantages to purchasing bonds. It's an easy way to invest, and maturities can be synchronized with college-planning needs. The major disadvantage to this investment method is the modest rate of return. Although the rate is not too bad if the bonds are tax-free, tax benefits only apply to families with a low AGI.

QUESTION?

What is the implied interest rate on the U.S. Treasury savings bonds?

If you buy bonds with a seventeen-year maturity at half of their face value, you are essentially buying bonds that will double in value in seventeen years. According to the Rule of 72, that rate of return is 4.23 percent.

Educational IRAs

Educational IRAs, now known as Coverdell Education Savings Accounts, emerged out of 1997 tax legislation as an attempt to foster college savings in the same manner as existing retirement-savings plans. Unfortunately, this was a weak attempt—the annual limit was $500, there were AGI phaseouts, and participation made investors ineligible for other educational tax credits. Can you save much at $500 a year at any rate of return? No. Still, the 2001 EGTRRA act put some teeth into this savings plan, making it attractive for many more savers with the following options:

- Annual contributions to the account may now run as high as $2,000.
- The phaseout threshold was increased from $150,000 AGI to $220,000 (married, filing jointly, with a similar rise for those who file single).
- Tax-free eligible expenses have been broadened to include elementary and secondary education (for those contemplating private school before college or noncollege professional education).
- Eligibility for educational credits is preserved, but credits must be used first, which may ultimately make some portion of your savings taxable.

Educational IRAs are normally set up through banks, brokers, or other financial services providers. They can be funded with almost any type of securities investment. Funding amounts are "after tax"—that is, there is no tax deduction for what you set aside. If funds aren't used for education, they are taxed when withdrawn, and (as with other retirement plans) 10 percent in penalties may apply. The advantages of tax-free compounding are worthwhile; moreover, educational IRAs offer the opportunity to be flexible in how much you invest, and they are low in cost if you manage your account yourself. One disadvantage of these plans, however, is that contribution and AGI limits still apply; if you can afford to contribute more than $2,000 per year toward your college-cost savings, you will need to look for an additional savings strategy.

Qualified State Tuition Plans

Probably the hottest college savings product on the market right now, qualified state tuition plans (or QSTP/529 plans) were created by recent tax legislation and got a big "step up" from the 2001 EGTRRA. The 529 plans (as they are most commonly called) allow each state to set up a savings plan, usually through a well-known investment company such as TIAA-CREF or Fidelity. Accounts are set up for each eligible child, and up to $50,000 can be contributed each year.

ESSENTIAL

The 529 is an especially powerful tool if there are wealthy family members in the picture. More than one account can be opened for a given child, so you and your parents can each open and control your own accounts. For now, a special gifting exemption allows an accelerated gift up to $55,000 to be transferred to these accounts free of gift tax, exceeding the normal annual $11,000 gift exclusion. Significant total funds—up to $250,000 per account in some states—can be transferred to these accounts.

Each state has its own plan and rules, and the rules do vary. (Just recently, the last few "holdout" states have adopted plans, so now all fifty states have 529 plans.) Each state has its own annual and total contribution amount, chosen program provider (investment manager), and available investment vehicles and expense ratios. In fact, it is worth shopping around from one state to another. For instance, many states offer state income tax breaks for proceeds used in the "home" state. There is no requirement to use the funds in the home state, but states may provide incentives, such as tax relief, to do so. The additional benefit added by EGTRRA is that gains are now tax-free instead of tax-deferred, and you can combine 529 plans with tax credits and Coverdell IRAs.

Better yet, these funds can be freely "rolled over" (transferred tax free) from one child's account to another, or even back to the parent, as long as they are used for educational purposes. Once a year, they can also be "rolled over" between states and within the investment plan. If the funds end up not being used for education, they will be taxed upon withdrawal and penalties may apply.

A chief drawback of the 529 plans is the lack of investment choice they offer. You can't invest the accounts in individual investments or even funds of your choosing. You must take what's available—each state allows from one to maybe ten investment choices. Most of these are conservative in style, and, at least in the past few years, many have been poor performers. Expenses can be high—as much as 2.5 percent—which eats into your earnings even if they are tax-free (which most are in the 0.50 percent to 1.0 percent range). Also, 529 savings can reduce eligibility for financial aid.

Still, 529s are probably the most powerful college savings vehicles around, particularly for wealthier savers or savers with wealthy family members. For most families, they provide a virtually unlimited, managed tax-free savings vehicle.

Information on 529 plans can be found almost everywhere. Newspaper and magazine articles on 529s appear almost daily. Notable Web resources include a Morningstar "529 center" at *www.morningstar.com* and the College Savings Plans Network, a nonprofit site run by the National Association of State Treasurers, at *www.collegesavings.org*. Both of these sites furnish good state-to-state comparative information, questions and answers, and links to state program sites.

Prepaid Tuition Plans

Still available, though fading from the scene somewhat, are state "prepaid tuition" plans. States allow you to prepay tuition for one of their state schools, allowing you to lock in rates. They work well as an inflation guard, but they generally lack the flexibility of 529 and other plans. If your kids decide to go out of state, do something else completely, or blow their grades and can't meet admission requirements, you can usually get your money back, but that's about it. Shop carefully, but if you don't have a very good crystal ball on family matters, you may want a more flexible savings plan.

UGMA

UGMA, which stands for Uniform Gift to Minors Act, is a common vehicle for transferring funds to a child while still keeping some parental control. UGMAs are useful for starting child savings and transferring something into their accounts to teach financial responsibility. However, they have lost their popularity as a college savings tool.

Years ago, the government closed the "lower tax rate" loophole and imposed the infamous "kiddie tax," making income above a certain (low) threshold for anyone under fourteen taxable at the parent's rates. Once the child reaches legal adulthood, he or she gains control of the assets, which can be used in any way.

E ALERT!

The danger with UGMA accounts is that once your child grows up, she is free to do with that money as she pleases. But even if she chooses to spend the money on a shiny new convertible, the amount is considered to be an asset and will decrease her chances to receive financial aid.

Tax Relief

Powerful savings vehicles make it logical to save as much as you can yourself. But there are still other "footholds" available to everyone, with or without the resources to save or invest. Tax credits have for years provided some assistance to lower-income taxpayers, and they are now being stepped up to help out in higher-income situations and situations where other resources are available. (Recall from Chapter 17 that credits are more powerful than deductions.)

Hope Credit

The Hope Credit, a product of the 1997 Taxpayer Relief Act, applies to qualified tuition and fee expenses for the first two years of undergraduate education, and up to $1,500 in credit can be claimed—100 percent of the first $1,000 paid and 50 percent of the next $1,000.

The Hope Credit is available for each child involved, but it is phased out for AGI over $50,000 (single) or $100,000 (married, filing jointly). The 2001 EGTRRA allows for more resource overlap, so Coverdell and 529 plans won't eliminate eligibility for credits. The Hope Credit works best for lower and middle-income families.

FACT

Let's take another look at the power of tax credits. If you have a total family AGI of $60,000, after deductions and exemptions you might face a tax bill of $8,000. If you land a $1,500 credit, that gives you a 19 percent reduction in your taxes. At that income level, it would take $7,500 in deductions to give the same savings.

Lifetime Learning Credit

The Lifetime Learning Credit is similar to the Hope Credit, but it is for any type of education at an accredited institution and can be claimed only once per taxpayer, not once per eligible child. In 2001, students could deduct 20 percent of qualified educational expenses. (The maximum qualified expenses were $5,000, so the maximum credit was $1,000; in subsequent years, this amount will likely be increased.) You cannot have a Hope and a Lifetime Learning Credit for the same child, and similar phaseout rules apply.

"Above the Line" Deductions

New and extended educational expense deductions are now available "above the line"—that is, for determining AGI. ("Above the line" deductions, if you recall, are better because AGI is used as the "standard" to index floors, ceilings, phaseouts, and cutbacks.) Deductions include the following:

- Student loan interest deduction, with new AGI phaseouts starting at $50,000 (single) and $100,000 (married joint).
- Qualified higher education expenses deduction, which allows up to $3,000 in 2002 (and increasing to $4,000 in 2004). Similar phaseout rules apply.

Financial Aid

It is your responsibility as a parent to prepare the funds to pay for your children's college education. However, to help parents with the sky-high costs of colleges and universities, financial aid is available to students who qualify.

Financial aid can be either "free" (no payback required) or offered as a series of subsidized or unsubsidized loans. Most of the loan programs are attractive because payback doesn't start until education is completed; interest rates are low; and terms are long, usually ten years or longer.

ALERT!

Financial aid—particularly the free kind—is great if you can get it, but it's better not to rely on it. It really shouldn't be part of the financial planning process, but you should know about it anyway.

Eligibility

There are some types of aid–particularly grants and scholarships–that aren't based on financial need. If your child is a whiz kid, a championship soccer player, or can kick a football accurately at 50 yards, you may be home free. However, most types of aid are based on financial eligibility.

The formula for eligibility is complex, and it depends on the family and its financial circumstances. Assets, income, and number of family members are considered; many assets, such as home and retirement assets, are excluded. The amount of money a student is eligible for is determined by subtracting your expected family contribution (EFC) from the total need (the cost of education).

For example, a family of four with $50,000 in eligible assets and $50,000 a year in pretax income might be expected to contribute $4,500, while a family of four with $150,000 in eligible assets and $100,000 annual income might be expected to contribute almost $25,000.

Normally, college students are considered to be dependents of their parents, and their eligibility for financial need is determined by their parents' income. However, your child may be considered as single if he or she is over twenty-three years old, married, enrolled in a graduate or professional program, has legal dependents, or is an armed forces veteran. Of course, this means you can't claim him or her as a dependent (for an exemption) on your tax return.

FACT

If you'd like to learn more about financial aid and eligibility, visit the College Entrance Examination Board's Web site at *www.collegeboard.org.* The Board provides a valuable handbook, the *College Aid and Financial Planning Handbook.*

Grant and Loan Programs

Most grant and loan programs are available from one of two sources: the federal government or the educational institution itself. Colleges and universities have a variety of grant and loan programs designed to attract the kinds of students they want. Many are funded by alumni contributions and endowments, and there may be state funding involved (especially true in public institutions). Other sources of aid include various civic organizations and even companies employing the student's parent. For instance, if you work for a college, your child may be qualified for a tuition reimbursement.

Government Assistance

When it comes to federal grants, the two types you should be aware of are Pell grants and Armed Forces aid. Pell grants are available to achieving students with strong financial need. They cover up to $3,125 in eligible expenses per year. Armed Forces aid includes several aid and scholarship programs for people coming out of armed forces service. Some are loans; others are grants, such as the recently revived GI Bill. These can be very attractive, financially.

Like most other government programs, student loan programs have evolved into a complex patchwork of overlapping offerings so complex that it is next to impossible to develop any lasting expertise on them. There are three main forms of federal and federally backed loans to be aware of: Stafford, PLUS, and Sallie Mae loans.

Stafford loans include a family of loan programs provided by the U.S. Department of Education. Typical repayment terms are up to ten years, with a minimum repayment of $50 per month. Interest rates are variable but are capped at 8.25 percent. There are subsidized and unsubsidized loans, based on EFC (expected family contribution) eligibility:

- **Subsidized loans:** These loans don't accrue interest and don't require repayment until six months after graduation or after the student is no longer studying full-time.
- **Unsubsidized loans:** These loans accrue interest right away, although the interest can be capitalized—added to the loan balance—until payments are required. Students who don't qualify for need-based aid may get unsubsidized loans.

Borrowing limits for dependent students vary from $2,625 (undergraduate first year) to $8,500 (graduate) per year. Independent students (those without parental financial support) have higher loan limits than dependent students: up to $7,500 per year for undergraduate and $18,500 per year for graduate students.

ALERT!

Remember that student loans are due and payable even if you don't graduate. If you or your child drops out of school and stays out for longer than six months, the repayment process will begin.

Some Stafford loans are "direct"—that is, issued directly by the Department of Education. These are known as FDSLP loans. Local private lending institutions or the college itself can also lend "indirect" Stafford loans. These are known as FFELP loans.

PLUS loans, or Parent Loans for Undergraduate Students, are similar to Stafford Loans except the loan is made to the parents. PLUS loans must come after other financial aid, and they are generally available to parents with good credit ratings. Terms are similar to Stafford loans except the loan is repaid by parents and the interest rate cap is 9 percent.

ESSENTIAL

Watch out for loan fees. With many loan programs, and particularly the Department of Education loan programs, there may be substantial loan origination fees taken right from the loan proceeds. With Stafford and PLUS loans, fees may be as high as 4 percent.

The Student Loan Marketing Organization, or Sallie Mae, is a government-backed private organization that borrows money on the open market by issuing bonds and then uses the proceeds to make higher-education loans. Sallie Mae offers a variety of loan products and features, and these loans are worth your consideration if you're in the higher-education loan market. To learn more about this program, visit *www.salliemae.com.*

It Can Be Done!

In conclusion, there are many tools available to help plan and finance a college education. For the most part, you are better off saving for college using any of the newly expanded savings programs than relying on financial aid to make up the difference. But remember, saving for college should not displace your retirement savings. You can borrow for college, but you can't borrow for retirement. Remember this, save what you can, keep track of tax laws and Federal program changes, and you'll make it (financially) to your kids' graduation.

Chapter 20

Planning for Retirement

Sooner or later, most of us will retire. For decades, retirement wasn't a problem. If you made it to retirement without debts, you could rely on a defined benefit pension and Social Security, which would provide a fixed monthly income for the rest of your life. But today, we live longer and have higher retirement lifestyle expectations, and Social Security benefits haven't kept up. On top of that, most of us are in charge of our own retirement savings. To prepare for your retirement, the first step is to know what your needs are.

Reasons to Worry

People worry about retirement with good reason. With the advances of modern medicine and the improved quality of life, people live long past retirement age. If you expect to survive thirty years past your retirement date, you will need quite a lot of money to support yourself and lead a comfortable lifestyle—even if you have the assistance of government entitlements.

But the very survival of the Social Security system is in question as demographics and the tax base change. Although it probably will survive in some form, you may not be able to rely on it for much.

ESSENTIAL

Of course, it's hard to visualize your retirement; there are so many unknowns. How long will you live? What will your health be like? What will the economy and inflation be like? Where will you be? Will you be able to produce any income?

The responsibility for planning your retirement lies on your shoulders. Not only must you furnish the funds to finance your retirement, but increasingly, you are in charge of managing them. Slowly disappearing are the days of defined benefit pension plans, when your monthly retirement was secure and the company or government bore the investment risk. Today's more popular defined contribution plans, such as 401(k)s, put you firmly at the helm of managing your own retirement assets—and destiny. And if you mismanage your funds, there are no retirement loans or financial aid available to help.

FACT

According to one study, more than 40 percent of households headed by workers nearing retirement (ages forty-seven to sixty-four) don't have enough to replace even half their retirement income, and nearly 20 percent don't have enough to keep themselves above the poverty line.

A Master Plan

Your retirement plan may well be one of the most carefully thought-out portions of your overall financial plan. You can "blow" a budget, or forgo budgeting completely. But if you don't do something for retirement, you may be in for long-term financial pain. Personal finance books and magazines hit the issue of retirement planning hard and often. You can find easy reads on determining the best places to live, making the most of your retirement savings plans, and covering medical costs in retirement. But what you can do here is the most important part—developing a comprehensive financial retirement plan.

What's in that comprehensive plan? It's pretty simple, really. There are three elements:

1. **Total resource need.** How much income you will need per month and how long you expect to live will determine the total financial resources required for retirement.
2. **Projected entitlements.** By now, you are probably eligible—or on track to be eligible—for Social Security. How much of your gross income need will Social Security meet? And if you have a pension or other "defined" benefit, how much will that provide?
3. **Net resource need.** You will have to come up with the difference between total income need and projected entitlements on your own. This amount of money should be available at retirement to distribute year-by-year during retirement.

A good retirement plan starts by assessing these three items objectively, then adds a little "what-if" scenario planning to cover possible outcomes. Then it proceeds to build the savings vehicles required to achieve the net resource need as a goal. Many people go straight into savings plans without first assessing needs. Saving towards an unidentified goal is good, but saving towards a more specific goal is much better.

Choose Your Retirement Style

A recent research study by AIG SunAmerica, a financial services subsidiary of a large insurance company, identified four different classes or styles of retirement, which seem to occur in about equal numbers:

1. **Ageless Explorers.** These retirees see themselves in an exciting new phase of life and keep busy to avoid boredom. They are healthy, travel a lot, and often seek completely new careers or ventures in retirement. Naturally, they need—and have—the most financial resources, with an average income of $65,000 per year and an average net worth of about $470,000.
2. **Comfortably Contents.** These retirees live the traditional postretirement leisure lifestyle. Their resources are adequate ($61,000 per year in income and a net worth of about $367,000) and they do travel, but more modestly. Generally, Comfortably Contents are less interested in new work or contributions to society.
3. **Live for Todays.** These retirees want to be like Ageless Explorers, but don't have the financial resources to achieve the type of lifestyle they would have liked. Because their average income drops off to $46,000 and net worth drops to $223,000, the Live for Today folks often continue working and worry about their finances.
4. **Sick and Tireds.** This group struggles with retirement and may have been forced into it. Their average income is a mere $32,000; their average net worth is $161,000.

E ALERT!

As you can see, unless you prepare for your retirement in advance, you are in danger of being left behind in the Live for Today or even the Sick and Tired group. To aim your retirement lifestyle more in the direction of the Ageless Explorers or Comfortably Contents, you must take control of your retirement today!

What's Enough to Live On?

The first step in considering what your retirement needs are is to figure out what will be enough for you to live on after you retire. This is a daunting task. After all, many of you probably have trouble establishing your budget for next month! But we have to start somewhere, so let's take what's known as the "replacement ratio" approach.

Living on 75 Percent

Rather than build a detailed "bottoms up" budget, with obligations, necessities, allowances, and other considerations that you can't project that far into the future, most planners recommend starting with a percentage of current income as a "base" retirement-income need. Will you take a pay cut in retirement? Yes, that's realistic for most of us. The kids will be gone, you'll have more time to deal with less money by shopping frugally, and you won't be commuting to work or buying expensive lunches or clothes associated with work. And you won't be saving for retirement any more! So if you make $60,000 a year today as a household, you'll need about $45,000 a year in retirement to support the lifestyle you've become accustomed to.

Upward and Downward Adjustments

The more realistically you can project your circumstances, desires, and tastes, the better job you'll do establishing your retirement needs. It's "crystal ball" time—you need to try to picture your retirement lifestyle choices.

ESSENTIAL

> Try to envision where you will be and what kind of living circumstances you'll be surrounded with. Are you planning to travel and live large? Or are you planning to live a quiet life, residing next to your children and grandchildren and taking the young kids out for ice cream cones once in a while? If you're dead set on a luxurious retirement, that will naturally require a bigger stake all the way around.

Starting with the 75-percent-of-income replacement ratio benchmark, here are some factors that may require you to make upward or downward adjustments to your projected retirement needs.

- **Frugality:** If you are able to live successfully on a budget, stay out of debt, and control spending, you'll need less in retirement. If you're happy driving a compact sedan, you'll do well; if it must be a luxury car, look out. If you plan to spend every other day shopping at the mall, you'll need more.
- **Location:** Different locations entail different costs of living. Retiring in Manhattan will clearly require more money than moving down to Florida. If you are willing to live in a retirement community that offers good retirement amenities without a huge cost burden, you will certainly need less money to retire. Most popular personal finance magazines have annual "best places to retire" articles. If you can stay away from the "big name" places, you'll be better off.
- **Health:** Although it's not something we can predict, health is an important factor in planning for retirement needs. If you have a chronic illness, if family members are subject to certain diseases, or if your health is weakening, you are likely to need money for prescription drugs, copayments for doctor visits, and so forth.
- **Mortgage:** Housing costs are one of the biggest retirement cost factors. If you plan to stay in your house and pay off the mortgage, or if you can buy your retirement home with cash, that will relieve an enormous cost burden—maybe a quarter or third of your retirement needs.
- **Long-term care insurance:** See Chapter 16.
- **Other factors:** Think through your lifestyle, hobbies, distance to the rest of your family, and need for activity. Some retirement planners like to guess on the high side, creating a bonus situation if the expenses do not indeed occur.

You should be able to gauge your monthly (or annual) income needs by starting with 75 percent of today's income and working up or down. Perhaps, as an example, you earn $60,000 today. Seventy-five percent is $45,000, and you plan to pay off your home, sell it at retirement (using the capital gains exclusion), and buy another for cash in a small town in Virginia. Once you subtract your mortgage payment from your base income need, you may be left with something like $33,000. But two of your kids live in California, and you want to go on at least one cruise per year. Add back $6,000 as a travel budget and $2,000 for long-term care insurance. This means that you will need about $41,000 per year.

And what about inflation? After all, you may be planning for thirty or even forty years into the future. Well, once you get to the actual planning of your retirement, you have two options. You can ignore inflation and project needs forward in today's dollars, but you must also take inflation out of investment returns. That is, if your investments earn 7 percent and inflation is 3 percent, your growth in real (today's) dollars is 4 percent. To use consistent dollars, you would have to earn 7 percent total, but you use only 4 percent in your wealth accumulation calculations. The other approach factors income needs upward in "day one of retirement" dollars—and factors each year after that accordingly. This second approach may be a little more accurate (especially because the rates can be variable) but it is also more difficult to calculate.

The Length of Your Retirement

Okay, so to stick with our example, you need $41,000 per year for each year in retirement. But for how many years? The length is important for several reasons. The first one is obvious: You need to know how much money you should be prepared to accumulate to cover all the years of your retirement. Plus, the longer you live, the greater your annual expenses will be. Though you may not travel as much or go shopping as frequently (if at all), your medical costs will rise significantly.

QUESTION?

Want insurance against living too long?
Try an annuity. Annuities do have their drawbacks, particularly if you find one with a high commission or if you have to access it prior to maturity. But they do provide insurance against living too long—and outliving your money—payments are guaranteed until you die. So if you plan to live to eighty-five or longer, then toss an annuity into your retirement portfolio just in case.

The average male lives about seventy-five years; the average female lives about eighty years. But through the miracles of modern medicine, these numbers are rising. Assuming you'll retire at sixty-five, for planning purposes let's suppose you'll need $41,000 each year for twenty years of retirement.

Relying on Social Security

How much of that annual income of $41,000 will be provided by Social Security? In times past, Social Security was a big part of retirement planning. Today's reality is that while Social Security is not to be ignored, it most likely will provide for only a fraction of your needs.

There is neither the time nor the need to go into the details of Social Security—what kinds of benefits are available, how they are calculated, and so forth. Many programs fall under the larger umbrella of Social Security—retirement, disability, survivor benefits, Medicare, and so forth. Here the focus is on retirement benefits. Suffice it to say the Social Security system is complex and has complicated formulas for determining benefits and eligibility.

Let's assume you meet (or will meet) the minimum qualifying criteria of forty working quarters (ten years) with at least $780 in wages. If such is the case, you can count on receiving income when you retire. If you were born before 1937, full benefits are available at age sixty-five; those born after that date don't get full benefits quite that soon. If you were born in 1960 or thereafter, full benefits don't start until age sixty-seven. If you were born between 1937 and 1960, your "full-benefit" age is prorated in two-month increments between ages sixty-five and sixty-seven; for instance, if you were born in 1956, full benefits are available at sixty-six years and four months. For your exact full-benefit age, refer to your Social Security statement or to the Social Security Administration Web site (✐ *www.ssa.gov*). You can also retire "early"—at age sixty-two—but you will suffer a monthly payment reduction of 20 to as much as 30 percent, depending on your year of birth.

What Can You Count On?

Monthly Social Security benefits are calculated based on your average indexed monthly earnings (or AIME), a weighted, inflation-adjusted average income level that the Social Security Administration calculates for every retiree. The average income level is divided into tiers, or "bend points," and benefits are calculated by adding three numbers, as follows (these calculations vary each year; the data given here is for the year 2000):

1. 90 percent of the first $531 of AIME
2. 32 percent of the amount over $531, up to $3,202
3. 15 percent of AIME over $3,202

So if your AIME is $5,000 a month, reflecting a $60,000 annual salary at retirement, your monthly Social Security benefit would be $(531 \times .90) + ([3202 - 531] \times .32) + ([5000 - 3202] \times .15) = \$1{,}602.32$ per month (or $19,227.84 a year). That means Social Security will only provide you with about 32 percent of your monthly gross income ($58,000).

The bottom line in the Social Security game is this: It helps, but it isn't the answer. Social Security benefits must be taken in stride with other retirement resources to meet total projected needs. To find out what you can expect, try doing an online estimate—the Social Security Administration provides calculators at *www.ssa.gov*.

FACT

Studies show that average wage earners can only count on Social Security to provide 42 percent of their preretirement income. Low-wage earners can count on as much as 60 percent; high-wage earners can only count on 26 percent of preretirement income.

Defined-Benefit Pension Plans

Social Security benefits form one part of indefinite retirement income entitlement. Another—for those fortunate enough to have one—is the defined-benefit pension plan. Pensions pay a monthly stipend, usually based on a percentage of your income at the time of retirement. Older, traditional companies and government agencies pay pensions. You should get up-to-date on how much pension income you can expect—typically, your pension plan administrator can provide you with this data.

How Much Do I Need to Save?

Now you know how much you will need for retirement and how much you can expect to receive from Social Security and, perhaps, from your defined benefit pension. So, what's your net resource need? How much do you need to save? In our example, you need $41,000 in annual income, and you can count on $19,224 in Social Security income. That means you need to save $21,776 for each year of retirement. How do you provide for your net resource need?

Recall from Chapter 4 the concept of accumulation and distribution annuities. Your retirement planning model should use both models in a "back-to-back" combination. The next two sections will show you how.

The Distribution Annuity

The distribution annuity takes a lump sum and distributes it in equal increments over a specified time period. The assumption is that the remaining declining balance continues to earn money, until it is finally gone.

In our example, what lump sum, available at day one of retirement, will pay $21,776 each year for twenty years? Referring to **FIGURE 4-4** in Chapter 4, the factor for a twenty-year annuity at, let's suppose, 5 percent, is 12.5. So you would need 12.5 times the yearly distribution amount saved up and available, or $272,200 (disregarding inflation for the moment).

For a more luxurious retirement, or if you think you won't have paid off your house by the time you retire, you might need $50,000 a year, for a total of $625,000 to start off your distribution annuity. For a longer retirement (let's say, for thirty years rather than twenty), the distribution annuity would be $335,319 for the basic retirement or $770,000 for the luxury version.

The Accumulation Annuity

If you know that you will need to have $272,000 for the distribution annuity on day one of your retirement, how much do you have to save today in order to get there? Now is the time for the accumulation annuity. If you recall, the accumulation annuity can help you figure out what you have to save each month or year, at a given return rate, to achieve a given lump sum at the end of a certain time period.

Suppose you plan to retire in twenty years. Take a look at **FIGURE 4-3** to find the factor for the investment with an aggressive 7 percent return—it's 41.0. To get your $272,000 in twenty years, you divide $272,000 by 41.0, and find that you need to save $6,634 a year, or $552 a month. If you want to consider inflation, do the same calculation at 4 percent (considering the other 3 percent lost to inflation). In this case, the factor in **FIGURE 4-3** drops to 29.8 and so the annual savings required is $9,127. That's quite an increase just to overcome the effects of modest inflation.

QUESTION?

What about taxes?
The assumption here is that your savings are tax-deferred through qualified retirement savings tools—that is, you pay no taxes as your savings accumulate. If this is not the case—if your investments are not in retirement accounts, the effective rate of return drops still further. Can you now see why tax-free retirement savings is so important?

Now you can see that the longer you have until retirement, the easier it is to save up enough money. If you're thirty-five and thirty years from retirement, the 4 percent factor jumps from 29.8 to 56.1—that means you need to save just $4,848 per year (as opposed to $9,127, from our example).

If you're already nearing retirement, on the other hand, things get ugly. If you have little to nothing saved, and you decide you need $272,000 with only ten years left to go, the factor is 12.0—implying an annual savings requirement of $22,667. The moral here should be clear: Start early, and keep on saving.

Putting It Together

The basic retirement planning model consists of a back-to-back distribution and accumulation annuity. The back end—the distribution annuity—is calculated first, to discover what you need on the first day of retirement, and then you work backwards to determine what you need to save to accumulate that sum, your retirement savings goal.

Using this model and the tables provided in Chapter 4, it's easy to build retirement plan scenarios. You may choose to do it this way, or you can use any of the various retirement planning calculators available on most financial Web sites, which operate on the same principles. Regardless of how you proceed, it helps to have a firm understanding of the model and how different factors—rates of return, length of retirement, and retirement income needs—affect the results. Ⓔ

Chapter 21

Choosing Your Retirement Plan

In Chapter 20, you figured out the amount of money you need to save for your retirement. Now, you need to know which retirement savings strategy and plan will work best for you. This chapter offers an assortment of savings tools and programs—some individual and some provided by employers—to make it all happen, and a few important retirement planning tips to help you along the way.

The Tax-Free Advantage

You have now observed the challenges in providing needed financial resources for retirement. If your savings and returns were continually taxed, the task would be a lot more difficult. Fortunately, the U.S. government is also well aware of the challenges and has furnished a wide assortment of tax-preferred savings vehicles to help you.

Tax preference is the underlying characteristic of all retirement savings vehicles. With most of them, both you and your employer can exclude the amount of money used to fund savings from your current income. Further, the investment earnings inside these savings plans are tax-deferred, which means that the money you save in these plans is not taxed until you withdraw the funds, usually during retirement.

ESSENTIAL

Deferring taxes helps a lot, for two reasons. First, compounding is allowed its full effect, since the money that would have been lost on taxes is retained for growth. Second, when you do withdraw funds in retirement, you're likely to be in a lower tax bracket and pay less in taxes.

Retirement Plan Classifications

When it comes to retirement plans, you have many options to choose from. Retirement savings plan provisions are defined by the U.S. Internal Revenue Code. As such, they have evolved into a patchwork of ideas and amendments, and the rules are detailed and complex. This book will provide you with an overview of what's available. Once you decide what type of plan will work best for you, make sure you do more research on the rules and restrictions of each plan.

Individual and Employer Plans

Some plans are set up, funded, and managed entirely at the individual level, while others are provided and managed by employers. Traditional and Roth IRAs are set up and managed by individuals. Employer plans—

pensions and profit-sharing plans, including the popular 401(k) plan—are set up and managed according to stringent guidelines on behalf of the employee. Amounts contributed by the employer into these plans are tax-deductible for the employer and are tax-deferred for the employee. In defined benefit plans, employers manage the assets themselves (more often through third parties); in defined contribution plans, your employer provides the platform for you to manage the assets yourself.

FACT

Falling in between employer and individual plans is a small assortment of self-employment and small-business plans. These include Keogh, SIMPLE, and SEP-IRA plans.

Pension and Profit-Sharing Plans

Pension and profit-sharing plans are both employer plans. Pension plans are structured to promise a specific sum to be paid at retirement, and they require mandatory employer funding to do so. That is, the plan must be funded even if the employer does not make money in a given period. Pension plans thus place more burden and risk on the employer; on the other hand, if the employer invests wisely, the pension recipient won't get the full benefit of the investment. Pension plans include traditional defined-benefit pensions, plus a small group of defined-contribution plans known as "money purchase" plans, where the employer buy-in amount is fixed each year.

Profit-sharing plans, on the other hand, have flexible employer contributions, often based on a percentage of profits generated. The legal promise of the profit-sharing plan is to defer taxes, not to provide a specific retirement benefit.

Defined-Benefit and Defined-Contribution Plans

Defined-benefit plans have a specific and promised retirement payout. A defined-benefit pension plan usually promises to pay a contractual portion of your terminating salary, regardless of the amount of money set aside or its investment performance. As an employee, you don't have a specific account or balance in a defined-benefit plan—rather, you get a promised share of a larger investment pool or trust fund upon retirement. The amount deposited by the company is determined by actuaries and is of no consequence to you, since the payout is guaranteed.

The defined-contribution plan, on the other hand, depends on the success of the investment choices you make. In this case, the employer guarantees what goes in but not what comes out.

ESSENTIAL

Defined-benefit plans are becoming more rare, as they are gradually being replaced by defined-contribution plans. Employers are getting out of the guaranteed-retirements business because with a defined-contribution plan, the employer transfers the investment-performance risk to the employees.

Some Retirement Plan Basics

It's a good idea for you to become familiar with the principles and common terminology of basic retirement savings plans. For instance, it is important to understand the vesting period of the retirement plan. Vesting is your entitlement to retirement funds (that is, the effective ownership of those funds), which prevails regardless of whether you switch jobs. The "vesting period" is mandated by the federal government: for most plans, all funds must be fully vested in either five years ("cliff vesting") or on a sliding scale in which increasing percentages are vested in years three through seven of your sustained employment. Vesting periods can be shorter than these government mandates—and it's a good thing if they are. Note also that eligibility to begin participating in the retirement plan can vary up to one year.

Contribution Limits

All retirement savings plans have annual contribution limits to qualify for tax-preferred status. (The limits are in place to avoid giving huge tax breaks to high-income workers and corporate executives.) These limits vary widely—many profit-sharing plans allow up to $40,000 to be set aside each year. In 2001, the popular 401(k) allowed a maximum employee contribution of $11,000 (a number that increases each year, under the 2001 EGTRRA tax act), while IRAs were increased to $3,000 each year (and more for taxpayers age fifty and over.) Pension plans, while not faced with contribution limits per se, allow pension benefits to be based on salaries up to $160,000 each year—a generous sum.

Salary Deferral and Employer Match

Some plans are built around employee salary deferrals, with a corresponding employer match. The 401(k) is the prime example. Employees are allowed to set aside a portion of their salaries before taxes—up to 17 percent—and the employer matches a percentage, usually up to 3 percent. This way the employee enjoys reduced taxes on current earnings *and* gets additional funds from the employer added into the retirement fund. Again, the employer contributions are tax deferred.

QUESTION?

Have you ever heard about ERISA?
ERISA, or the 1974 Employee Retirement Income Savings Act, requires employer plans to be fair and not discriminatory (biased towards senior executives); it approves employer plans, and stringent adherence is required.

Required Withdrawals

Many retirement savings plans require a certain amount to be withdrawn as income each year once you have turned seventy and a half. Why? Because the government has generously granted tax deferral, but it wants to collect its taxes eventually! You aren't supposed to use a retirement plan to build an estate for your heirs. A notable exception is the Roth IRA, which requires no withdrawals and can be used to pass tax-deferred savings to your heirs.

Individual Retirement Plans

In this and the next section, employer-sponsored and individual retirement savings vehicles are discussed in more detail. It's impossible to cover all plans or all the details involved. If you need more information about a specific plan, you need to do some basic research. Fortunately, that information is readily available from the pension plan providers.

When it comes to individual retirement plans, the two that most people rely on are traditional IRAs and Roth IRAs. Let's examine these more closely.

Traditional IRAs

IRA stands for "individual retirement arrangement," and it is just that—a retirement plan you fund yourself and manage yourself, all the way to retirement. IRAs are set up through any bank or brokerage house, and funding and investment choices are entirely up to you. Basic features of a traditional IRA include the following:

- You can contribute $3,000 each year, with that limit to increase to $4,000 in 2005 and $5,000 in 2008; in 2003 and after, you can contribute somewhat larger amounts if you are fifty years old or older.
- The amount contributed is tax deductible if you're not covered by another qualified employer plan and if your AGI is less than $44,000 (single) or $64,000 (married filing jointly).
- The working spouse may open a spousal IRA account for the nonworking spouse, effectively doubling the couple's annual IRA contribution.

ESSENTIAL

Whether or not you're eligible to deduct IRA contributions, you still get tax-preferred treatment on investment growth, so traditional IRAs can make sense even if you don't qualify for the deduction.

Roth IRAs

A Roth IRA is a special type of IRA set up in the early 1990s. Contributions to Roth IRAs are never tax-deductible, but earnings from a Roth IRA are tax-free (not just tax-deferred, like in most other plans). Additionally, original principal can be withdrawn with no penalties or taxes, and there is no requirement to withdraw funds at age seventy and a half. As a result, many planners recommend Roth IRAs as a way to accumulate tax-free wealth, particularly if you aren't eligible for a tax-deductible IRA.

A Roth IRA is also a better option for those of you who aren't sure you can set aside savings permanently. If you contribute to a tax-deductible IRA and then are forced to withdraw before age fifty-nine and a half, you will not only pay income taxes on the amount withdrawn (which you deducted earlier), but you will also pay a 10 percent penalty. This can be expensive. With a Roth IRA, such deductions of original principal carry no penalty and no taxes. Regardless, it isn't a good idea to kill the goose that lays your golden retirement eggs, so these "emergency" withdrawals should be avoided regardless of the type of IRA you have.

FACT

Annual limits apply to your individual contributions regardless of the plan or plans you have; that is, your combined traditional IRA and Roth IRA contributions can't exceed $3,000 each year. However, subject to certain income limitations, you can supplement employer-sponsored savings plans, such as the 401(k), with individual savings plans.

The 401(k) Plan

The number of employer plans far exceeds the number of individual plans, particularly when self-employment and small-business plans enter the picture. The basic plan offered by employers is the 401(k). (For those of you working in the public sector, the 401(k) has a virtual equivalent known as a 403(b).)

The 401(k) allows you to defer a percentage of your salary, sometimes up to 17 percent and always within an $11,000 maximum (this applies to investments made through 2003), and is usually matched up to 3 percent by the employer. The 401(k) is clearly the most popular "self-reliant" employer plan. Employers have migrated to this plan to minimize their risk (as it carries no pension payout requirements). Employees benefit from the high annual contributions, size of pretax savings, and employer matching. It is possible to accumulate sizable wealth even with no salary increases and with relatively small employee outlays.

Employees do, however, take the burden of managing their own investment portfolios. Usually they receive a fairly wide assortment of aggressive and conservative investment choices, like stock and bond mutual funds. Employees often have a chance to invest in their company's own stock, but the "all eggs in one basket" risk is high—if your company fails, your retirement savings will lose their entire value.

Wealth Accumulation with a 401(k)

Following the earlier example, suppose you earn $60,000 a year. You're thirty years from retirement, and you decide to set aside 8 percent of your salary in a 401(k). Further, your employer matches 3 percent, and you invest with a goal of earning 6 percent on your money. Effectively, your annual contribution will be $5,400 (6 percent of $60,000 plus 3 percent of $60,000). Once again, looking at the accumulation annuity table (**FIGURE 4-3**), the factor for 6 percent at thirty years is 79.1. So you take the annual contribution ($5,400) and multiply by 79.1 to get accumulated wealth of $427,140 on the first day of retirement. Do a little better on your investments—say, 8 percent—and the factor rises to 113.3, giving you $611,820 upon retirement. Wealth accumulation will be greater with higher contributions and/or higher investment returns.

What about inflation and its effect on 401(k) wealth accumulation? Earlier we discussed moderating investment returns to account for inflation, but here you don't need to, because your salary and annual deferral should rise with inflation. So the 8 percent rate of return figure used in the example is more realistic.

ESSENTIAL

The 401(k) is an excellent way to leverage your savings. Take note that your original investment in the example is a mere $108,000—6 percent of $60,000 over thirty years. You can see how, with employer contributions and proper investment management, the 401(k) magnifies your original savings amount.

Retirement Savings Strategies

You can read books and magazines or talk to financial advisors and brokers to learn more about retirement savings and savings plans. Some brokers offer excellent literature explaining these plans, and there are resources on the Web. This chapter concludes with a list of strategies and tactics to help you finance your retirement plans most effectively:

- Take advantage of what is available to you in terms of what your employer has to offer. If your company matches your contributions to a 401(k), make sure you are enrolled and are putting in as much as you can to get the matching funds.
- Contribute to your retirement plan as much as you can, and do it consistently. Remember, you can't borrow your retirement, so retirement savings should normally come before other financial goals.
- Manage your retirement investments. Wealth accumulation depends on investment returns, particularly over the long haul (because of compounding). Although they are long-term investments, retirement assets should be managed well and actively. Particularly while you're young, these investments can be more aggressive. If there's a reason to switch investments, go ahead and do it. There are no tax consequences, and negative returns in a tax-free environment are particularly unfavorable.
- If you're older and have insufficient savings for retirement goals, use the new "catch-up" higher IRA contribution limits to build your retirement base.
- Pay off your mortgage so that when you retire, you find yourself living in a house that you own, with no monthly mortgage payment to worry about.

- Plan to supplement your retirement income. Set yourself up to work in some capacity—it will keep you busy, keep your mind fresh, extend your contributions in your field or profession, and help out a lot financially.

ALERT!

Keep up with the tax law changes; you may discover new benefits to help foster retirement savings. We got Roth IRAs and 401(k) plans a few years back and in 2001 got a big boost in contribution limits. Your retirement savings strategies and plans should adapt to these changes.

Chapter 22

Leave Your Mark with Estate Planning

Sooner or later, your assets must be transferred to someone—preferably someone of your choosing. Excel at personal finance all your life and you'll leave a sizable estate. But estate taxes can take a big bite if you plan poorly or not plan at all. Even if your estate isn't big, liquidity and ease of transfer are still important to avoid hardship for your loved ones during this difficult period. This chapter explores the key elements of estate planning and estate-planning strategies.

Why You Need Estate Planning

Your estate is all that you own and leave behind at the time of your death. At that time, you must transfer your property—your assets—to something or someone, usually your loved ones. When you plan your estate, you are planning how you want your assets distributed at death (or, in some cases, before death).

If you die without a will or an estate plan, you die *intestate*. The state you lived in will essentially provide a will for you, dividing assets among closest of kin. It can take a while to determine what assets go where. Meanwhile, your family may have trouble paying the bills (including the funeral, medical bills, and so forth).

Furthermore, your estate may be large enough to be subject to estate taxes, which can take as much as 55 percent of your wealth over certain limits. The laws have changed, and this issue now doesn't come into play until your net taxable estate exceeds $1 million, but still—all that hard work and well-thought-out asset accumulation, and half of it gets confiscated by the government!

Estate Planning Is for Everyone

Estate taxes are, for some of us, a very good reason to do estate planning. But for the many of us who don't have large enough estates to trigger estate taxes, there are reasons aplenty to do estate planning:

- **Providing for specific family needs:** Making sure the right heirs get the right assets—and income from those assets—is important. If you're married (once) and intend to leave everything to your spouse, your estate planning will be pretty straightforward. But if you had a prior marriage and want children from that marriage to receive some assets but provide other assets and maybe income to your current spouse, you need to plan your estate accordingly.
- **Avoiding probate:** Probate, the legal disposition of your assets, takes a long time—in many cases, up to a year or more. And it can be expensive. For ordinary estates, legal fees of $5,000–10,000 are not uncommon (and they are set by statute, which makes them

unavoidable). Finally, probate is a matter of legal record, so anyone has access to the size, nature, and distribution of your assets.

- **Providing liquidity:** Without a proper estate plan, all your assets could be tied up in probate, so your family members may have little or nothing to pay ongoing bills or meet costs associated with your death, let alone estate taxes, if these are due. Emotional considerations in this time of life can make this particularly devastating.
- **Achieving charitable intentions:** Many people have worked hard through life and wish to give something back. Charitable contributions at death are often desirable, particularly if estate taxes are an issue.

ESSENTIAL

Estate laws vary quite a bit from one state to another. In this chapter, you will learn the general terms common to all states. For details, you need to find out what your state laws are, and the best way to do that is to get professional help.

Transfer of Property

Estate planning involves planning the transfer of your assets—your property—at death. Does it make a difference what kind of property it is, and how it is owned? Absolutely. The way property is owned can determine whether it must go through probate or whether it is part of the taxable estate at all. There are three ways to transfer your property: by contract, by ownership, or by will.

Transfer by Contract

Certain types of property require you to designate a beneficiary as part of establishing ownership. Retirement plans, insurance policies, and trusts are examples. When you die, property transfers automatically to your designated beneficiaries. These properties do not go through probate even though they are part of your taxable estate.

Make sure your beneficiary choices are up-to-date. If you set up a trust thirty years ago listing your wife as the beneficiary, but you are now divorced and would like the funds to go to someone else, make sure you take her off the beneficiary designation. If you don't, there isn't much your intended beneficiaries can do about it.

Transfer by Ownership

Suppose you own property jointly with someone else. Transfer will happen according to how the ownership is set up. Let's take a real estate property as an example. If you purchased property as a joint tenancy with right of survivorship (JTWROS), your share transfers automatically upon your death to your joint survivors and does not have to go through probate. If you are a single owner or if you share the property as tenants in common, your interest in the property will transfer according to provisions in a will.

If you and a spouse own a home together, the cleanest, easiest way to own is with a JTWROS, with ownership transferring immediately and freely upon death. The same applies for bank and brokerage accounts, providing convenience and liquidity during your family transition. But you would set up a "tenants in common" agreement and use your will if you wanted your interest to pass to someone other than an existing owner. Why? Well, you might want to pass your share of an owned business to someone in your family, not to the other business owners. If you are in a situation where this is an important consideration, you will do well to do more research into various types of ownership and what will happen to your property when you are deceased.

Transfer by Will

All your other possessions may be passed down to your survivors by a will. The will is a signed document declaring your asset distribution choices for assets not already transferred by contract or by ownership. It is an important document and will be discussed in further detail in the following section.

ESSENTIAL

Good estate planning means making sure it's possible to carry out your best intentions. Take inventory of each property you own, and understand how that property will transfer. Make sure the transfer is set up correctly to achieve your intentions and avoid problems, and make sure you do it today. When you're gone, your family will be in no position to fix things themselves.

Where There's a Will There's a Way

A will is, simply, a written and legally executed document that states to whom you want to leave your possessions. It may be very specific, listing each one of your belongings and to whom they are bequeathed, or it may be general. Your will may also grant powers of attorney to allow others to handle important decisions, financial as well as medical, for you as you become incapable of making these decisions yourself. The will must be written, and, in most states, executed–signed and witnessed by at least two other people. (Some states do allow handwritten, or holographic, wills.) Once written and executed, a will can be amended by executed updates known as codicils.

What's in a Typical Will

In your will, you are the testator–the person who makes the will. When the testator dies, he or she is referred to as the decedent. As the testator, you name an executor, who is left in charge of managing your estate and its assets until they become legally distributed. Typically, you would assign this role to a family member, but this isn't necessary. What's more important is to have a competent administrator with time to take care of everything. The executor identifies assets, works with the probate process to establish value, and also pays the bills and manages the daily affairs of the estate until it is officially distributed to the beneficiaries (specific people or entities designated by your will to receive your assets).

FACT

An estate is a legal entity under the law. When you die, the estate comes into being through the probate process; when asset distribution ceases, the estate ceases to exist. While in existence, the estate pays taxes on income like an ordinary citizen and is liable for bills and obligations created before or after death. The executor is in charge of managing this legal entity and may be entitled to some compensation for doing so, especially if he or she is not a family member.

Children cannot be beneficiaries until they reach adulthood. If you have children, your will should appoint a legal guardian for them. Make sure you get agreement from your designee before assigning this role.

In the will, you transfer your properties by making bequests. These may be tangible (real and personal) or intangible (financial, intellectual, or investment) properties. Bequests can be specific, clearly identifying individual items by name and description, or more general, as in "the home I am living in at the time of my death." There may or may not be a specific asset inventory in a will. Assets already bequeathed by contract, such as insurance or retirement accounts, need not appear in a will. Bequests can also be residuary—for instance, a clause may state that all assets not specifically identified go to a particular beneficiary.

What Is a Probate?

Probate is the legal administration of a will by a court, which opens the probate process after a citizen's death. For those who left a will, the probate is governed by it; for those who die intestate (that is, without a will), the probate is conducted in accordance with state law, and the court will appoint the executor and legally establish the estate as an entity.

The court can grant permission to convert certain assets to cash to meet estate needs or pay off liabilities. The court will also ensure that property is evaluated correctly and fairly for transfer. If there is a discrepancy in a will or some portion of it is impossible to execute—perhaps an heir or guardian is deceased—the court will resolve this. If challenges are brought by heirs or would-be heirs, they are heard and decided in court. The probate process can be long and expensive and may cause headaches for those family members and heirs that must await completion. Good estate planning can minimize the impact of probate, but it usually cannot be avoided altogether.

The probate process incurs probate fees, which are based on the size of the estate and set by state statute. Statutory fees vary from state to state, but might be $3,000–4,000 for a $100,000 estate, $5,000–6,000 for a $200,000 estate, and $20,000 for a $1 million estate. The fee is set by size—not the complexity—of the estate, so if you've planned your estate well but haven't taken steps to avoid probate—such as setting up correct ownership or contractual transfers, including trusts—your estate will lose a lot of its value to fees.

A Few Common Problems

If all you need is a simple will that bequeaths everything to a spouse or an individual heir, you can probably put it together yourself, as long as it's properly signed and witnessed in according to your state's estate laws. However, if your estate is large or complex, you would do well to avoid the following problems:

- **A will that's too vague:** A will that names certain property to go to heirs but has no residuary clause will tie things up while residual property is assessed and heirs are identified. Furthermore, unless you specify the possessions you are talking about, you might cause a family squabble as your heirs fight over *which* Oriental rugs or diamond rings were meant for whom. As a good estate planner, try to picture whether, with little to no knowledge of the assets or the heirs, you could figure out your own intentions.
- **Poor choice of executor:** An executor should have the time and administrative ability to manage the estate and assist in the probate process. Get your executor candidates to agree to the job, and think through whether they are really capable of doing it.
- **Improperly executed will:** You get mad at your oldest son and decide to disinherit him. You rewrite your will in anger on an airplane and stick it into your briefcase, but you don't get proper witnesses or signatures. Guess what—your son still gets his inheritance.

- **No simultaneous-death clause:** If your major heir or heirs die at the same time (as in an accident), or worse, within a short time of each other, property may have to transfer twice, incurring more effort, cost, and taxes. A typical strategy is to require beneficiaries to survive you by a minimum number of days (for instance, thirty, forty-five, or sixty) to become eligible.

Estate Taxes: Concepts and Principles

Estate taxes are a good news/bad news story. The bad news is that estate taxes are among the highest and most complex forms of taxation. Effective marginal estate tax rates start at 45 percent and go quickly to 55 percent. The good news is that the government offers a generous exclusion, known as the unified credit. In 2002 and 2003, for example, estate taxes were negated on estates worth up to $1 million. Recent legislation has increased this amount to $3.5 million; in fact, the estate tax is scheduled to be repealed in 2010.

ESSENTIAL

The tax law (EGTRRA) that was passed in 2001 made major changes to estate taxes that will be valid until 2010. However, we don't know what will happen after 2010—the law may certainly change again. Trying to guess which way the law will go is a full-time occupation in the professional estate-planning community.

Most of you won't have to worry about estate taxes, but if your estate grows beyond these thresholds, or if your financial planning includes possible inheritances that might trigger the estate tax, you should understand how estate taxes work and how they are changing, and then build a precise estate plan to keep them at a minimum. Particularly when estate taxes enter the picture, it makes sense to get professional help with your estate plan.

Your Taxable Estate

In calculating income tax, first you must assess your taxable income, and only then can you figure the tax. The same holds for estate planning. For estate tax purposes, your estate will include certain items and exclude others—and it's good to know which is which.

Inclusions are assets owned in your own name (like real estate, bank and investment accounts, life insurance, and retirement accounts); half of everything owned jointly with your spouse; all properties owned jointly with anyone else, unless they paid for it (you can't just "give" ownership away to get something out of your estate); amounts owed to you; assets in trusts over which you have direct control; and your share of partnership or business assets. Excluded from your taxable estate are debts or other obligations, taxes owed (this excludes the estate tax), as well as estate administration and funeral costs.

A complete inventory of these items gives us the gross taxable estate, analogous to the adjusted gross income (AGI) used for income taxation. From this figure, you can subtract deductions and adjustments are made for gifts.

Marital Deduction

At one time, property passing between spouses was subject to estate tax. The government decided this was a bad idea, and since the 1980s, property passing without qualifications to a spouse can be deducted from your gross taxable estate. Most estate plans call for simple tax-free transfer from one spouse to another. But in divorce-remarriage situations, some estate owners may want to pass a portion to direct heirs (children) and other portions—or maybe just the income from certain assets—to a spouse. To accomplish this, you will most likely need to rely on a trust.

ALERT!

Don't forget the charity deduction: Transfers to federally qualified charities, done by will or trust, are deductible from the gross estate calculation and may help you avoid estate taxes.

The Unified Gift and Estate Tax System

While estate transfers are property transfers occurring at death, gift transfers are transfers of property to a willing recipient before death. If Grandma writes you a check for $50,000 to buy a new house, or makes you a joint tenant and part owner of her house by title transfer, you just received a gift. Are gifts taxable? And if so, who pays the tax?

In fact, gifts are taxable, and they are treated as part of the taxable estate. Because the government has created a unified taxation scheme for gifts and estates, transfers before and at death are taken together and taxed together, so the unified credit ($1 million in 2002 and 2003) applies to both the gift and the estate values. If Grandma gives you a million dollars during her lifetime, she can apply the unified credit to that sum and owe no taxes on that gift. But when she dies, that second million she wishes to leave you as an inheritance will be fully estate taxable, since the unified credit is used up. If Grandma chooses to pay gift tax at the time the gift is made, that will preserve some or all of the unified credit to shelter estate taxes.

FACT

Gift tax rates are the same as estate tax rates, and so is the unified credit, at least for now. The EGTRRA rise in the estate tax exemption does not apply to gift taxes after 2004—the gift exemption stays at $1 million, so we may not be calling the credit/exemption "unified" for long.

If you are married, both you and your spouse get the unified credit. That means that in 2002 and 2003, you can actually get $2 million of your estate exempted from taxes.

Annual Gift Exclusion

One of the critical features of gift/estate tax law is the annual gift exclusion. The law says that individual donors can give up to $11,000 to one or more individuals each year without incurring gift taxes. So if you're sitting on a $1.5 million estate, you might want to start giving away $11,000 per year to your favorite nephew. Over the course of ten years, you will pull $110,000 out of the estate, saving $45,000–55,000 in estate taxes.

But the real power of the gift exclusion surfaces in the concept of gift splitting. The $11,000 exclusion is for each donor (married or not) and each recipient. Mom and Dad are two donors. If Mom and Dad wish to give to Josh and Natalie, they can give $22,000 to each recipient. Since there are two recipients, a total of $44,000 can be excluded from the gift tax. In large families with lots of heirs, an estate can be taken down below the tax "radar screen" pretty quickly.

ESSENTIAL

If there is any possibility of paying estate tax, a good estate plan will make the most of the gift exemption to get under the threshold. If you are a possible recipient in someone else's estate, make sure they understand the gift exclusion—you can present a compelling case to get it sooner and tax-free!

Gifts of Appreciating Property

If the property is likely to appreciate in value and estate taxes are on the horizon, it can make sense to transfer the property as a gift, not as part of an estate. Why? Because transfer valuation for the property is established at the time of the gift, and is often the basis of what the donor paid for it. If transferred at death, it is valued at its full girth (market value), so the tax liability may be much greater. (Note: Any gift given in the last three years does not get the favorable tax treatment).

A good estate plan in a taxable situation will pass property by gift sooner, to enjoy a lower valuation and to capture the exclusive nature of the gift tax. But what if you don't want to surrender your assets completely to your kids just yet? What if you still need some of the income from those assets for your future needs? Look into "grantor" trusts, which effectively transfer the assets while retaining an income interest for you–as much as you want for as long as you want. Grantor trusts are complex, but if what they offer sounds appealing, by all means get more information on how they work.

Inheritance Taxes

In addition to estate and gift taxes, you also have to consider inheritance taxes. How do inheritance taxes differ? Well, estate taxes (and gift taxes) are taxes levied by the federal government on the right to transfer property to someone or something else. They are paid by the transferor (the former owner), not the transferee (the recipient). Inheritance taxes, on the other hand, are levied and collected by the state from the recipient.

The good news is that not many states charge an inheritance tax, and state taxes paid are credited against federal estate taxes (although this favorable treatment is being phased out). Usually, the unified credit/exemption applies just as for estate taxes. If you're in an inheritance tax state, you need to figure inheritance taxes into your estate plan.

The Truth about Trusts

Trusts are legal entities designed to "own" assets to accomplish a long list of estate-planning objectives. Among those objectives are the following:

- **Facilitation of asset transfer:** Trusts are contractual transfers that avoid the probate process, saving your inheritors time and money and avoiding unnecessary publicity.
- **Management of finances** for beneficiaries who are unable or unwilling to do so.
- **Providing a shelter for your assets from estate and gift taxes:** Certain types of trusts may help shelter assets from taxes. Although assets used to fund these trusts may be subject to gift taxes when they are taken out of the estate, taxation may be on a smaller base and at a lower rate.
- **Splitting assets** (and income from those assets) between different beneficiaries.
- **Controlling the direction of assets after your death:** For instance, if you want your assets to go to your kids once your spouse remarries, you can set up a trust to make that happen.
- **Achieving charitable objectives** by setting up charitable trusts.

Setting up a trust involves several people who play different roles. The person who creates (and funds) the trust and establishes the beneficiary (or beneficiaries) and the trustee is known as the donor or trustmaker. The beneficiary is the person or organization that receives either the assets or the income—or both—from the trust. The trustee is the person or entity in charge of managing the corpus (assets), investments, and the payout of the trust. The donor may serve as his own trustee, or he may appoint a family member or a fee-based professional organization to do the job for him.

FACT

The trust donor, together with trustee, puts together trust documents to define the trust and its terms and conditions; any specifications are valid, as long as they are legal. The "control from the grave" concept gets quite interesting with some more creative trustmakers.

Living Trusts

Living *(intervivos)* trusts are set up while the donor is living and are a part of the donor's estate. (That is, they cannot help you avoid estate taxes.) The living trust defines asset and income distribution to a named list of beneficiaries. The main purpose of setting up a living trust is to bypass probate and set up asset management after you're gone. As they are living trusts, you retain ownership of these assets until your death. You also have the option of changing the terms and conditions at any time.

Irrevocable Trusts

Irrevocable trusts, as the name implies, cannot be changed. They involve a transfer of ownership. The transfer of ownership is made according to your terms, but once you set up the trust, you cannot change it or benefit from the assets. When you fund an irrevocable trust, you effectively make a gift to its beneficiaries. If kept within the annual gift exclusion, or if used to buy a life insurance policy owned by the trust, irrevocable trusts can be used to reduce or minimize estate taxes.

Testamentary Trusts

This fancy-named trust actually comes into existence when you die because it is triggered by the probate process. Testamentary trusts are created by will and are usually used to provide asset management and control asset direction once you die.

Qualified Terminable Interest Property Trusts

The Qualified Terminable Interest Property (QTIP) trust is designed to control asset direction. A QTIP trust is usually used if the donor wants to leave an estate to a spouse in trust but have the assets revert to children from a previous marriage. Typically, the spouse receives income from the trust but can't touch the assets. The interest terminates when that spouse dies or (if specified) remarries.

Bypass Trusts

These trusts are set up to pass assets outside the marital pair to take advantage of the unified credit available to each spouse. The trust can pay income to the spouse who is still alive—it simply separates the corpus from their estate. This type of trust also avoids estate taxes on increased trust value after the first spouse's death.

Charitable Trusts

Charitable remainder and charitable lead trusts are designed to transfer a portion of an estate to a charity or charities before or upon death. A charitable remainder trust pays an annual sum back to the beneficiary (who may be the trustmaker or another party), then transfers any remaining assets to the charity upon death. The donor gets a charitable income tax deduction up front, and since the corpus goes to charity, there is no estate tax on this amount. The charitable lead trust pays the annual sum to the charity, then reverts the remainder principal to the beneficiary. Either way, these trusts are powerful tools to achieve charitable objectives and reduce taxes.

Life Insurance Trusts

Sometimes carrying the heady name "Irrevocable Life Insurance Trusts," these trusts are irrevocable trusts designed to own a life insurance policy. Usually the policy is set up to pay heirs as beneficiaries. As they are irrevocable and uncontrollable by the grantor, they pass outside the estate and avoid estate taxes. Funds used to pay premiums can be subject to gift taxes, but only if they are above exclusion amounts. Life insurance trusts can be powerful tools to pass on a large, tax-free sum with relatively low cost to the donor.

ALERT!

As you can see, trusts can be used to do just about anything. They do more than save estate taxes, and some of these trusts could be considered by almost anyone, regardless of wealth. But they are complex and require help to set up properly, and they can be expensive to set up and maintain if complex.

Additional Estate-Planning Strategies

To conclude this chapter, here are some principles and strategies to keep in mind as you do your estate planning:

- Understand estate-planning principles even if you're not wealthy. They can help your family in the time of crisis.
- Envision the future, think your desires through, and figure out exactly what you want to happen with your assets. Then set up a will (and trusts, if appropriate) accordingly.
- Think through the special situations like multiple marriages and business ownership.
- If your estate goes beyond the unified exemption amount ($1 million in 2002 and 2003), it can really pay to plan ahead. Keep track of your net worth not only to measure your progress but also to manage your estate. Use bypass trusts to preserve both unified exemptions. Remember that the exclusion amount rises through 2010.

- Take advantage of the gift exclusion and favorable tax treatment if you're above the unified exemption amount.
- Make the most of estate-planning tools to achieve charitable objectives.
- Use life insurance wisely to provide liquidity, pay estate taxes, or replace gifted assets.
- Don't try to do this yourself. Of all the areas in personal finance, this one is the trickiest and hardest to learn, so get professional help.

Chapter 23

E Be Prepared for Life Transitions

Life is full of events and surprises, and it is easy in times of bliss—or of great stress—to lose control of your finances and make decisions that could stand in your way for a lifetime. Getting married, having kids, changing jobs, and going through divorce require proper focus on finances. This chapter introduces some helpful ideas and principles for managing these transitions.

Nothing Stays the Same

Everybody goes through life transitions, from the time we are born to the time we die. People grow up, get married, and have children. Some get divorced, remarry, and have stepchildren. Gone are the days when a man takes a job right out of high school or college and works with the same company for the next forty years, until retirement. Today, your career is likely to change several times along the way—you may lose your job, start your own business, go into consulting, and take an early retirement.

ESSENTIAL

Throughout your life, there will be periods of steady income and gaps between those periods. There will be times of unusual or abnormally high expenses—a college education to pay for, weddings, family moves, divorce, an early death of a spouse. All that affects your personal finances and personal finance planning.

It's hard to keep your financial wits about you when going through an emotional transition such as a layoff or an exciting transition like a wedding, and it is common to lose the awareness, commitment, and control needed to stay on top of your finances. During these times, you need to remember that if you apply some financial wisdom during a period of crisis and change, you will emerge better off in the long run.

Love and Marriage

Financially, getting married can be one of the best things to happen to you. Your "sole proprietorship" becomes a partnership, with two productive entities working together to achieve goals, whatever they might be. Even if your spouse doesn't have a job and does not contribute to your income, the effort provided in caring for property, raising children, and managing affairs so that you can be more productive represents a great value.

ALERT!

If the two partners don't clarify their roles in the marriage, the seeds of failure begin to sprout. In this context, the financial roles are what's important, and it's worth examining some of the ideas and principles that make for an effective financial partnership in marriage.

Set Joint Goals

It's great if you've already discussed your financial goals prior to getting married. An open and friendly discussion of short-, medium-, and long-term financial goals is healthy and necessary—otherwise, both partners may be marching to a different tune. If one spouse wants to save for retirement and pay off the home, and the other spouse doesn't care about retirement and would rather spend the money on a vacation home, that's a problem. As a couple, you need to sit down and discuss your goals, and then find a way to compromise.

ESSENTIAL

Jennifer Openshaw, a leading authority on women's and family financial issues, recommends making an occasional "financial date" to discuss your finances. It's a good way to set aside conversation time in a neutral, mostly uninterrupted setting—as long as you don't blow your budget on a $40 bottle of Chardonnay.

Decide Who's in Charge

It is usually more efficient and effective for one spouse to take the lead—to pay the bills, construct the budget, get agreement, track progress against the budget, and monitor performance against goals. It doesn't make sense to have each spouse write every other check during a bill-paying situation.

However, there's no need for your family to become a financial dictatorship. Having one spouse totally in control of the family finances is rarely a good idea. Furthermore, the person not responsible for family finances will soon lose touch with what's going on, financially—as their awareness diminishes, so will their commitment and control. Meanwhile, the controlling spouse gets tired of having to worry about the details and grows resentful of having to be the responsible one.

Make sure that the approach you pick is right for you. Here are three different ideas on how to deal with the leadership issue:

1. **Divide duties.** If you track performance against long-term goals, your spouse can be in charge of setting the budget. If you manage investments, your spouse should manage the checkbook. One of you can take responsibility for retirement assets, the other for non-retirement assets—and so on.
2. **Switch off.** Switching off not only helps with the stress on the part of one spouse and the loss of interest on the part of the other, but it can also bring a fresh perspective and new ideas to the process.
3. **Keep it one person.** In some partnerships, one partner simply has the tools and the interest to do it, and the other doesn't. That's okay—so long as it is agreed to and deliberate. The "managing" partner has a duty to keep the other informed, and the "nonmanaging" partner has a duty to stay aware and committed.

Build a Joint Budget

Obvious problems emerge if only one of you is living on a budget. Instead, there should be a single budget for both of you. Does it mean that every single expenditure for a Coke or candy bar has to be agreed to or "signed off" by your spouse? Hardly. If you recall the principles of budgeting outlined in Chapters 2 and 3, there are portions of the budget set aside for individual needs and discretion. Still, the majority of a budget should be a joint exercise that both of you agree and commit to—otherwise it becomes nothing more than a meaningless sheet full of numbers.

As a couple, you will also need to consider your retirement savings. Retirement accounts are, by nature, individual, so getting married has no effect on them. However, if one spouse stops working, she can either become the beneficiary of the working spouse's IRA account, or the working spouse may open a spousal IRA for her.

QUESTION?

Should you protect your own credit in marriage?
Yes. If something happens to one spouse, or there is a divorce, the second spouse will have trouble establishing credit. Here's a good recommendation: Keep at least one charge account in the name of each individual spouse, and use it once in a while. Why not use this credit card as your PAL (personal allowance) account? For a review of managing multiple accounts as a family, see Chapter 5.

Having a Baby

Congratulations! You are starting a family. Having children is one of the most rewarding experiences of life, and as a blissful parent, surely you want to provide the best of everything for your children. But you also need to keep in mind the financial realities of raising children, or that little bundle of joy will cost you a bundle. If you aren't careful, you may never get on your feet again for retirement, and if you teach your kids bad financial habits, their financial well-being will be in jeopardy as well.

When it comes to expenses associated with having a baby, it's important not to go overboard. Your baby's room should be cozy and comfortable, but there is no need to call in an interior decorator. Similarly, you can purchase baby gear at garage sales or consignment stores—the beauty of buying baby stuff is that babies grow up quickly, and many secondhand products look almost new. You may also get things from other family members—they are usually only too glad to share their sentimental favorites within the family.

Consider Your Child Care Options

Child care will be one of your biggest baby expenses, and at $500 a month or so in many places, it may be one of your biggest expenses overall. You must budget for this, and take advantage of any tax savings through "cafeteria" or dependent care reimbursement plans through your work, or through dependent care tax credits. Know the tax rules: Tax-preferred treatment can be for up to $5,000 a year in such expenses, resulting in tax savings of $2,000 a year (at a 40 percent combined marginal bracket)—not a trivial amount. Also think about creative—and less costly—child care solutions: grandparents, neighborhood day care co-ops, and so forth.

Of course, one option is for one of the spouses to stay at home with the kids. This is a tough decision to make. Leaving work—even if it's only temporarily—can be costly in terms of income and career development. But it can make sense, especially considering day care costs (not to mention the bonding with your children). There are ways to take time off or work part time to span the period of early childhood, and many employers realize that flexibility means happier parents and improved productivity—less unplanned time off, for one thing. It's worth discussing options with your employer, as well as keeping tabs on parent-friendly employers in your area.

Insurance: Check Your Coverage

Insurance needs change dramatically when you have your first child, and they will change again with each child you have. In a nutshell, you have more to protect, and you need to make sure beneficiaries are set up properly. Consider the following:

- **Life insurance:** You should consider adding life insurance for each child born. Some studies say it costs about $100,000 to raise each child in a normal family, so term coverage in this amount is good, if you can swing it. Consider making your spouse a beneficiary, with a trust or a grandparent as a contingent beneficiary—it is dangerous to put 100,000 tax-free dollars in a young child's hands!
- **Disability coverage:** The need for disability coverage grows when children enter the scene. If you become disabled, not only does it affect your income stream, but you may incur additional expenses to take care of the children!
- **Health insurance:** If you're insured by an employer, adding family members costs money. And if you're paying for your own insurance, know that kids are less likely to have catastrophic health problems but that they tend to have more doctor visits. You can moderate insurance costs by "self insuring" the little stuff and taking a higher deductible

on catastrophic coverage. If self-employed or working for a small firm, medical savings accounts (MSAs) can help a lot.

ESSENTIAL

When you get a new addition to your family, take the time to set up a new savings account for your little boy or girl. It'll feel great to walk into a bank and create an account for this new person, and who knows? That savings account could one day grow into a full college savings fund.

As Your Kids Get Older

As they enter the cartoon-watching phase, your kids start to develop a consciousness of things, money, and the things money will buy. How you manage this phase will have great bearing not only on your finances but on their own financial habits when they get older. Here are a few bits of advice:

- **Build a sense of what money is.** Make it possible for kids to have and spend some of their own money, which they earn or receive as a monthly allowance. When they want something, give them a feel for how much it costs. Reward good habits, and point out bad ones.
- **Don't spoil your kids with buying stuff.** Your money can't buy you love, and this applies to your kids as well. Don't just buy things they want—your purchases should be reasonable. Some parents buy stuff for kids as a reward for their accomplishments or achievements. Although this method works, you might find difficulty convincing them to do something without the benefits of your reward.
- **Teach your kids about commercialism and the power of advertising.** A kid who is taught how advertising works and the value of money is more likely not to be swept up in advertisements' extravagant claims.

As kids get older, their needs shift from inexpensive toys and candy to considerably more costly wishes and needs. At the same time, they are more capable of managing money, and, hopefully, of earning it.

Teenagers should pay for at least some of their expenses. Parental matching can send the right message of helping and rewarding them—not doing everything for them.

E ALERT!

Keep your kids away from credit cards. Some of the worst debt problems happen because kids don't know how to use credit cards correctly. Charging stuff is exciting and wonderful, especially the first few times, and it quickly turns into a habit that is hard to get rid of. If a kid must have a credit card—and these days, with e-commerce and such it is hard not to—monthly payoff should be mandatory.

Facing a Career Change

Sooner or later, it's going to happen. You and/or your spouse are going to switch jobs or even change profession. There are a lot of financial considerations that need to be made before, during, and after such a transition.

The most obvious financial consideration is income, especially if you quit, get fired, or are laid off. While you search for a job, your expenses may actually increase. Furthermore, in today's job market, you also need to be prepared for relocation expenses, which aren't always covered by the new employer.

Other considerations include benefits and insurance coverage (especially health insurance) and the interruption of retirement and college savings. The latter isn't usually too much of a concern, unless the transition lasts an extended period of time or retirement assets are consumed to meet expenses during the hiatus.

Luckily, you *can* prepare for a job change in advance. In particular, you need to build an income reserve to cover your expenses, which means identifying all the costs of unemployment and being prepared to deal with them. You also need to consider actions that would help you find another job: Keep on building and diversifying your skills to keep up with the job market, and maintain a professional network that you can rely on in times of need.

FACT

COBRA is a federal act that obligates employers to provide health insurance to former employees at discounted group rates for a period normally up to eighteen months. Under COBRA, although you will have to pay the entire rate yourself, you will at least retain your health insurance, which is still 30 or 40 percent less than the individual rate you can get on your own.

The Divorce Disaster

Divorce is a disastrous occurrence, both emotionally and financially. The emotional part is obvious. But what about the finances? Divorce is a costly undertaking that splits or destroys family finances. It occurs against a highly charged emotional backdrop that makes rational financial planning and decision-making next to impossible. There is no way to make divorce not hurt—emotionally or financially—but again, if you keep your wits about you, and separate emotions from facts, some of its impact can be reduced.

Divorce proceedings usually consist of three phases: a pleading phase, a discovery phase, and a trial (unless settlement is first reached). There are substantial legal expenses at every step of the way, and it is important to know how you can minimize these expenses and preserve your finances.

QUESTION?

What about a prenuptial agreement?
Prenuptial (and postnuptial) agreements can be a handy tool to "manage" divorce before it ever happens. If one spouse brings significant assets into the marriage, many of the asset distribution laws will preserve those assets, and the "prenupt" will simply make the distribution faster and more certain. Check the laws in your state before deciding if a prenupt makes sense.

Effective Redistribution of Assets

If you divorce, you and your spouse will have to figure out a way to split up your assets. To do that, you should first create an inventory of all your assets and place a value on them, being as thorough as possible. Take careful inventory of each asset in each account, and try to establish how much that asset has changed in value during your marriage. Get outside appraisals where it makes sense. The more rational your property valuation is, the more rational the decisions will be about who gets what.

When it comes to legal asset division, laws vary by state. In most states, the court distributes assets according to what they think is fair, depending on what is provided into the marriage and what each spouse's needs and children's needs are. Nine states—mostly in the West—use community property rules, where all assets acquired since marriage are automatically divided fifty/fifty. Deciding what has happened since marriage can be tricky, and so is dealing with the family home—unfavorable sales are often forced. Finally, one state (Mississippi) divides according to name on title—period. In all cases, you can agree among yourselves how you want to divide assets before getting a court decree.

Distributing assets calls for title changes, which will require a lot of your attention. Here is what you will need to do:

- Retitle jointly owned assets, particularly those with rights of survivorship.
- Change beneficiaries on contractually transferred assets—insurance policies, retirement plans, and trusts.
- Review your estate plan, and draw up new wills and trusts.
- Appropriately redistribute retirement assets, including pensions. For defined benefit pensions, where there is no specific account balance in your name, a QDRO (Qualified Domestic Relations Order) will legally split benefits.

A Real Estate Concern

Be careful how you manage your house. If a jointly owned primary residence property reverts to a single owner, the $500,000 total capital gains tax exclusion once available to the two co-owners drops to $250,000, the amount for a single owner.

Depending on how large a gain you may have on your house, you can suddenly take a big tax hit if forced to sell. You may want to consider selling the house during the year of the divorce settlement to guarantee a full deduction.

Paying Alimony and Child Support

With divorce come alimony and child support payments. Determining what is "proper" alimony and child support is beyond the scope of this book. However, it might be helpful for you to learn their impact on your taxes. While alimony is deductible for the payor and is taxable income for the payee, child support is generally not deductible to the payor (though he or she may be able to claim an exemption), and it is not taxable income to the payee.

ESSENTIAL

This just scratches the surface of some of the issues you'll encounter in divorce. Again, even under the best of circumstances, divorce is disruptive to any financial plan or achievement of financial goals. Assets are split up, and family costs increase as more households are created. Tax benefits can be lost. But beyond that, the sheer emotional storm of divorce can wash even the most rational and stable financial ships under.

Chapter 24

Building Your Financial Plan

Now it's time to start building your own personal financial plan. This chapter gives an overview of how a good financial plan is created—by setting goals and developing strategies that will work best for you. However, you don't need to do it alone. If you would prefer to get some help along the way, this chapter will also explore ways you can receive professional assistance and find additional do-it-yourself resources.

Where to Begin

Every financial plan is different for each person, with varying amount of detail. Some individuals may need a high-level framework, with a single page of goals and maybe a few strategies or general guidelines. Others, especially those who have had little previous experience managing and controlling their finances, may prefer to create a more detailed plan with specific strategies, checklists, and frequent progress reviews. Here are some of the factors that most influence your financial needs and plans:

1. **Starting point:** This point is pretty obvious: Where you are now, financially, will determine your financial planning. If you're already a millionaire, your position is far different from that of a $40,000 credit-card debtor. Likewise, if you're already saving money from each paycheck and have a retirement plan, your situation is different from the person with no savings who is just making ends meet. Often, your current position depends on whether you've set the right goals and how much you've already achieved.
2. **Stage of life:** Referred to by marketers as "lifestage," your age, marital status, family status, and career stage all play a big role in your personal finance plan. If you're three years from retirement, your main concern should be wealth preservation; if you are twenty-five and single, your emphasis should be on wealth accumulation.
3. **Life needs:** Every individual and family has a different lifestyle and different commitments. Most people need a home, dependable personal transportation, health care, and college education for their kids. A good financial plan should maintain existing lifestyles and, in the long run, improve them. But occasionally personal financial planning may involve a reduction in commitments and a "downsizing" in lifestyle. This is perfectly okay; in fact, a planned-for downsizing is a whole lot better than an unplanned one!
4. **Aspirations:** Most lifestyle and financial aspirations are centered upon the need to improve the family lifestyle or attain significant personal goals—more travel, more education, starting one's own business, making a charitable contribution, and so forth. The financial plan should address these aspirations just as it addresses the more

traditional financial goals like retirement and college education requirements.

Here's the point: All these factors influence your goals and the financial plan you create. They must be taken in balance—a life experience in which basic life needs or aspirations are continually suppressed will not only be dissatisfying, it will cause your financial plan to go "off track" as you struggle and, perhaps, give up. And if you deceive yourself about the starting point—that is, fail to take proper financial inventory or brush your financial problems under the carpet—the likelihood of success diminishes.

ESSENTIAL

Even if you can't achieve your aspirations at this point, it makes sense to include them in your plan. This way you are aware of what you have to do, and the plan has a greater sense of purpose. Eventually, as you grow and your financial habits improve, your aspirations will take center stage.

Three Stages of Financial Planning

Where you and your family are in life has a lot to do with where you're going financially. Think of your adult life as divided into three stages: the accumulation phase, the preservation phase, and the distribution phase. At the risk of oversimplifying, most people under fifty are in an asset accumulation phase, where the emphasis of planning is on aggressively saving and investing assets to build as big a net-worth base as possible. Between fifty and sixty-five, the nest egg should already be established, so the emphasis shifts to preservation—more conservative investments, reduced spending—to keep the nest egg intact. The closer to retirement you are, the more preservation oriented, or conservative, your financial plan should be. Finally, at retirement, as you switch to living on the nest egg, the emphasis turns to distribution—how to disperse your assets to meet lifestyle goals while still preserving as much of your net worth as possible.

FACT

Before retirement, most people choose a financial plan that is a mix of accumulation and preservation strategies, determined in part by risk tolerance and specific family situation (number of kids, special needs, location, and cost of living). After retirement, the strategy usually shifts to a mix of distribution and preservation.

Setting Financial Goals

Setting financial goals is an expansive and creative exercise. The goals you come up with are highly dependent on your situation and what you think you can achieve. There can be big goals and small ones, or you might prefer to set up a lot of small goals that would lead up to a big one. Goals can be short-term or long-term, and a good financial plan usually includes both. Here are a few common rules for goal-setting:

1. **Goals must be specific and viable.** "Achieve a net worth of $1 million by age fifty" is a viable financial goal. "Get rich" or "become wealthy" is not. Every goal should have a specific time frame as well as a specific, measurable criterion for achieving it. Note that the "measurable criterion" need not be an amount of money; it can be something like "Set up a detailed record keeping system by June 1."
2. **Goals must be realistic.** "Become a millionaire by age fifty" may be specific enough, but it is not a viable goal if your net worth is a negative $40,000 at age forty-eight. Unrealistic goals can cause undue stress or discourage the person who set it—if you know it can't be done, why bother trying? Good goals are set in context of the financial situation at hand. For the negative $40,000 person, getting out of debt is a good goal. For someone with a good job and a net worth of $300,000, becoming a millionaire is a reasonable aspiration, as long as the time frame is realistic.
3. **Goals can be personal or task-related.** Task-related goals involve achieving a certain task, such as reaching a specific number in net worth or paying off all your debts. Personal goals, which are just as valid, are more about developing awareness and control over finances.

"Know within $50 how much I've put on my credit card every month before the statement comes" is a good personal goal.

4. **There should be short-term and long-term goals.** Long-term goals are set for a five-year term or longer; short-term goals are meant to be accomplished in less than five years. If you only set long-term goals, there are no milestones along the way by which to measure your progress. That makes the task more vague and less urgent, and it leads to procrastination. And without long-term goals, you have no overlying strategy in your personal finance plan.

ALERT!

There is certainly more than one way of reaching your goals. As you construct your own set of personal (or family) goals and strategies, make sure you look at the alternatives, and choose those that are most effective and efficient.

Preparation

Setting good financial goals and building a financial plan around them requires good preparation and a knowledge of where to start. First, you need to take inventory of your situation: Examine your income, expenses, assets, and liabilities—and where all those things came from (see Chapter 2 and 3)—to form a good understanding of your finances and financial habits.

Second, you need to take inventory of your planning. Capture existing financial planning building blocks that may already be in place—previous goals, savings plans, insurance policies, employee benefits, and so forth. If you are married, make sure you have all the records for all the members of your family.

Then, it's time to apply the SWOT analysis. SWOT stands for Strengths, Weaknesses, Opportunities, and Threats, an analysis framework that provides a way to inventory and classify what is good and bad about your personal finances situation. The four quadrants making up the SWOT diagram in **FIGURE 24-1** are fairly straightforward.

FIGURE 24-1

Strengths	**O**pportunities
Weaknesses	**T**hreats

▲ SWOT analysis.

1. **Strengths:** These are areas of your finances where you are doing well or are ahead of the plan—zero debt, accumulated wealth, and a retirement plan ahead of schedule are all strengths. Don't forget to include personal attributes: good awareness, commitment, and control are all strengths.
2. **Weaknesses:** The opposite of strengths, weaknesses are areas where you have trouble or are behind.
3. **Opportunities:** These are identifiable opportunities in your finances or in the external environment—an improving economy or career prospect, a possibility to get rid of a certain expense, such as day care or a car payment. Opportunities can signal a step forward in wealth accumulation or goal achievement, and it's worth getting them on paper to make the right moves when the time is right.
4. **Threats:** Threats that may thwart a financial plan may include loss of income, increase in expenses, or external factors such as inflation or reduction in retirement benefits.

Once you have completed your SWOT analysis, you should be able to identify the most important issues in your finances and build viable goals around them.

A Few Examples

The best way to learn is by example. Following is a set of simple examples of financial goals, as well as the strategies and tactics to achieve them. Please note—these are by no means the only way to outline your goals; it's fine if your approach happens to be totally different.

Example #1

Personal goal: Retire early (by age sixty).

Financial goal: Accumulate $1 million in net worth by age sixty.

Strategy: Contribute maximum amount to 401(k) plan and pay off mortgage by age fifty.

Tactics:

- *Take 5 percent take-home pay cut to increase savings (total $3,000).*
- *Reduce expenses.*
- *Cut $1,200 per year out of vacation budget by eliminating two three-day weekend trips each year.*
- *Take care of lawn and garden, save $600 a year on landscaping fees.*
- *Take lunch to work three days a week, save $1,200.*
- *Increase mortgage payment from $900 to $1,100 a month.*

Example #2

Personal goal: Take one year off work to pursue education in a new field of interest.

Financial goal: Accumulate $34,000 ($24,000 for expenses, $10,000 for a reserve).

Strategy: Create off-the-top savings and learn to live on less.

Tactics:

- *Switch growth investments to income investments.*
- *Learn to live on 80 percent of current take-home pay.*

Example #3

Personal goal: Create a worry-free retirement at the expense of more risk now.

Financial goal: Get retirement assets (RAs) to achieve 80 percent of current income retirement at reasonable return.

Strategy: Increase 401(k) contributions and build investments faster, save more outside of 401(k), and take on more risk to increase investment returns.

Tactics:

- *Increase 401(k) by 2 percent.*
- *Start an "off-the-top" credit union payroll deduction.*
- *Increase allocation of investments to 75 percent aggressive growth investments.*

Example #4

Personal goal: Mitigate risks of catastrophic losses in case one or both income producers die or become incapacitated.

Financial goal: provide ten years' income in life and disability coverage for both spouses for the next twenty years, reduce to five-year coverage after that.

Strategy: Build one year's income in reserve savings accounts, purchase insurance for the rest.

Tactics:

- *Buy $150,000 in life coverage for each spouse to supplement insurance provided by employers.*
- *Buy disability insurance to provide one-half of income coverage; use savings and lifestyle reductions to make up the gap if one or both become disabled. Construct a "what-if" budget if one or both spouses become disabled.*
- *Meet with insurance broker to figure out best way to structure and pay for these coverages and provide coverage in later years.*

Getting Help with Your Financial Plan

If you decide that you need help with achieving your financial goals, there are many types of financial professionals who can help you. Choosing the right person can be critical—there are good service providers as well as charlatans out there. One problem is that a financial advisor's best interest may not be your best interest, so the fee-based (as opposed to commission-based) advisors are a surer bet—at least you know that your advisor is not being paid according to the amount of product he or she sells you.

ESSENTIAL

It may be true that you're better at achieving goals that you set for yourself, and good financial planners will allow you to set them yourself, too—but with a little assistance.

The financial industry has gone through a hectic transformation in the past twenty years as legal barriers have come down and financial management has become more democratized, particularly through the Web. Just ten or fifteen years ago, buying securities or getting insurance quotes could not be accomplished without professional assistance; today, you can do it yourself online.

Furthermore, changes in the financial industry's strategies have caused diversification among various providers, who now try to offer a broader set of services for their customers. As a result, many brokers sell insurance, insurance agents and banks sell mutual funds, CPAs are doing asset management–and so forth.

Professionals in the Financial Sector

Each of the major financial-service sectors has its own set of professional standards, credentials, and licensing. There is a whole "alphabet soup" of lettered credentials in all fields, and licenses–often granted by federal and state agencies–to go with the credentials. The credentials usually arise from a rigorous educational curriculum, including a certification exam and required continuing education. Take the following examples:

- Insurance agents and brokers may have a CLU (Chartered Life Underwriter) or CPCU (Chartered Property/Casualty Underwriter), and should have a state-granted insurance license.
- Investment advisors may have a CMFC (Chartered Mutual Fund Counselor) or an RIA (Registered Investment Advisor) designation. RIAs are more common for fee-based (as opposed to commission-based) investment advisors and managers; they are registered with the SEC and must meet varying state requirements.
- Tax advisors may have their CPA (Certified Public Accountant) and/or a state-granted tax preparer's license.

- Estate lawyers have legal degrees and credentials; there is no corresponding professional credential specifically for the estate-planning specialty.

This is just a sample of the more common licenses and certifications, which are numerous and constantly evolving.

In addition to the financial professionals that have a specific area of expertise, there are general financial advisors, known as Certified Financial Planners (CFPs) and Chartered Financial Consultants (ChFCs). These planners are familiar with all fields in financial planning–investing, tax, estate planning, risk management, money management–and can offer broad perspective and advice, often on a fee basis, to help you manage your financial needs. The financial planner acts as sort of an architect and general contractor–he or she can tell you about wills and trusts but will refer you to a specialist to draw up a will or trust.

ALERT!

Watch out for show-offs. Some financial professionals are so intent on convincing you of their wizardry that they purposely talk fast and use confusing language and mathematical terms. If a planner isn't willing to talk to you on your own terms, move on. Don't be afraid to say you don't understand—that's why you're there.

Choosing a Financial Professional

To get good professional help, you want to shop around as carefully as you would for a doctor, lawyer, or any other professional. The most important point is to find an advisor who is competent and who does not have a conflict of interest. Furthermore, you should look for a person who has the right education and credentials, has experience in the industry, knows how to communicate, is able to provide references, and can clearly state the costs and fees associated with the service provided. Interview several advisors to see which one will best suit your needs. You can tell a lot from a person by how he or she talks to you. Promptly returned phone calls, follow-up, good phone manners, and good body language are all signs of genuine interest and professionalism.

Putting Your Goals into Action

The best-laid plans are worthless if they aren't used. Once you have an outline of your goals, strategies, and tactics, it's time to take action. Here are a few final pieces of advice to get you started on the right path:

- **Don't go it alone.** Make sure all family members are aware of the goals and actively participate in trying to achieve them—everyone in your family should know his or her role.
- **Measure results.** The best way to get sustained performance is to check progress periodically and perhaps grade yourself on how you're doing; a quarterly review may be a good idea.
- **Reward achievements.** People are motivated by rewards. If you and your family have stayed aware, committed, and in control, you should be rewarded. But don't go overboard and spend all the money you have been saving up toward your goals on your reward!

Appendix A

E Financial Worksheets

You can use the following financial worksheets to review your own finances as they were explained in Chapter 2 (and throughout the book). The financial self-assessment you make is critical to your understanding of where you are and where you would like to be headed financially.

Net Worth Worksheet

Date:

ASSETS

Nonretirement current assets (NRAs)		
Cash, checking		
Savings, credit union		
Securities, brokerage accounts		
Mutual funds		
Life insurance, cash value		
College savings, savings plans		
Other		
Total NRAs		
Retirement assets (RAs)		
401(k)		
IRA(s)		
Other RA's current value		
Total RAs		
Real property		
Home		
Second home		
Investment property		
Collectibles		
Personal property		
Other		
Total real property		
Business interests		
Other		
Total business interests/other		
TOTAL ASSETS		

LIABILITIES

Current liabilities

Credit cards	
Installment debt (car loans, etc.)	
Home equity loans/credit lines	
Student loans	
Margin loans	
Other	
Total current liabilities	

Long-term liabilities

Home mortgage	
Second home mortgage	
Investment property mortgage	
Business loan or share	
Other	
Total long-term liabilities	

TOTAL LIABILITIES ______

NET WORTH ______

Cash Flow Worksheet

Year:

Income	Period Jan	Feb	Mar	Apr	May
Earned income					
Salary, wages (regular)					
Bonuses, commissions (irregular)					
Tips					
Other					
Total earned income					
Self-employment income					
Own business					
Freelance income					
Income from partnerships					
Rental income					
Royalties					
Other					
Total SE income					
Investment income					
Interest					
Dividends					
Capital gain distributions					
Other					
Total investment income					
Retirement income & other					
Social Security					
Pension					
Income from other retirement plans					
Alimony					
Child support					
Family trust(s)					
Disability or other insurance					
Other					
Total retirement/other					
TOTAL INCOME					

Jun	Jul	Aug	Sep	Oct	Nov	Dec	TOTAL

EXPENSES

Obligations (fixed)	Jan	Feb	Mar	Apr	May	Jun
Home (mortgage or rent)						
Installment loans						
Car loans						
Student loan payments						
Other loan payments (not credit cards)						
Credit card interest						
Household operation						
Utilities						
Energy						
Telecom						
Water/Sewer/Disp						
Insurance premiums						
Auto						
Life						
Home/renters						
Health/dental						
Disability/LTC						
Taxes						
Federal						
State						
Property						
Vehicle						
Self-employment						
Other						
Dues, owners' association						
Other						
Total obligations						

Jul	Aug	Sep	Oct	Nov	Dec	Total

Necessities (manageable)	Jan	Feb	Mar	Apr	May	Jun
Food						
Clothing						
Transportation						
Auto						
Gas						
Maintenance/repair						
Parking, tolls						
Non-auto						
Fares						
Other						
Household						
Maintenance, repair						
Home improvement						
Furnishings, fixtures						
Garden						
Supplies						
Other						
Child care & tuition						
Day care						
Tuition						
Summer school/camp						
Babysitting						
Financial/professional services						
Accountant						
Legal						
Bank fees, etc						
Other						
Medical care (not covered by insurance)						
Co-pays						
Dental						
Eyeglasses, contacts, etc.						
Other						
Personal care						
Haircuts, styling						
Cosmetics						
Other personal care						
Total necessities						

Jul	Aug	Sep	Oct	Nov	Dec	Total

Discretionary	Jan	Feb	Mar	Apr	May	Jun
Recreation and entertainment						
Health, other clubs						
Restaurants						
Subscriptions						
Other/miscellaneous						
Recreational equipment						
Purchase						
Maintenance/upkeep						
Supplies						
Travel and vacations						
Charitable contributions, incl. church						
Other						
Total discretionary						
Small stuff						
Meals at work						
Small family expenses						
Small individual expenses						
Total small stuff						
TOTAL EXPENSES						
NET EARNINGS/CASH FLOW						

Jul	Aug	Sep	Oct	Nov	Dec	Total

Financial Summary

Net Worth	
Net Cash Flow	

Assets		
Nonretirement assets (NRAs)		
Retirement assets		
Real property		
Home		
Personal property		
Total assets		
Liabilities		
Current liabilities		
Long-term liabilities		
Total liabilities		
NET WORTH		
Income		
Earned income		
Self-employment income		
Investment income		
Total income		
Expenses		
Obligations		
Debt service		
Necessities		
Discretionary		
Small stuff		
Total expenses		
NET INCOME (CASH FLOW)		

Appendix B

Risk-Tolerance Questionnaire

Many different questionnaires are used by financial planners, investment counselors, and even psychologists to help determine individual tolerance to risk. Some are short and simple; some are more elaborate. Some evaluate only feelings and behavior towards risk; others look further into your life situation and lifestyle. Appendix B is a brief questionnaire that explores both psychological and situational risk factors.

Risk-Tolerance Analysis

Answer each question. Be as honest as possible.

1 = strongly disagree
5 = strongly agree

Question	Response
1. Expected return: Given historical returns on different kinds of investments, my desired level of investment return is above average.	☐
2. Risk tolerance: I am willing to bear an above-average level of investment risk (volatility). I can accept occasional years with negative investment returns.	☐
3. Holding period: I am willing to maintain investment positions over a reasonably long period of time (generally considered ten years or more).	☐
4. Liquidity: I do not need to be able to readily convert my investments into cash. Aside from my portfolio, I have adequate liquid net worth to meet major near-term expenses.	☐
5. Ease of management: I want to be very actively involved in the monitoring and decision-making required to manage my investments.	☐
6. Dependents: There are none or only a few dependents that rely on my income and my investment portfolio for support.	☐
7. Income source: My major source of income is adequate, predictable, and steadily growing.	☐
8. Insurance coverage: I have an adequate degree of insurance coverage.	☐
9. Investment experience: I have prior investment experience with stocks, bonds, and international investments. I understand the concept of investment risk.	☐
10.Debit/credit: My debt level and my credit history are excellent.	☐
	☐
	Divide by 10 = ☐

The higher the number the greater your risk tolerance.

Appendix C

E Classification of Mutual Funds

Following is a classification of different available mutual fund types commonly found in major financial publications such as the *Wall Street Journal*. This classification is based on one furnished by Lipper, Inc., an investment research firm.

Stock Funds
Code—*Category* • Description
LG—*Large-cap growth* • Invest in large companies (with market cap over $5 billion), with long-term earnings that are expected to grow significantly faster than the earnings of stocks in major indexes. Above average P/E ratios, price-to-book ratios, and three-year earnings growth.
LC—*Large-cap core* • Invest in large companies with wide latitude in their holdings. P/E ratios, price-to-book, and three-year earnings growth are comparable to average of U.S. diversified large-cap funds.
LV—*Large-cap value* • Invest in large companies that are considered undervalued relative to major stock indices.
MG—*Mid-cap growth* • Invest in midsize companies (market cap $1–5 billion) with above-average growth prospects, P/E, price-to-book, and three-year growth rates.
MC—*Mid-cap core* • Invest in midsize companies with wide latitude in their holdings. Key ratios are in line with other U.S. diversified mid-cap funds.
MV—*Mid-cap value* • Invest in midsize companies that are considered undervalued relative to major stock indices.
SG—*Small-cap growth* • Invest in small companies (market cap less than $1 billion) with above-average growth prospects, P/E, price-to-book, and three-year growth rates.
SC—*Small-cap core* • Invest in small companies with wide latitude in their holdings. Key ratios are in line with other U.S. diversified small-cap funds.
SV—*Small-cap value* • Invest in small companies that are considered undervalued relative to major stock indices.
XG—*Multi-cap growth* • Invest in companies of all sizes with above-average growth prospects, P/E, price-to-book, and three-year growth rates.
XC—*Multi-cap core* • Funds that invest in companies of all sizes with wide latitude in their holdings.
XV—*Multi-cap value* • Funds that invest in companies of all sizes considered undervalued.

Stock Funds *(continued)*

EI—*Equity income* • Seek high current income (dividends) and growth of income through investments in equity securities.

SP—*S&P500 Index* • Funds that replicate the S&P 500, passively managed.

SQ—*Specialty equity* • Invest in all market-cap ranges, with no restrictions. May have strategies specialized or distinctly different from other funds.

EM—*Emerging markets* • Invest in emerging market equity securities in countries identified as "emerging markets" according to GNP and other economic measures.

EU—*European region* • Invest in companies concentrated in European region.

PR—*Pacific region* • Invest in companies concentrated in Asia/Pacific region.

LT—*Latin America* • Invest in companies concentrated in Latin American region.

GL—*Global stock* • Invest in securities outside of United States, may have U.S. securities as well.

IL—*International stock* • Invest only in international (including Canadian) securities.

AU—*Gold-oriented* • Invest in gold mines, gold industry, gold coins, or bullion.

HB—*Health/biotech* • Invest in companies related to health care, medicine, and biotechnology.

NR—*Natural resources* • Invest in natural resource stocks.

TK—*Science/technology* • Invest in science, technology, telecommunications.

UT—*Utility* • Invest in utility stocks.

Taxable Bond Funds

Code—*Category* • Description

SB—*Short-term bond* • Short-to-intermediate term bonds (usually less than five years), usually investment grade.

SU—*Short-term U.S.* • Short-to-intermediate term U.S. Treasury securities.

IB—*Intermediate bond* • Intermediate-term bonds with weighted average maturities between five and ten years, usually investment grade.

IG—*Intermediate U.S.* • Intermediate-term U.S. Treasury securities.

Taxable Bond Funds *(continued)*
AB—*Long-term bond* • Invest in corporate and U.S. Treasury securities, usually with long (greater than ten year) maturities, usually investment grade.
LU—*Long-term U.S.* • Intermediate-term U.S. Treasury securities.
GT—*General U.S. taxable* • Invest in a wide universe of U.S. corporate and Treasury bonds.
HC—*High-yield taxable* • Invest to achieve high yields, often through lower-grade securities.
MT—*Mortgage* • Invest mainly in agency bonds FNMA (Fannie Mae), GNMA (Ginnie Mae), etc., representing mortgage portfolios.
WB—*World bond* • Invest in international debt securities.

Municipal Debt Funds
Code—*Category* • Description
SM—Short-term muni • Short-to-intermediate term state and local government or government agency securities.
IM—Intermediate-term muni • Intermediate-term state and local government securities.
GM—General muni • State and local government securities, all maturities.
SS—Single-state muni • Invest in securities of specific states to achieve maximum tax advantage.
HM—High-yield muni • Invest to achieve high yields, often through lower-grade securities.
NM—*Insured muni* • Invest in insured securities.

Stock and Bond Funds
Code—*Category* • Description
BL—*Balanced* • Primary objective is to conserve principal by maintaining a balanced portfolio of both stocks and bonds.
MP—*Stock/bond blend* • Multipurpose funds with a mix of stocks and bonds; can also be convertible securities funds.

Appendix D

Additional Resources

An ever-increasing array of resources is at your disposal to make and execute your financial plans. Appendix D offers a list of books and Web sites that may answer your general personal finance questions, give you more information on investing, and approach specific financial topics that you may need to understand in greater detail.

Further Reading

Making the Most of Your Money, Jane Bryant Quinn (Simon & Schuster).

The Millionaire Next Door, Thomas Stanley and William Danko (Longstreet).

What's Your Net Worth?, Jennifer Openshaw (Perseus).

The Wall Street Journal Guide to Understanding Personal Finance (WSJ/Lightbulb Press).

The Pocket Idiot's Guide to Living on a Budget, Peter Sander, Jennifer Sander (Alpha/Pearson).

Smart Women Finish Rich/Smart Couples Finish Rich, David Bach (Broadway).

The Motley Fool Investing Guide, Tom Gardner and David Gardner (Fireside/Simon & Schuster).

Rule Makers, Rule Breakers, Tom Gardner and David Gardner (Fireside/Simon & Schuster).

One Up on Wall Street, Peter Lynch (Fireside/Simon & Schuster).

Wall Street on Sale, Timothy Vick (McGraw-Hill).

Value Investing for Dummies, Peter Sander (Hungryminds/Wiley).

Best Intentions, Colleen Barney, Victoria F. Collins (Dearborn).

Retire Worry-Free—Smart Ways to Build the Nest Egg You'll Need, (Kiplinger Books).

Web Sites

www.quicken.com—General personal finance site with emphasis on investment analysis. Supports Quicken personal finance software and bill-payment products.

www.smartmoney.com—General personal finance site from Dow Jones & Co.

www.money.com—General personal finance site from CNN/AOL Time Warner; this site is especially good for beginners.

✐ *www.msmoney.com*–General personal finance site originally targeted to women. All personal finance topics covered, with strong focus on life transitions like marriage and divorce.

✐ *quote.yahoo.com*–The Yahoo!Finance portal features well-packaged investment and other personal finance information, and links to other sites and resources.

✐ *www.cnbc.com*–Investing site offering investing news and commentary.

✐ *www.morningstar.com*–Primarily an investing site, with a strong focus on mutual funds and strategies on investing, such as college 529 savings and retirement plans.

✐ *www.bloomberg.com*–Investing site that offers investing news and commentary.

✐ *www.irs.gov*–The IRS site: the definitive resource on income taxes. It includes complete tax-planning information, forms, and information on new laws in a surprisingly reader-friendly style.

✐ *www.taxplanet.com*–Independent tax site that offers tax tips, quick reference, summaries of new laws, and laws that are pending. A newsletter is also available.

✐ *www.rushforth.net*–Private estate-planning attorney explains estate planning in readable English.

✐ *www.insweb.com*–This site is an insurance portal and marketer that offers insurance quotes and general information about insurance.

✐ *www.einsurance.com*–Insurance portal and marketer, insurance quotes, and general information about insurance.

✐ *www.myfico.com*–Public access site for Fair, Isaac, & Co., credit and credit-rating analysts. The site offers excellent credit-management advice and provides individual credit rating and explanation for $13.95.

✐ *www.eloan.com*–Loan portal, where you can get latest rates and shop for a variety of loans. Comparisons of loans are also available.

✐ *www.list.realestate.yahoo.com*–Complete real estate portal that offers real estate pricing, recent sales by location, real estate buying and selling strategies, loans, and links to other services.

Index

I

J, K, L

P

Q, R

S

T

U

V

W

Y, Z